66 CHAPTER

DR. GEORGE W. WESTLAKE JR.

Debbie

"God Bless you".

[signature]

12/8/19

Scripture quotations identified KJV are from the King James Version of the Bible.

Scripture quotations identified as NASB are from the New American Standard Bible © The Lockman Foundation, 1960, 1962, 1963, 1971, 1973, 1975, 1977.

Scripture quotations identified NIV are from THE HOLY BIBLE NEW INTERNATIONAL VERSION © NIV© 1973, 1978, 1984 by International Bible Society. Used by permissions of Zondervan Publishing House. All rights reserved.

Scripture quotations identified as NKJ are from the New King James Version of the Bible, copyright © 1979, 1980, 1982, Thomas Nelson Inc. Publishers.

Scripture quotations identified as ESV are from The Holy Bible English Standard Version ©Permanent Text Edition © 2016 copyright ©2001 by Crossway Bibles, a publishing ministry of Good News Publishers.

Scripture quotations identified as NLT are from The New Living Translation of the Bible, ©Copyright 1996, 2004, 2015 by Tyndale House Foundation.

Scripture translations from Greek are from the Nestle Auland Greek New Testament, 27th Edition, United Bible Societies.

Cover design by Graphic Artist Kevin Williamson: kevinwilliamsondesign.com

Cover artwork "The Opening of the Sealed Scroll is by Pat Marvenko Smith, ©1982/1992 – www.revelationillustrated.com

Dr. Westlake's book, The Most Often Asked Questions on Sunday Night Alive is available by contacting Sheffield Family Life center 5700 Winner Rd, Kansas City, Mo 64127., phone 816-241-4831

The textbook I wrote on Daniel and Revelation for Global University may be available by contacting Global University 1211 S Glenstone Ave., Springfield, Mo 65802. Phone 800.443-1083, 417-862-9533.

Introduction and Foreword

As the title of the book, CHAPTER 66, indicates, the Book of Revelation is the final chapter of the story given to us of God and creation. Of course, there is much more that has not been revealed following the events of Revelation. Without Revelation the Bible is like reading a mystery story with the last chapter missing...a *Who done it ?* without finding out *who done* it.

Hebrews 1:1 points out, God spoke through the prophets in *different ways and at different times-bits and pieces* (of course the author goes on to show that Jesus, Himself, is the ultimate revelation of God).

Revelation takes the bits and pieces and puts them together where they belong. I am aware that there are those who believe all prophecy was fulfilled in AD 70, and others see it only as a Spiritual Allegory—*We Win!* Others try to see various characters from History such as Napoleon, The Huns, Islam...it seems that no two agree as to whom each picture represents. It is stated in the opening phrases of the book, and the closing phrase calls the book a PROPHECY. The events and persons in the Book are real events and real persons: That does not mean the Anti-Christ has 7 heads; but he will be real and the events surrounding him will be real., as will all the other characters and events to complete CHAPTERS 66 OF GOD'S STORY.

I have had the privilege of teaching the entire Bible College Level, All of it Under Graduate, much of it at Graduate Levels for over 40 years, and New Testament Greek, levels 1-4 for 25 years. I have been teaching Revelation in Colleges and Seminaries in 10 different countries for 30 years and have been teaching Prophecy Seminars in Churches, and Pastor's Seminars for longer than that. Having read between 150-200 books on Bible Prophecy over the last 60 years, I have done my best to understand all the various interpretations of Revelation and coming events. I also wrote, in 1987, the textbook: Daniel and Revelation for Global University, which has been translated into many languages, and used in many countries. As of this writing, I am 87 years old, and because of God's grace am still teaching and preaching here at home and in other countries. I also have taught Graduate Hermeneutics (How to properly interpret Scripture) at many Bible Colleges.

The purpose of this writing is not to present all the various theories or interpretations of Revelation, but to present what I see as the consistent interpretation of the book as it puts the pieces of prophecy together to present CHAPTER 66.

In addition to pastoring all this time, I had the privilege of doing a live Bible Question and Answer program on local radio for a few years. Then on local television for 24 years, did the same, with my wife, Jean, and others sometimes, on a program we called *Sunday Night Alive,* from 10:30 pm to Midnight for most of the time, then, because the station was sold, we changed the name to *Living Answers for Today,* and were live on Saturdays and rebroadcast throughout the week on other stations. While on Sunday nights, Neilson indicated we had the largest audience in the city many times during the broadcast. I have a book entitled, *The Most Often Asked Questions on Sunday Night Alive*

There are many great scholars and Christian Brothers and Sisters who hold different interpretations of Revelation and Bible Prophecy as a whole, many of whom I highly respect. We all *see through a glass darkly* now, and some day *face to face.* It's fine to disagree without being disagreeable.

I have tried to keep simple language in the book. As a Pastor most of my life, I had a sign on my pulpit, *KISS.* When guest speakers asked me what that meant, I told them *It is for my benefit and means KEEP IT SIMPLE STUPID!*

There are many issues in the book that scholars disagree: i.e., Regarding The Authorship and the date of writing, I will not present the arguments in this book. I will defer to the textbook I wrote for Global University on Daniel and Revelation in 1987 for that. Based on all my reading of early church writers and others, Internal evidence in the book itself, and secular history, I am thoroughly convinced the Author of the Book of Revelation is John the Apostle of Jesus, and the date was during the reign of Domitian between AD 91 and 96

I prefer to use italics rather than quotation marks, and I will not always give specific chapter and verse references to well known Scriptures. Most Bible quotes are from KJ, NASB, and my own translations. Frequently a mixture of which one I feel is best, plus my own wording which is based on my 60 years of studying the Greek and Hebrew Texts. I will reference other versions such as the NIV, ESV, NLT. Frequently, when people asked me, *What version of the Bible do you quote when you are preaching?* I would answer, *The Westlake James Version.* I will not use verse numbers in the discussion if the Chapter title is a Chapter number of Revelation. All verses in that chapter will be from that chapter unless otherwise indicated.

It is my prayer as you read this different presentation of the Book of Revelation, you will have a increased awareness of the greatness and majesty of Jesus Christ, a renewed passion that all may come into a relationship with Jesus Christ as Lord and Savior and a fresh understanding of the future. Please Read Revelation through at a Single sitting (all 22 Chapters without a break 4 or 5 times before using this book). Please read in either the King James, New King James, New American Standard, or English Standard Versions. Why? These are word for word translations. The newer versions are Dynamic Equivalents...meaning the translators put the thought of the verse in their own words, and sometimes the preconceived theological viewpoint of the translators shows up. They are all good to read, but not really for serious study. Read it like a newspaper, like a whole story. That is the best way to begin studying any book of the Bible. Then, do the same with Daniel.

George W. Westlake, Jr., DMin.

Dedication

First, to my wife Jean of over 59 years, and my coworker in God's ministry. She traveled all over the world in ministry with me.

She was everything a man would want in a wife and mother of their children. She loved God, her family—loved being a wife and mother, and the ministry of serving other people. I never heard her complain when we pastored very small churches and had little income. I never heard her complain about being a Pastor's wife. She received a phone call from a lady working on PhD and writing about the difficulties of being a pastor's wife. Jean's answer was, *I cant think of one.* She loved everything she did, especially praying for people. She loved teaching young ladies, playing the organ and the piano.

She met Jesus Christ when she was 5, was baptized in the Holy Spirit when she was 7, and knew she would be a pastor's wife when she was 10. As a teen ager she played the piano for her church in Akron, Ohio, and as a teacher of children she knew she should attend Central Bible College in Springfield, Missouri. But, for three years after High School, God told her to wait another year. Why? There was someone she had to meet who had been serving in the army .

When I went to Central Bible College, after the Korean War, I told the other guys, *I'm not even going to look at a girl until I am a Senior.* I had plenty of girl friends prior, and met a lovely Korean Christian girl, and thought maybe God will lead me back to her when I graduate.

I was preaching and playing the piano at Walnut Grove Assembly of God, and if you ever heard me play the piano you know we were desperate. I stood up in the Freshman Orientation Class and asked or a pianist. I got a note advising me she had been her church pianist since she was 13 and we could meet after class. I met her and thought *She is a silly kid* and she said she thought, *He is an old stuffed shirt.*

We were thrown together on Sundays, Wednesdays, and Saturdays when a group of us did street meetings around the area; She would play the accordion while a group of us sang, and I would usually preach. We frequently ate together as a group. One day I couldn't study. All I could think about was this 4 foot 10 in, bouncy girl who bubbled all the time and loved God so much. I finally got the courage to tell her, *I think I like you!* That was the understatement of the year. We were married that Spring and pastored the Assembly of God Church in Fristoe, Missouri, a town of 100. The church had 54 members. We drove back and forth to school 70 miles.

She had power in prayer as well as public ministry. God would give her a name to pray for and she would meet them later. We were in Australia and going to the Great Barrier Reef to swim and had to take a 2 hour boat trip to get there from Hamilton Island. We met an Australian couple who knew absolutely nothing about Christianity. So we had 2 hours to talk about it. He and I swam 3 or 4 hours, and the ladies talked. So on the way back I started to ask, *Do you want to receive Jesus Christ?* And the Holy Spirit told me, *Shut up!* I started to ask again an hour later and heard, *what part of shut up don't you understand George!* God wouldn't let me ask them. The lady wrote her name, including her middle initial, and address in Jean's bible

After we got home, three weeks later, God reminded Jean to check her diary. 10 months before meeting this couple she had written this lady's name down, including her middle initial, and prayed for her. And something she never did before, she looked at the clock and wrote down the time. We sent a letter to Australia. We received a phone call from the lady. *We have checked the exact time, and that's when I had a head on collision and was not expected to live.* As a result of that she and her husband became Christians. She was a published author and began writing Christian poetry. She would frequently call Jean and talk for 3 hours at a time.

I got a lot of attention on the platform of churches, but I sang to her at Sheffield Family Life Center on her 70th birthday, *You are the wind beneath my wings.* I could honestly tell her daily, *I love you forever* and mean it. I even have asked God, since He took her home, *I don't know if you do this but please remind her I love her forever.*

She touched so many lives, and truly our children are serving God because of their praying mother. So many people have told me how she influenced their lives to be what God wanted them to be. Even though the last few years of her life on earth, she was legally blind, had Alzheimer, and was diabetic, she came alive at church. I would lean over and say, *That's your son George preaching* She would say *I know it!* She would pray for people and they would get healed. The Sunday before God took her home there was a lady in service for the first time who had been told by 4 doctors she had cervical cancer. Her friend brought her down for Jean to pray for her. The next day the doctors could not find any cancer.

She may have been short in stature, but a giant spiritually. I am so grateful God gave her to our children, grand children, great grand children, to many people her whole life, and, especially to me.

To our four children, Linda, Debbie, Tina and George, who are all serving God in various ministries. If I never would have had any other blessings from God, having Linda and George as children and having all four as teen agers and young adults, and our family today, would have been blessing enough. Also to Kevin, Peter, Marcelo and Annett who God prepared for our children. Three strong Christian son in laws who are all involved serving God, Kevin as a leader in Men's ministry and other areas and who can fix anything that needs fixing, Peter who is a senior pastor, Marcelo a musician, and a beautiful diamond, Annette, who serves along side of George as the First Lady of Sheffield Family Life Center.

Then God gave us something special to love when he gave us grandchildren: Tabitha, Stephanie, Roger and his wife, Brooke, Chance, Laura, Thomas, Danielle, Bethany Geo (George IV) and his wife Amy, Sarah and her husband Alberto, Austin and His wife Lauren, Spencer, Blake, Alexis and Brooklyn; and wonderful great grandchildren, Payton, Wyatt, Layla Mae, Seylah, Milan, Miliyah, Luciana Jean, Jude (the only one with last name Westlake) and Natanya Jo

To Angel Burress, my adopted granddaughter, whom we have known since she was 4 years old. She moved into our house to take care of Jean the last five years of Jeans life. She took care of her with such love, patience and understanding. Without her I would not have been free to travel the world and teach. I could leave knowing Jean was in good hands. Many people commented on how well Angel took care of Jean.

Acknowledgments

First, to God who transformed my life when I was 19, called me by His grace and gift into the ministry, which I have loved every part of all these years. He gave me a fantastic wife and children, and has supplied every need over the past 68 years.. As I have mentioned in sermons, we pastored some small churches, with so little income, we had to pray socks in for our children, but they never did without socks, and everything else they needed. His Grace has sustained me during difficult times and great times. I thank Him for His Amazing Grace to our family and to me.

To the congregation, staff, board and pastors of Sheffield Family Life center who have allowed me to serve this congregation for 46 years, 33 as Senior Pastor and the last 13 as Pastor Emeritus, and who support my ministry around the world teaching in Bible Colleges and Seminaries.

Pastor Orie Robinson, Pastor of Revival Tabernacle in Detroit, who led me to the Lord when I was 19, and had so much patience with me since I became extremely legalistic. There were 3 of us, one 20, the other 21, and myself, who became the *Spiritual Three of the Youth Group, (Youth groups in that day went as high as age 35)* and were quick to condemn the rest of the group for even playing baseball. We felt everything we used to do had to be classified as *worldly*. People in the church asked Pastor Robinson what he was going to do with me. He told them, *He is spending so much time in the word, he will get straightened out.* I was asked to preach to the youth one Friday, and my Sermon was *not all who say Lord Lord will enter the Kingdom of heaven, but he who is doing the will of my father. You're not, we 3 are.* As soon as I finished my 20 pages of notes, that took about 7 minutes, I knew I was wrong. I went into the prayer room in the farthest corner, heard someone coming and took a peek, and it was Pastor Robinson. I knew he was going to really chew me out. He came along side, put his arm around me and said, *We have to preach it straight sometimes, don't we!* He became the example of what I wanted to be in the ministry. As Albers Switzer said, *Example is not the main thing in influencing people it is the only thing.*

At 20 I was drafted into the Army during the Korean War, started preaching in Korea, but got involved with a lot of Christians who were anti-education. So, when I went to Bible College I was skeptical about what I could learn there since, *I knew it all!* The first day in chapel Dr. Stanley Horton preached, and I thought *wow and He is highly educated, what a great sermon!* The next day I sat in his class and found out *I really don't know anything about God's word.* I still don't. It's a living word, and today I am a day older so it speaks to me as a day older. It is always new!

Pastor Albert Pyle who pastored Eastside Assembly of God in Springfield while I was attending Central Bible College. He was a example of what a pastor should be. I became his unofficial assistant as I was with him while he was fulfilling pastor duties. He invited me to preach my first Revival anywhere in his church, and was a constant encourager, advisor and friend.

I want to acknowledge all of the Professors at Central Bible College, and Fuller Theological Seminary who challenged my thinking and taught so well, and Dr. Julius Mantey, co author of the second year Greek textbook, *A Manual Grammar of the Greek New Testament*, and professor of Greek at Northern Baptist Seminary. I never met him but after 3 years of Greek at undergraduate level, and 1 year at Graduate level, I wanted more, so I took courses from him by correspondence. He not only challenged my thinking in many areas, but emphasized translating the Greek text as it is accurately even if it disagrees with our theological assumptions.

Dr. Stanley M. Horton, the most brilliant man I ever met, became a mentor and friend. I had the privilege, among other classes he taught, to take Hebrew. The second year there were only four of us who took it, and the third year I was the only one taking it. I served as his teaching assistant grading Hebrew papers and teaching his first year and second year classes when he had to be out of the City at times. He challenged me not to accept everything I heard, but to closely examine Scripture. He was my Faculty Advisor on my Master's Thesis. For many years after I graduated he was always available by phone or e mail to discuss areas of the original languages I was questioning, and about theological issues. He ministered in every church I have pastored since 1960 when he came to Bad Axe, Michigan and taught a course on Science and The Bible for the whole community. He came to our Bible College, Sheffield School of the Bible, in Kansas City, Missouri and taught Isaiah, and preached at Sheffield on Sunday Morning, when he was in his 90's. His Home Going Celebration Service, and My wife, Jean's were the same day in 2014. In 1987, he was teaching in Singapore and was asked if he knew anyone else with a doctorate they should invite to teach. He recommended me, and as a result I have traveled all over Asia and The South Pacific for the past 30 years teaching and preaching.

Dr. Donald Johns Sr. I sat in his Gospels class as a freshman like a little bird with an open mouth. I had never heard such teaching. He was professor of Philosophy also, and I took a minor in Philosophy just to be in his classes. Not only could he keep you on the edge of your chair while he was teaching, he taught us to examine the writings of the philosophers, such as Plato, Aristotle, etc., and discover their basic assumptions on which their philosopher were based. As a result, I have been able to quickly discover the basic assumptions of Christian writers and teachers. He challenged my theology in many places. In addition, while I was in College my heart was acting strange. The specialist told me he knew there was something wrong, but was having trouble knowing exactly what. In Brother Johns class I had an attack: Pain shooting down both arms and my chest, couldn't breath. Brother Johns walked over, touched me and simply said, *God in Jesus Name heal him.* Pain was gone instantly and I could breath. Have never had heart problems since. According to my Doctor, my heart is still great at 87.

Dr. Robert Cooley. He taught a course called, *Creative Bible Teaching,* during my first Master's study. He totally revolutionized my bible study methods to the point the method is automatic with me even today. After he became President of Gordon Conwell Seminary, I was being led by God's Spirit to get a Doctorate. I couldn't decide whether to attend were he was president or Fuller Theological Seminary. His advice was, *George, Gordon Conwell is more academic, and Fuller is more practical. You don't need the academics.* Following his advice I went to Fuller. The courses there were exactly what I needed as a pastor.

40 years after taking the course mentioned above, I was asked to teach it in Malaysia. My notes from that course had been burned in the trash can with a stack of magazines by mistake. I called him, and he had just taught it again, and not only sent me his outline for the course, he sent back my papers I had written for the course 40 years earlier.

Dr. Ray Anderson. He was my adviser while working on my Doctorate. He challenged my thinking also as I sat in his classes and read his books. One of the greatest thinkers of our time, and I have recommended his book, *The Soul of Ministry* every place I have taught since.

Dr. Gary Seevers, President of Global University, and others responsible , for releasing the copyright of the material in the textbook I wrote for them in 1987 On Daniel and Revelation. They have to have the copyright on materials written because they are in so many countries and have to edit it to meet requirements in that culture. It was a thrill for me many times to go to a country, such as Samoa, and have the professor tell me they were using my book to teach.

Pat Marvenko Smith, who has allowed me to use her magnificent drawings of Revelation in my Power Point Presentation teaching seminary classes and churches throughout Asia, Europe and Latin America, as well as at home; and my favorite ever, the cover picture of this book.

C. M. Ward, The International Revivaltime Radio speaker who was on stations all over the world. I have still seen signs in other countries on churches saying, *A Revivaltime Church.* I had heard you had to have a big church to have him come and preach. I was pastoring the First Assembly of God in Kennett Missouri in 1963. We had the largest church building in the city and a congregation at that time of a little over 100. Brother Ward came for an area wide Youth Conference so our building was used. After service I asked him, *Brother Ward, how big does a church have to be for you to come and peach* He responded, *If its big enough for you to put your life into, its big enough for me to preach in.* I was privileged to have him speak for a week in every church I pastored on into the 1980s. He was truly a mentor. Eating meals with him was equal to several years of education in practical ministry. When I was pastoring at Cape Girardeau Missouri, in my late thirties, He said to me one day, *God is getting you prepared for the most important ministry of your life in your early forties.* I came to Sheffield when I was 41. I have always remembered his statement, *if its big enough for you to put your life in, its big enough for me to preach in.* I never ask the size of a church when I'm invited by a pastor to preach and never put a price on my ministry.

There have been so many pastor friends who have influenced my life, I could go on and on; like the Presbyterian Pastor who became a mentor to me while I was only 29 pastoring in Bad Axe, Michigan; and church members who have been encouragers and helpers down through the years, such as the ladies who helped take care of my wife her last years so I could travel and teach around the world.

And a great THANK YOU to my oldest granddaughter, Tabitha Horne, who found time in her busy schedule to edit this manuscript, and make many of he charts; and My oldest daughter Linda for helping with chart making.

The Name of the Book and Basic Information

Names of the books of the Bible are important. For example, , In our English bibles it is called *Genesis*, a word that comes from the Greek language and means *generations*. The phrase *these are the generations of* occurs over and over in the book and actually marks divisions in its outline. In Hebrew, the language in which the book was originally written, the name of the book is *Bereshith*, and means *in the beginning*. This phrase is used in the first sentence of the book. The name of the final book of the Bible is also found in its first sentence.

The word *revelation* is a translation of the Greek noun *apokalupsis*, which means *that which is unveiled*. The verb form *apokalupto, to unveil*, is also found in the Greek New Testament. These words are used in various Scripture passages to express two main ideas. First, they refer to God's action of revealing things to our understanding. Second, they refer to the visible appearing of Jesus Christ. A third usage can also be seen in1 Pet 1:13, *Therefore gird up (prepare) the loins of your mind, be sober (well balanced...thinking correctly) hope (a command) on the basis of the grace that is <u>continuously</u> being brought to you by (the) revelation of Jesus Christ*. The truth expressed is that there is a constant unveiling of Jesus Christ to us as we walk with Him. We meet Him as Savior, then gradually as strengthener, provider, friend, miracle worker, healer, etc. etc. It is a lifetime of knowing Him better and with more understanding.

The second main idea, the visible appearing of Jesus Christ, is the theme of the book of Revelation. This theme is sounded like a trumpet in chapter 1, verse 7:

BEHOLD, HE IS COMING WITH THE CLOUDS, AND EVERY EYE WILL SEE HIM, EVEN THOSE WHO PIERCED HIM, AND ALL TRIBES OF THE EARTH WILL WAIL ON ACCOUNT OF HIM. EVEN SO. AMEN.

The Primary Subject

As you may have noticed, the title of the book of Revelation is not simply *The Revelation*; rather, it is from the first verse, *The Revelation of Jesus Christ*. So it is an unveiling, a making manifest, a revealing of a *person*, Jesus Christ.

It is important to understand that the Bible is a book about Jesus Christ? From the *In the beginning* of Genesis until the final *Amen* of Revelation, there is one majestic figure who walks on every page of God's book, and that is God's Son. On the road to Emmaus (Lk 24:13ff) He spoke to two individuals and *beginning at Moses and all the Prophets, He expounded to them in all the scriptures the things concerning Himself*. He is the subject and the object of it all. Moreover, in its final chapters, He is seen in the fullness of His person, position, and accomplishments—past, present, and (most of all) future. In the book of Revelation, Jesus Christ is active. He *speaks, moves, conquers, judges,* and *rules.* He *commands* John to copy His dictation and to send it to the seven churches. He *commands* John to *Come up here* He *takes* the seven-sealed book out of his Father's hand. He *opens* the book. He *stands* on Mt. Zion with converted Israel. He *reaps* the harvest of the earth, *rides* on a white horse, *tramples* the winepress of the wrath of God, and *rules* throughout eternity.

The book of Revelation is not only a revelation of Jesus Christ, but also the revelation from Him to His servants of the series of events that will take place to complete the plan of God.

THE MEANINGS OF THE WORD ANGEL

In the Old Testament, the Hebrew word, **malak,** is used to describe *any kind of a messenger, human, or angelic.* The last book of the Bible **is Malachi** , which means *My Messenger.* In the New Testament the Greek word, **anggelos,** is the same; it can refer to any kind of *Messenger.*

Obviously, in many, many places it is referring to an *Angel.* But many times to a *Human Messenger*: Some examples include: Mt 11:10, Mk 1:2, Lk 7:27 regarding John the Baptist; Lk 7:24 *Messengers* sent from John The Baptist to Jesus; 9:52, about *Messengers* Jesus sent ahead to Jerusalem; II Cor 12:7 *Messenger* of Satan; Ja 2:25 The *Messengers* (spies) connected with Rahab; and in Rev 17:1 an *Angel* begins speaking with John and in 19:10 John tries to worship the *Angel* and the *Angel* says to him, *see that you do not do that! I am your fellow servant and of your brothers who have the testimony of Jesus. Worship God!*

It is unfortunate that this word is translated always as **Angel** in Revelation. Remember the importance of context in determining the meaning of the word. In Revelation the context clearly indicates frequently John is giving a picture of Jesus as will be indicated throughout this study. In Revelation Jesus is seen as: **THE**

Judge of His Church	**Ruler of the Kings of Earth**
Alpha and Omega	**Son of Man**
First and the Last	**Living One**
Amen	**Owner of The Earth and Sea**
Beginning and the End	**Wielder of The Harvest Sickle**
Firstborn from the Dead	**Son, Male of Israel**
Owner of the Keys of Hades and Death	**Trampler of The Winepress of**
Faithful and True Witness	**The Wrath of God**

Lion of the Tribe of Judah	Rider on The White Horse
Root of David	King of Kings
Lamb	Lord of Lords
High Priest	Morning Star
Possessor of the Seal of God	Light of Eternity

AND THE PRIMARY PICTURE OF JESUS IN REVELATION IS...,,,,,,,,,,,,,,,,,,,,
THE *GO'EL-OUR NEAREST RELATIVE-OUR KINSMAN/REDEEMER*

REVELATION 1:19
JESUS HIMSELF GIVES THE OUTLINE OF THE BOOK OF REVELATION IN

I.   The Prologue, (Introduction), 1:1–8

WRITE:

II.   Things You Have Seen, 1:9–20 (The Vision of Christ)

III.   Things Which Are, 2:1–3:22 (The Messages to the Churches)

IV.   Things Which Will Take Place After These Things (*Gk: Meta Tauta*) 4:1–22:6

    A.   The Church in Glory, 4:1–5:14

    B.   The Great Tribulation, 6:1–19:21

    C.   The Millennium, 20:1–6

    D.   Gog and Magog, 20:7–10

    E.   The Great White Throne, 20:11–15

    F.   All Things New, 21:1–22:6

V.   The Postscript, 22:7–21 (Be Ready)

SPECIAL FEATURES OF ITS FORM

As you know, the Bible contains writings on many different subjects and in many different forms. For example, it contains the psalms of David, the proverbs of Solomon, the prophecies of Isaiah, and the letters of Paul. Some of the prophetic writings in the Bible are given in a form called *apocalyptic*, a style that has several distinctive features. Even though Four books of the Bible that are considered to be especially apocalyptic in form, the prophecies of Daniel, Ezekiel, Zechariah, and Revelation; all prophetical writings in the Bible use some apocalyptic style writing.

The following paragraph presents the three main features of the apocalyptic style found in the biblical books, along with examples from the book of Revelation:

1. *In the apocalyptic writings, signs and symbols are used to convey spiritual truth.* For example, notice the expression *made it known*, which occurs in Revelation 1:1. This is a translation of a Greek word which literally means *to signify, to show with signs.* Signs and symbols are used throughout the book. John states *I saw* over sixty times (see 1:12 and 14:6 for examples). He states twenty-eight times *I heard* (see 5:11 and 12:10 for examples). In addition, he specifically indicates that he was *shown* something (see 4:1; 17:1; 21:9–10; and 22:1 for examples).

REVELATION IS A PICTURE BOOK

2. *The apocalyptic writings show future victory for the forces of God against the forces of Satan.* See, for example, the victory over Satan that is presented in 12:7–12 and 20:7–10.

3. *In apocalyptic writings, angelic beings intervene to explain events.* This is illustrated by the appearance of the angel in 10:9–11 and 17:15–18.

The apocalyptic style was also used by non-biblical writers. Though their writings resemble those of the biblical books in some ways, there are some important differences. For example, non-biblical apocalyptic books contain an extremely pessimistic view of the life of the godly. By contrast, the biblical writers are optimistic. They show that although the godly suffer persecution, God blesses His people with peace and joy in the midst of tests and trials of faith. They have a relationship with Him that nothing can destroy.

PRINCIPLES FOR INTERPRETING ITS MEANING

There are five important principles to follow when one interprets the prophetic message of the book of Revelation. We have listed them below.

Principle Number 1: Let the Scriptures interpret themselves. In Revelation John recorded the pictures and scenes which he saw, and it is our task to interpret these signs based on the teachings of the rest of the Word of God.

Three things to remember when we interpret these signs are these:

(1) THE BIBLE IS ITS OWN BEST INTERPRETER,

(2) WHEN THE OBVIOUS SENSE MAKES THE BEST SENSE, ANY OTHER SENSE IS NONSENSE.

(3) A TEXT WITHOUT A CONTEXT IS A PRETEXT AND IT BECOMES A PROOFTEXT.

Cults pull Scriptures out of their context and make them say what they do not say. A Scripture means what it means in that sentence, in that paragraph, in that chapter and that book, and it must agree with the teaching of the rest of the Bible.

Well meaning Christians sometimes do the same thing. If, for example, Someone from a different country who knows little English goes to a Zoo and tells his American English speaking friend, friend, *I want to see an elephant with a Big Nose.* The American replies, *in English it's a trunk not a nose.* Later they are walking through the Zoo and the Foreigner hears two men talking, *I just bought a new car and it has the biggest trunk I've ever seen.* He calls his wife on the phone and says, *These Americans sure are strange. They drive cars with big elephant noses on them, can't wait to see one.* What some people do with scripture is equal to that.

THE CONTEXT OF THE BOOK OF REVELATION IS THE WHOLE BIBLE. EVERY SYMBOL IN THE BOOK OF REVELATION IS EXPLAINED SOMEWHERE IN THE WORD OF GOD.

Principle Number 2: *Apply the rule of prophetic perspective*. One of the best examples of this passage is to compare Is 61:1-2 with Lk 4:16-21.

The Spirit of the Lord God is upon me, Because the Lord has anointed me To bring good News to the afflicted. He has sent me to bind up the brokenhearted, To proclaim liberty to captives and freedom to prisoners; To proclaim the favorable year of the Lord and the day of vengeance of our God, To comfort all who mourn. (NASB)

In The Synagogue in Capernaum, Jesus quoted this passage and *stopped reading* after the phrase **the favorable year of the Lord** He then goes on to say, **this day is this scripture fulfilled in your ears**. He stopped reading in the middle of a sentence because the **day of vengeance of our God** <u>was still future then and it is still future today.</u> That is what the Book of Revelation is all about. **There has been over 2,000 years pass in the middle of a sentence. .** In the day Jesus read that there was hardly ever punctuation between verses, and the few that did have punctuation had it after *The Day of Vengeance of our God.*

The rule of prophetic perspective teaches us that **THE PROPHETS SAW THE EVENTS BUT RARELY THE TIME GAPS IN BETWEEN.** Look at Is 9:6ff:

For unto us a Child is born, Unto us a Son is given; And the government will be upon His shoulder. And His name will be called Wonderful, Counselor, Mighty God, Everlasting Father, Prince of Peace. Of the increase of His government and peace There will be no end, Upon the throne of David and over His kingdom, To order it and establish it with judgment and justice From that time forward, even forever. The zeal of the Lord of hosts will perform this. **He has been born, but the throne is still future.** Peter, preaching on the Day of Pentecost quoting Joel 2:28ff says:

And it shall come to pass afterward, that I will pour out my spirit upon all flesh; and your sons and your daughters shall prophesy, your old men shall dream dreams, your young men shall see visions And also upon the servants and upon the handmaids in those days will I pour out my spirit. **this all happened on Pentecost, but the next phrases are still future......** *And I will show wonders in the heavens and in the earth, blood, and fire, and pillars of smoke. The sun shall be turned into darkness, and the moon into blood, before the great and the terrible day of the Lord comes.*

There is no Scripture that states the Messiah will come to earth, die, go back to heaven, and after a couple thousand years or so come back to rule. However, both events are in Scripture even though Scripture does not specify how much time is involved between the two events.

The only place we find time given in these prophetical books are Dan, chapters 7, 8, 9 and 12, and Rev 11, 12, 13, which will be discussed later.

Principle Number 3: Recognize the possibility of double fulfillment of prophecy. The prophets whose messages are recorded in the Old Testament were primarily preachers to their own generation, not foretellers of the future. They warned the people of their day about an impending Day of the Lord that would shortly come as a judgment for sin and idolatry. Yet their messages often point beyond what happened in their own time and forward to the great Day of the Lord that is described in the book of Revelation. For example, the prophet Joel mentions the Day of the Lord (Joel 1:15; 2:1–2, 11, 31). In Joel's day, judgments certainly were coming upon Judah in the near future; however, there is a final Day of the Lord yet to come, the one pictured in Revelation 19. Thus, Joel's prophecy will have a double fulfillment. An example, which will be discussed later in this book is found in Dan 9:27, 11:31 and Mat 24:15. Both passages in Daniel refer to the same event which took place in the past, and Jesus, in Matthew 24, 200 years later, refers to the same event as being in the future. The Holy Spirit, as the Author of the Bible, can intend for a scripture to have a double fulfillment and, at times, give it a totally different meaning in the New Testament. That does not give us the right to make a something a double fulfillment, or to apply a different meaning to Scripture that has not been done in Scripture itself, by the Holy Spirit.

Principle Number 4: Understand the use of signs and symbols. Many signs and symbols such as animals, colors, numbers, and objects appear throughout the book of Revelation. They are used to express certain meanings. According to J. B. Smith, there are forty-six symbols the book itself interprets. Other important symbols are explained elsewhere in Scripture. The symbols most commonly used in Revelation are given below with the meanings expressed through them.

NUMBERS

One	God
Two	Confirmation
Three	Trinity
Four	Earth
Six	Man, Evil
Seven	Divine Fullness/Completeness (occurs 54 times)
Ten	Political Completion
Twelve	Final Completion/Fullness

COLORS

White	Purity, Ancientness
Pale (Chlorine Color)	Death
Red	Bloodshed, War
Purple	Imperial Luxury
Emerald Green	Rest, Refreshment
Black	Calamity, Distress

ANIMALS

Lion	Jesus
Lamb	Jesus
Horses	Military Might
Wild Beasts	Antichrist and False Prophet
Frogs	Demons

Principle number 5: *Understand the use of parenthetical enlargements.*

In writing, a *parenthetical enlargement* is a close-up view, a fuller description, of one part of a subject that has already been mentioned. For example, one may view an entire town from a distance and receive an overall view. Then he may walk up close to one individual house and notice its details. The close-up view of the house is like a parenthetical enlargement. They are used throughout the Bible, and there are several in Revelation.

There is a good example of a ***parenthetical enlargement*** in the account of Creation in Gen 1 and 2. In chapter 1, all six days of Creation are presented, including the creation of man and woman, given in verses 26–30. Then God, in chapter 2:1-3, rested on the seventh day-the rest of a completed task. Then in verses 4–25, there is a longer, more detailed description of one event of day six: the creation of man and woman.

An important note: God is called in Gen 1 simply *Elohim, God!* In Gen 2 He is called *YHWH-Elohim.* The powerful creator God of Genesis one is, in fact, the personal, covenant keeping God, *YHWH.*

There is a false teaching, that God created men and women prior to Adam and Eve. The first ones were created in Genesis one, then Adam and Eve after a destruction of the earth. But Genesis 5:1 states: ***This is the book of the generations of Adam. In the day that God created man, in the likeness of God made he him; Male and female created he them; and blessed them, and called their name Adam, in the day when they were created.* (KJV) THIS MAKES IT VERY OBVIOUS AND CONFIRMS THAT ADAM AND EVE WERE THE FIRST HUMANS CREATED, AND THEREFORE BOTH DESCRIPTIONS , GENESIS ONE AND TWO, ARE OF THE SAME PERSONS.** In addition, this other theory translates Genesis 1:2 the earth *became* shapeless and uninhabitable, claiming the same word means *was* or *became.* However it's the verb *to be.* But like English, when the verb *to be* means *was* its spelled *was,* when it means *became* its spelled *became.* The word translated *became* is different than the Hebrew word *was.* The word here is **hayah**, *was*; *became* is **yehaye**, or **haya le**. The Septuagint, The Greek Old Testament, translated by Hebrew Scholars, translates the verb into Greek as **en**, *was*, not **egeneto**, *became.* I had taught Genesis one in our College, and pointed all this out. The following week we had a Hebrew teacher from Israel in our class as guest of our Jewish Outreach Leader. He did not know what I had taught the class, and I asked him publicly, *Youse, is there any way possible to translate the form of hayah in Genesis one as became?* His reply, *Of Course Not!*

A second example is Gen 10:25 states that *in the days of Peleg the earth was divided*, and the narrative continues with no reason given. Then Ch 11 is a **parenthetical enlargement** which explains why: *The Tower of Babel!*

The book of Revelation is presented in the same way. John gives a narrative in proper order. Then he enlarges on important subjects that he has already mentioned. To interpret the book of Revelation accurately, it is important to place these parenthetical enlargements properly. With one exception, Ch 14, the parenthetical enlargements give additional details of events already stated. Ch 14, however, looks forward or anticipates major events that are to follow. . Many books this author has read have difficulty with chapter 14, as did I, until one day the Holy Spirit spoke to me, *Why do parenthetical Enlargements have to only discuss the past, why not the future?*

PARENTHETICAL ENLARGEMENTS OF THE BOOK OF REVELATION.

CHAPTER 7 . . . . . .The 144,000 of Israel and The White-Robed Multitude

CHAPTER 10 . . . . .The Mighty Angel with The Scroll

CHAPTER 11:1-14 . .The Two Witnesses

CHAPTER 12 . . . . .The Woman, Her Son and The Dragon

CHAPTER 13 . . . . .The Two Wild Beasts

CHAPTER 14 . . . . .The 144,000 of Israel again, The Final Preaching of the Gospel
                    The Announcement, Babylon Has Fallen, Babylon Has Fallen
                    The Final Harvest, The Winepress of The Wrath of God

CHAPTER 17 . . . . . .The Two Wild Beasts and The Great Prostitute

CHAPTER 18 . . . . .Babylon, emphasizing especially Commercial Babylon

CHAPTER 1
The Things Which You Have Seen

The Revelation of Jesus Christ, which God gave unto him, to show unto his servants things which must soon (or suddenly) come to pass; and he sent and signified it by his angel unto his servant John:

The first verse makes known to us that God is the source of the truth contained in the book. It also shows us the purpose of proclaiming that truth in this book. It shows that Jesus has the authority to reveal, but also to accomplish and control the events that take place in this book. And He has sent his Angel/Messenger to John, to *signify/show with pictures*, these *things which are going to take place* to fulfill the truth that is prophesied throughout Scripture.

It is impossible for people who are not servants of God to understand the book of Revelation. It is foolishness to them just as *the word of the cross is folly to those who are perishing*"(1 Co 1:18). To those of us who are God's servants, however, Revelation is a great book of victory and rejoicing in Jesus Christ our Lord!

The opening phrase reveals not only the nature and purpose of the book but also the character of Christ's coming. The Greek phrase translated *soon* in this verse is **en tachei**. This phrase is translated *speedily* in Lk 18:8 and the NLT gives an alternate as *suddenly* which fits the context of the paragraph better. It is translated *soon* in Rom 16:20, and In 22:7 Jesus is translated as saying *behold I come quickly. Soon* in 1:1 would refer to God's time—not ours. God's timing is not the same as ours. II Pet 3:8 teaches that God views everything as *now*, as *in the present, He has foreknowledge.* The word *must* **(dei)** *in* 1:1 has led many scholars, who hold different views of Revelation, to believe the term **en tachei** indicates *certainty of fulfillment*, and **en tachei** is used to mean *imminent*, which indicates the possibility these events taking place at any time. Jesus, Paul and Peter indicate, they will come **as a thief in the night (not knowing when)**; thus the **en tachei** in the context of Revelation primarily means *suddenly*; therefore, it does not mean that *the things that must soon (suddenly) take place* had to occur immediately after Revelation was written. **It is obvious Jesus has not come yet.** Although the primary emphasis of Revelation is Jesus returning as King of Kings and Lord of Lords, the book contains a series of events, beginning suddenly in 4:1 which will climax in that Great Event and the things which follow presenting God's Plan for Eternity. **So the use of it here is that once these events begin suddenly, without warning, there will be no delay in them as they happen quickly, even the Millennium and following, Showing clearly it's a reference to God's time, not ours. to close CHAPTER 66.**

SEVEN BEATITUDES OF REVELATION

The best-known beatitudes are found in Mat 5:1–12. It is the first of The Seven Beatitudes . The other six are found in 14:13, 16:15, 19:9, 20:6, 22:7, and 22:14.

Observe especially the nature of this first beatitude. First, a blessing is pronounced on the one who *reads* this prophetic book. Second, and most important, the blessings are promised to those who hear and *apply* what is written. The Bible is not given to fill our heads with knowledge, but to teach us how to live day by day. That this prophetic word is important to believers is seen in the blessings promised to those who receive and apply its message to their Christian experience.

John begins with two commonly used New Testament greetings: *grace* and *peace.* We who are Christians are aware that a person must experience God's grace before he or she has real peace. Grace and Peace are given from Him *Who Is and Who Was and Who is coming*; (The last phrase is not the verb, *to be.* It is a verb of motion. *He is coming!) and from the seven Spirits which are before his throne.* There are two opinions regarding the identity of the *seven spirits* First, since angels are called *ministering spirits* in He 1:14, some believe these seven spirits are angels. Some Jewish traditions indicate seven angels stand in the presence of God. Lk 1:19 refers to Gabriel *who stands in the presence of God.* Some traditions hold that the *angels of the presence* are *archangels.* But only one angel is called an *archangel* in the Word of God (1 The 4:16; Jude 9). But why would angels be squeezed in between the Father and the Son? The New Living Translation says, *The sevenfold Spirit.* My contention, along with many others, is that seven spirits symbolize the fullness of the ministry of the Holy Spirit. Is 11:2-3 speaks of the sevenfold ministry of the Holy Spirit which would rest upon the coming Messiah, The Branch (Hebrew **netzer**); Jesus was from Nazareth..*Branch.* In Zech 4. He sees the 7 fold candlestick and is told it means, *It is not by might, nor by power, but by My Spirit says The Lord of Hosts. And from Jesus Christ,*

Notice the three descriptions of Jesus:

1. *He is the faithful witness.* A witness is one who gives evidence, one who testifies for a cause, one who has personal knowledge of something, one who gives public affirmation by word or example. How can we understand God? As we behold Christ, hear His words, and witness His compassion, we see God (Jn 14:9). How can we know God's power? We know it by seeing Jesus as He heals the sick, raises the dead, and cleanses lepers. How can we know God's patience? We witness patience as we see Jesus in His longsuffering with His disciples. How can we know God's love? God's love is revealed in Jesus as He reaches out to every needy person and as He says, *Father, forgive them, for they know not what they do* (Lk 23:34). Thus Jesus is the perfect witness; He presents the character and attributes of God faithfully to His people.

Now, notice what Acts 1:8 indicates that the coming of the Holy Spirit on believers would cause them to *receive* and *be.* They were to be baptized in the Holy Spirit, and the Spirit's indwelling presence would dramatically change their lives. Disciples of Christ would *receive power* to *be* witnesses for their Lord. The emphasis here is on what believers *are* rather than on what they *do,* for what believers *do* results from what they *are.* Just as people look at Jesus and see the Father, we are to be so filled with the Holy Spirit that people will see Jesus Christ in our lives and want to know Him as their Savior.

2. *Jesus is the firstborn from the dead.* Firstborn does not mean Jesus was created at some point in time, because God the Son has always existed (Jn 1:1–3, 14). The term *firstborn* is clarified in Col 1:14-19 as *Preeminent.* (see Appendix A). He is over everything. Jacob made Joseph, his eleventh son, *Firstborn.* (I Ch 5:1-2) The Nation of Israel is called *Firstborn.* (Ex 4:22)

3. *Jesus is the ruler of the kings of the earth.* He is in absolute control. Satan temporarily appears to be in control, but the book of Revelation shows who is really in charge. We observe several important things. First, we see our Lord's attitude toward us: *He loves us.* Second, we note this love is active; *He loosed us out of our sins* (Rom, chapters 6,7,8) *by His own Blood.* Third, as a result of His redemptive love, *He has elevated us from the status of alien sinners to occupy the role of citizens of His kingdom and priests of God.* Thus **every believer is a priest** and has access to God through Jesus Christ and no other mediators are needed (Heb 4:14–16). In the New Testament, there is no separate office of a Priest in the body of Christ.

This paragraph ends with the first exclamation of praise to God in the Book of Revelation. To Him be Glory and Power (Dominion, Authority) into the ages of the ages (forever and ever)

The theme of the book is now sounded,

BEHOLD) HE IS COMING WITH THE CLOUDS, AND EVERY EYE WILL SEE HIM, EVEN THOSE WHO PIERCED HIM, AND ALL TRIBES OF THE EARTH WILL WAIL ON ACCOUNT OF HIM. EVEN SO. AMEN.

John consistently uses three different words for see. All three are use in Jn 20:1-8: Mary came to the tomb and *saw **Blepo** (See with the eyes.)* it was empty. She ran and told Peter and John. John comes first to the tomb and stooping down *saw **Blepo*** a number of things. Peter goes in and *saw **Theoreo*** (Sees with questions, theorizing). John goes in and *saw **horoo*** (Sees with understanding) and believes.

People see Jesus different ways today. Some as a good man, some as a deceiver, some as a prophet, but in that day The Word of God states: ***every eye will horoo him, (see with under-standing).*** That is **When every knee shall bow, and every tongue shall confess that Jesus Christ is Lord** (future tense of **horoo is opseomai**) (I Jn 3:2 indicates *We will be like Him when we see **(horoo)** Him as He is.*) Actually the word translated, *Behold*, in verse 7 is the command to see with understanding. We have some understanding now, but day by day, as stated earlier, He reveals himself to us. We need to be continually spending time in His Presence so He can transform us into His image, and teach us more about Himself, and enable us to be the proof to others that he is alive, and He loves them.

As Paul states, *We, with unveiled face,* (contrasting Moses who put a veil over his face) *reflecting the glory of the Lord as in a mirror are being changed into the same image from glory into glory.* (II Cor 3:18) The construction of the sentence means we are looking at his face in such a way that people looking at us see His glory reflected in us.

God refers to himself as *the Alpha and the Omega*. This figure of speech is like saying *the A and the Z* in English, because *alpha* and *omega* are the first and last letters of the Greek alphabet. Two further references to God as *the Alpha and the Omega* also contain the phrase: *the Beginning and the End* (21:6; 22:13). The Triune God is *the First and the Last* (21:6). Both the Father and the Son are referred to in Revelation as the *Alpha and the Omega*, and in Hebrews the same quality (eternal) is attributed to the Spirit (Heb 9:14). 22:13 refers more directly than do the other two verses to Jesus Christ as the *Alpha and the Omega*. God the Father created all things through His Son Jesus Christ (John 1:1–4, 10; Col 1:15–18; Heb 1:1–4).

John tells us where he was and why he was there. He indicates that he is *on the island called Patmos on account of the word of God and the testimony of Jesus.* The fact that he identifies himself as a *brother and partner in suffering* refers to him being banished to this island because of his faith.

Tradition tells us the Roman emperor Domitian had tried to cook John in boiling oil, but John would not cook. Therefore, the emperor banished John to the island prison of Patmos. Moreover, the manner in which John discusses suffering indicates this was a natural or common consequence of being a faithful witness of Jesus. The following Scripture passages indicate that suffering for the cause of Christ is normal and to be expected: Heb 10:32–39; 11:35–38; 12:4–7; Jam 5:10; 1 Pet 1:6–7; 4:12–19; 5:8–10.

In spite of his isolation on the island, John declares he was in the spirit (the Greek text says clearly that he *became in the Spirit on the Lord's Day*). Though physically barred from the crowds, his spirit was free to soar into the presence of God. Moreover, this occurred on the *Lord's Day*.

What does the phrase *the Lord's Day* mean in Revelation? Some people believe John was transported into the future and experienced the *Day of the Lord,* which is another name for the *Great Tribulation*. However, the Greek phrase translated the *Day of the Lord* (**he hemera tou kuriou**) differs from the phrase translated here as *The Lord's Day.* (**he kurioke hemera**) The latter Greek phrase refers to the first day of the week, Sunday. Thus, John's statement, indicates that it was on Sunday when *John became in the Spirit*. I am aware that there are well meaning Christians who believe a Christian must worship on the Jewish Sabbath Day, the 7th day, even claiming that a Pope changed Saturday to Sunday. There was no Pope until approximately AD 600, and records from the early church indicated they worshipped on resurrection day. In Acts 20, Paul was in Troas 7 days, and it is indicated that , *on the first day of the week when the disciples came together to break bread that Paul preached to them*. In addition, see the following quotes:

Ignatius, Bishop of Antioch in AD 110: *If, then, those who walk in the ancient practices attain to newness of hope, no longer observing the Sabbath, but fashioning their lives after the Lord's Day on which our life also arose through Him that we may be found disciples of Jesus Christ, our only teacher.*

Justin Martyr, AD100-165: *And on the day called Sunday, all who live in cities or in the country gather together in one place and memoirs of the apostles or the writings of the prophets are read as long as time permits. Sunday is the day on which we hold out common assembly because it is the first day on which God, having wrought a change in the darkness in matter, made the world. And Jesus Christ our Savior on the same day rose from the dead.*

Irenaeus, Bishop of Lyons wrote about AD 178: *The mystery of the Lord's resurrection may not be celebrated on any day other than the Lord's Day*

Others who made similar comments were, *The Epistle of Barnabas written between AD 120-150; Bardaisan, born AD 154; Cyprian, Bishop of Carthage, AD 200-258; Eusebius, about AD 315; Peter, Bishop of Alexandria, about AD 300.*

It is made clear in Romans 14 and 15 that it doesn't matter about which day. People used to call on the TV program I hosted, and ask, *Do we have to worship on the Jewish Sabbath, sundown Friday to sundown Saturday OR on The Lord's Day, Sunday?* My answer was *Yes!* A similar question was frequently asked, *Do we have to baptize in the Name of The Father, and The Son, and The Holy Spirit OR In Jesus' Name Only?* My answer was the same, *Yes!* I can give you all kinds of reasons why I baptize in the name of the three, **but we are not saved by what day we keep, or a baptismal formula, we are saved because we have received Jesus Christ as Lord and Savior and are following Him.**

If you want to keep Saturday, or Sunday, or Thursday.....keep it unto the Lord, but don't try to put your pet legalism on others. That is the teaching or Romans, Chapters 14-15. *Now accept the one who is weak in faith, but not for the purpose of passing judgment on his opinions. One person has faith that he may eat all things, but he who is weak eats vegetables only. The one who eats is not to regard with contempt the one who does not eat, and the one who does not eat is not to judge the one who eats, for God has accepted him. Who are you to judge the servant of another? To his own master he stands or falls; and he will stand, for the Lord is able to make him stand. **One person regards one day above another, another regards every day alike. Each person must be fully convinced in his own mind. He who observes the day, observes it for the Lord**, and he who eats, does so for the Lord, for he gives thanks to God; and he who eats not, for the Lord he does not eat, and gives thanks to God. .(14:1-7 NASB)*

The conclusion of the discussion by Paul concerning those who esteem certain days, and those who consider certain foods unclean, is to keep your conviction before God, but do not put condemnation on your brother or sister who may disagree. *Now may the God who gives perseverance and encouragement grant you to be of the same mind with one another according to Christ Jesus, so that with one accord you may with one voice glorify the God and Father of our Lord Jesus Christ. **Therefore, accept one another, just as Christ also accepted us to the glory of God.** (15:5-7 NASB)*

What do we do on the Lord's day when we go to church? Do we enter into the Spirit, or just go because it's the thing to do? Do we determine to truly worship God and draw near to Him? Because John became in the Spirit he heard the voice of the Lord, Saw His glory, and felt the hand of the Lord touch him. We receive a fresh touch when we are there to meet with Him.

As John was in the Spirit, he heard a loud voice like a trumpet behind him. The voice commanded him to *write on a scroll what he saw and to send it to the seven churches*. The seven churches were churches in seven cities of the Roman province of Asia, which we will discuss more completely in the next two chapters.

John turned to see (**Blepo**-with his eyes) who was speaking to him and he saw *seven golden lampstands*). We are told later, *the lampstands are the seven churches* and among them was the person whose voice he had heard. Here, John had a vision of Jesus, the person who had just commanded him to write.

His description:

- Clothing: Jesus' dignity as prophet, priest, and king
- Head and hair: Jesus' purity, wisdom, and eternity
- Eyes: Jesus' omniscience (all knowing) and insight
- Feet: Jesus' judgment
- Voice: Jesus' power and strength
- Right hand: Jesus' concern, assistance, and control
- Mouth: Jesus' completely authoritative word
- Face: Jesus' glory, majesty, and holiness

John's vision was graphic, majestic, and utterly overpowering. To see the glorified Christ among the seven golden lampstands, the Lord with whom he had fellowshipped so closely for some three and one-half years during His ministry, must have overwhelmed the apostle. He states *when I saw him (**horoo**-with understanding) I fell at his feet as if dead*. Believers in every period have been encouraged and inspired for service by a fresh vision of their Lord.

John's response to this marvelous vision is predictable. Daniel the prophet had responded in much the same way a few centuries earlier when he saw a similar vision (Dan 10:4–12). Jesus placed His hand on John and said, **Stop being afraid** The number one command in the entire Word of God is, **Don't be afraid and/or Stop being afraid!** It appears 366 times, one for every day of the year, and an extra one for leap year. The touch of Jesus removes fear and brings assurance. I pray as you study God's Word , the reality of Jesus' authority will so grip your life will know that the Christian has nothing to fear. A double negative in English is unacceptable. We don't say *I **don't** have **no** pencils*, because what you are really saying is you have pencils because what you don't have is no pencils. But in the Greek of the New Testament, a double negative means *I <u>absolutely don't</u> have any pencils*. Heb 13:5 uses 5 negatives in one short sentence: *I will no not leave you nor no not forsake you!* Bad English, but Good Greek!! It is obvious that John feels no fear as he sees these awesome, terrible scenes of judgment.. Jesus continues, "*I am The first and the last, even The Living One, And became dead, and see (with understanding) I am alive forevermore, and I have the keys of Death and Hades.*

When Old Testament people died, their soul/spirits went down into the earth, to **Sheol** (a Hebrew word). The Greek equivalent in the New Testament is **Hades**. *Once the KJ Bible translates **Sheol** as grave. This creates opportunity for some cults to say **Sheol** is only the grave. But the reference is Gen 37:25 when Jacob is weeping over Joseph, not thinking he is in a grave, but having been given the impression Joseph had been eaten by a wild animal says I will go* **to Sheol to him.**

Jesus described what Hades was like in Lk 16:19–31. This passage indicates that Hades was divided into two parts. One part was a place of torment; the other part was called paradise, a place of comfort. *When it describes Lazarus was in Abraham's bosom, it is not like the song, Rock My Soul In the Bosom of Abraham. John at the Last Supper was said to be Leaning on Jesus Bosom, which means he was the guest of honor at a feast sitting on the right hand of the host. Jesus had said, As Jonah was three days and three days in the belly of the fish, so must the Son of Man be three days and nights in the heart of the earth. He told the thief on the cross, Today you will be with me in Paradise.* Lk 23:42–43 and Mt 12:39–40 indicating Hades was *down in the earth* at this point. However, in 2 Cor 12:1–6, Paul indicates that paradise is now located *above*. In Mat 16:18, Jesus said, *Upon This Rock (Peter's statement, You are The Christ, The Son of the Living God) I will build My Church and the gates of Hades shall not prevail against it.* The primary meaning, in this case, is that for those who are part of His church, the gates of Hades will never close around them…… When Christians depart from this life, they do not go to Hades as godly people did who died in Old Testament times. What formerly was the paradise side of Hades is now empty. II Cor 5:6–10 (especially v. 8) and Phi 1:18–26 state, that when the Christian dies, he or she goes immediately to be with the Lord. I will discuss what happens to those in the torment side of Hades later.

We are told plainly what the seven stars and seven lampstands are in a clear and direct manner. *The seven stars symbolize the angels/messengers of the seven churches* and *The seven lampstands symbolize the seven churches.*

It has always impressed me that John saw the lampstands/churches first, the function of a lampstand is to shine forth or enlighten, then in the midst of them, Jesus. The purpose of the church is to reveal Jesus Christ, and unless He is in the midst, it is not a church. I. Moreover, the angels/messengers are in His Hand, He gives special strength to His Messengers to fulfill

His Commission. God help us always to remember our part in carrying out the purpose of the church. May we also remember that the Kingdom, the power, and the glory belong forever to Jesus! As I remind Pastors around the world, We are only in distribution, not production.

CHAPTERS 2-3

The Letters to the Seven Churches

Now we move to the second point of the outline: *"The Things Which Are:"*.

The Lord of the church addresses each of The Seven Churches in turn, and He speaks specifically to conditions that exist in each. Nothing escapes His attention, for the all-knowing One walks in their midst. He points to elements worthy of praise and offers commendation; He sees aspects unworthy of His church which He sternly denounces. In these seven churches we see qualities that have characterized the church throughout history. **This is Word For Word Dictation from Jesus.** No human personality interpreting.

Jesus stands in these two chapters as the Judge of the church. His opinion matters much more than the opinions of others. What does He think of us as He looks into our hearts and observes our activities? Let us allow the words of Jesus to speak to our hearts and note the things He approves and the things He disapproves. Observe His promises to the overcomer and His warning to the one who does not overcome.

We are given four reasons or a fourfold purpose for the seven letters. First, the seven churches addressed were literal churches in the Roman province of Asia. Furthermore, the situations our Lord described were actually occurring in these seven churches, and they needed to be dealt with by the Head of the church himself. Secondly, The book was also an encouragement showing ultimate victory in their struggle against Rome.

Thirdly, these seven letters are messages of encouragement, warning, and rebuke for all members of the body of Christ. This is indicated by the exhortation to all such individuals that is found at or near the end of each of the letters: *He who has an ear, let him hear what the Spirit says to the churches.* In these letters the Christian can see certain things to avoid and certain things that please the Lord. We can all examine ourselves in the light of these letters and the fact Jesus is coming quickly.

Fourthly, the word *mystery* is used in connection with the seven churches. *Mystery*, as used in the New Testament means something that has been hidden is now revealed. (Rom 15:25-26; Eph 3:1-6; Col 1:25-29) This indicates that there is more here than what seems to appear. Also, **the entire book is called a Prophecy**. So, along with many many others, I am convinced that the entire history of the church from its beginning on the Day of Pentecost in Acts 2 through its history to *the Day of the Lord* is pictured in the letters to the seven churches. The church, represents the visible Kingdom of God on earth, but often, what is called church is not in reality church. The church of Jesus Christ consists of Those who have received Jesus Christ as their Lord and Savior by Faith (Jn 1:12-13; have been Born Again by the Holy Spirit (Jn 3:1-6); Have the Holy Spirit bearing witness within them that they are Children of God (Rom 8:16, Gal 4:6 I Jn 3:24) and are living a transformed life (2 Cor 5:17); one that is continuously being transformed into the very nature of Jesus Christ which is demonstrated by the Fruit of The Spirit in his or her life. (Gal 5:16-25). Of course the entire New Testament teaches We now live by the power of the Holy Spirit within Who enables us to live as God wants us to live.

These seven actual, local churches were not selected because they were more important than other churches in that area at this time. They evidently were chosen because certain situations that existed in them would characterize the church at various stages throughout its entire existence.

Augustine, and many since, taught that the Millennium was an indefinite period of time in which The Church would convert the world, and when we got it converted, then Jesus Could return. But you will notice as you read the contents of the seven letters, that the opposite seems to have been taking place throughout history. Please read all of Mt 13. Two of Jesus' Parables indicate this trend: Jesus describes the Kingdom of God (the visible, Kingdom people can see is the church) *like a small herbal seed that becomes a great tree and the birds find lodging in it.* The pictures Jesus uses in His Parables are consistent. Birds, in this chapter, *devour the seed*, (v. 4) and in Jesus explanation (v.19) it is the *Wicked One* who *steals the seed*. The next Parable describes a woman hiding a little *Leaven* in 3 measures of meal until the whole was *Leavened. Leaven* in the Parables of Jesus, and throughout the Bible is a picture of evil. Armageddon, when Jesus returns does not show the world welcoming Him back, but, rather wanting to defeat Him.

THE CONTENT OF THE LETTERS TO THE CHURCHES

Greeting to the Angel/Messenger of the Each Church

Characteristic of Jesus Described to Confront/Encourage Each Church

What Jesus Knows about Each Church

What Jesus Approves in Each Church (Except Laodicea)

What Jesus Disapproves in Each Church (Except Smyrna and Philadelphia)

Special Exhortation and/or Promise to Each Church

Instruction to Each Individual to Hear What He says to Each Church

Promise to Overcomers in Each Church

THE PERIOD OF TIME EACH CHURCH DEMONSTRATES

Ephesus	Pentecost to the end of the 1st Century
Smyrna	End of 1st Century to AD 312
Pergamum	AD 312 to about AD 600
Thyatira	About AD 600 on into the Great Tribulation
Sardis	AD 1517 on into the Great Tribulation
Philadelphia	Late 1800s to the rapture of the Church
Laodicea	Late 1800s on into the Great Tribulation

The church at Ephesus represents the pure state of the apostolic church from its birth to about the end of the first century. Near the end of the first century, however, a marked change occurred in the cultural circumstances of the church that begins a second period. A hostile world initiated a series of persecutions that lasted for a little over two hundred years. Again, a marked change of peace occurred as the church became accepted by the Empire. These types of changes in various periods justify associating the characteristics of each church with a respective period of church history. As you read church history, you will see how all of this fits together.

Christians sometimes see something in the Bible they have never heard before and never heard anyone else talk or write about. And think, *I have a new revelation, something no one has ever seen before!* I had such a revelation, when having studied Revelation for years, *I saw that the last four churches mentioned will all be on earth when the Rapture of The Church takes place. Wow, I thought, wait till I get this message out. Wow, I've seen something no one else has! Wow! Wait till I tell people this! Wow!* **then,** I read Harry Ironside's Book on Revelation, written in 1923 and He said **the same thing 8 years before I was born.** Since then, I have read many authors, who lived long before me, and current ones who said the same thing. I tell students. *If its true its not new, and if its new its not true* If is true you will find people before you who have seen it, and if you can't find evidence in Christian writing about your *new* truth its not true.

WE ARE INSTRUCTED TO *HEAR* WHAT EACH LETTER SAYS TO THE CHURCHES, AND *APPLY* BOTH THE ENCOURAGEMENTS AND WARNINGS TO OURSELVES.

THE FIRST THREE CHURCHES OF THE CHURCH AGE 2:1-17

THE LETTER TO THE CHURCH IN EPHESUS

2:1-7-pentecost to last part of first century—Ephesus means Let Go or Allow

Ephesus was the leading city in the province of Asia. It had an ample harbor and it was located in a rich farming area. Moreover this city was exceedingly wealthy. The temple of Artemis stood in the city. It was one of the seven wonders of the ancient world. Ephesians honored Artemis, the many-breasted goddess of fertility, and they believed this image *fell from the sky* (Acts 19:35). They were proud that their city was called *The Temple Warden of Artemis*. Many priests were dedicated to Artemis, and as many as 3,500 priestesses were committed to serve the goddess. We know idolatry always produces immorality; therefore, it is not surprising the city was filled with immorality and debauchery, as well as religion, philosophy, and culture.

Unto the angel of the church of Ephesus write; These things says he who holds the seven stars in his right hand, who walks in the midst of the seven golden candlesticks. Jesus is active in the church at Ephesus. He walks in the midst of His people there, and He is acquainted with their activity and service. This is an excellent picture of the early church, where the presence of the Lord was seen constantly in power to save souls and perform other miracles.

Our Lord still desires to be present in such power in church services today. It is one thing to know He is there; it is another thing to allow Him to manifest himself in our church services. Our pattern ought to be to fit into His program—not to ask Him to fit into ours. He knows exactly what needs to be done and how to do it. *As we learn to depend on our Lord's guidance, He will continue to build His church through us* (see Mt 16:18).

In each of John's letters to seven churches in Revelation 2 and 3, Jesus states something He knows about the church. In five of them He states, *I know your works. He knows our activities also, as well as the motives behind them.*

Jesus approves five things in the church at Ephesus. The statement *I know your works* indicates the Ephesian church was an active church. While good deeds do not save a person, they are an indication of his or her spiritual vitality. We do well to remember that one is not saved by faith *and* works, but by faith *that* works. *Labor* means to the point of exhaustion-fulfilling His Commission in this world, *Perseverance*, another of this church's virtues, means determination to keep on going in spite of opposition. They held a standard of uprightness, could *not bear evil*, and they were careful to weigh every teaching against the Bible standard. They were an orthodox group and would not tolerate false apostles. Christians are to test those who claim to be sent from God. The Word of God is the standard for such testing. We may be sure that a person sent from God does not have a message contrary to the Word of God (2 Cor 4:5; 10:17-11:4; Gal l:6-10; 1 Jn 2:18-27). The Ephesian believers were correct to measure ones doctrine by a scriptural standard.

Jesus states, **You have endured, and borne because of My Name and have not fainted.**

BUT I HAVE AGAINST YOU BECAUSE YOU HAVE LEFT YOUR FIRST LOVE

He didn't say you have *lost* it. You have *left* it. He uses the primary word for Love, **agape**, 100 percent giving of self. I have told couples for years, Marriage is not a 50-50 relationship, it 100-100 percent giving. Then, He says, **Remember from where you have fallen, repent and do the first works (over). If not I am coming to you and will remove your candlestick out of its place unless you repent.** *Repent* simply means to change your mind and, as a consequence, your direction. If the relationship is to remain intact, we must purpose to live as close to Jesus as we once did. Our relationship demands that fervent love. Their first love had been lost like so many marriages. The best way to retain restore love in a marriage is to do the first works over again. Notice the word, **do.** Action is required to restore the love.

It is easier to act yourself into new feelings than it is to feel yourself into new actions.

If you wait until you feel like loving again it will never happen, but if you start doing loving things the feelings of love will return. This is true in a marriage and it is true also in serving God. If you are out of church, don't wait until you feel like going again, start going and before long you will want to go. If your not praying, waiting on God, start doing it, and before long you will feel like doing it...wanting to do it. If your not witnessing for Jesus Christ, start doing it and before long you will want God to lead you to some else.

Jesus also commended them because *you hate the deeds of the Nicolaitans, which I also hate.* There are two meanings of *Nicolaitans*. First, the word comes from two Greek words that mean *people conquerors*. These words may represent the beginning of the idea that ministers are to be elevated to a special place above other Christians. Although this idea became more popular later, We might say this represented the beginning of the institutional church ministry with a separate clergy and laity. There certainly is an authority connected with the ministry, but this authority is described in 1 Pet 5:1-4 as one connected with humility, service and example. Second, the name *Nicolaitans* referred to a group of people who claimed one could be a Christian and practice all kinds of immorality. Ignatius, a disciple of the apostle John, referred to these people as *impure Nicolaitans . . . who are lovers of pleasure . . . corrupters of their own flesh.* We do not know precisely what all their doctrines were, but we know the Lord hated their practices and commended this church for its stand against them.

THE OVERCOMER is promised a blessed place in the paradise of God. *Overcomer,* **Nikao** means to win the victory over. Who are overcomers? To some people overcomers are those Christians who have reached an advanced degree of maturity in Christ, *A Spiritual Elite.* To others, overcomers represent those who live very narrow lives—those whose lives are characterized by *dos and don'ts.* **BUT THE BIBLE IS ITS OWN BEST INTERPRETER**!

For whosoever is born of God overcomes the world. And this is the victory that has overcome the world—our faith. Who is he who overcomes the world, but he who believes that Jesus is the Son of God? (I Jn 5:4-5) **THE BELIEVER IS THE OVERCOMER!**

THE LETTER TO THE CHURCH IN SMYRNA

2:8–11-end of first century to AD 312-Smyrna is from Myrrh

Smyrna was described in its day as the *most beautiful city in the world.* Smyrna was located on a bay of the Aegean Sea and it was called the *crown of Ionia, the ornament of Asia.* The city was rich in architecture and culture. *Smyrna* comes from the word used for the spice *myrrh*, which was used to embalm the dead. You may recall that the wise men brought *Gold*-He is King of the Jews, for whom they came searching, *Frankincense*-an incense offered to Deity-He is God, and *Myrrh* –One Born to Die.

The Characteristic of Jesus presented here, *Jesus is the first and the last, the One who became dead and came to life (is Living).* Why does He Start this way? He is writing to a suffering church. *I know your works, tribulation, and poverty (but you are rich).* He is reminding them He, Himself, has been were they are. In Him, every believer is a victor. This period is associated with the persecution in the Roman Empire that became widespread and, at times, intense from the end of the first century until about AD 312. Christians in general have undergone persecution throughout the church's history. The entire New Testament indicates that Christians will have their faith tested by difficulties and persecutions. That God uses them to strengthen our faith, and bare witness to the world of our Faith.

Not only are the people of this church afflicted, they are also poor. However, their Lord says that their poverty is only apparent; actually, they are rich. The best and enduring riches are not material; they are spiritual. In this sense, then, the believers in Smyrna were rich. James reminds us that *the poor are rich in faith* (Ja 2:5), and Jesus taught in Lk 16 that if we are not faithful with our finances toward God, How can He give us the ***True Riches!***

The false teaching of our day about Financial Prosperity teaches one Gospel for the prosperous nations and another Gospel for the poor nations. Blame lack of faith on the part of the poor, and are ignoring what Paul says in I Tim says from verse 5:5-12. Yes God does give back financially, but the true riches are far beyond that. **I ask, in a sermon**: *Do you want to see a prosperous person? Front view, I turn, Side View, I turn, Back View, I turn Good Side. I've never had a lot of money, but I had a wife for almost 60 years to whom I said daily, I love you forever, and meant it. I have three beautiful, capable daughters who love and serve God and a spectacular Son who leads a great congregation of people, loving God and people. I Have three spectacular Son in Laws who love and serve God, and a beautiful Daughter in Law who, as First Lady of the church, loves God and people and serves them. I have 15 spectacular Grand Children, and 9 of the greatest great grandchildren in history, and I have been part of an exciting inner city church for 45 years, and get to travel the world and proclaim the Gospel of Jesus Christ and seen so many lives changed by his power...*

THAT IS PROSPERITY!!!!!!

They are being slandered by false Jews. *I know the blasphemy of those who say they are Jews and are not, but are a synagogue of Satan* These so-called Jews may have been Jews by virtue of their race and religion, but they were not truly Jews, for they rejected Jesus as their Messiah and persecuted His church. It is also possible these false Jews were Judaizers who demanded that all Christians keep Old Testament rules (such as circumcision, feast days, and not eating certain foods). The Whole book of Galatians is against that teaching, as are many other portions of the New Testament. Whoever they were, they were not God's people. Actually, they are identified as Satan's, and they slandered the people of God in Smyrna.

The church now receives two special exhortations and a general notion of what the immediate future holds: First, the Lord of the church says, *Do not fear any of those things which you are about to suffer! Conflict is coming, and the devil will test you to the limit. Prison and persecution are coming.* Second, the Conqueror—our Conqueror—exhorts: *Be faithful unto death,* Then follows with the blessed promise, *I will give you The Crown of The life.*

The special promise to The Overcomer/The Believer is *You will not be hurt by the Second Death.* This will be explained toward the end of Revelation.

A clear look at the approaching storm reveals the testing and persecution is limited to a specific period of time: *ten days*. There were ten distinct periods of persecution that the church suffered under imperial Rome from the end of the first century until the year AD 312. Beginning with Nero, AD54, Domitian AD81, Trajan AD98, Adrian (Hadrian) AD117, Septimius Severus AD193; Maximim AD235, Decius AD240, Valerian AD254, Aurelian AD270, Diocletian AD284 (beginning dates for the ten persecutions, under each Caesar)

The Emperor Constantine had a vision in AD 312 which caused him to make Christianity an official religion of the Roman Empire, and in AD 313, *The Edict of Milan*, which brought peace to the whole of Rome's imperial domain was issued; It resulted ultimately in making Christianity The Official Religion of the Roman Empire. Moreover, it introduced a new period that was marked by extremely different conditions. Whereas the suffering church in the second period fought for its life, the next period was set apart by extreme toleration in which the church gradually blended in with the secular world of which it was a part. Thus, it lost its distinctive purity and vision in the process.

IN THE SMYRNAN PERIOD THE DEVIL TRIED TO DESTROY THE CHURCH

IN THE PERGAMUM HE DECIDED TO DESTROY IT BY JOINING THE CHURCH

THE LETTER TO THE CHURCH IN PERGAMUM

2:12–17-AD 312-313 to about AD600-pergamum means elevation or marriage

The city of Pergamum, although not as important commercially as Ephesus and Smyrna, was more important as a political and religious center. On its acropolis, Pergamum had dedicated a high altar to Zeus and a temple to Athena. Pergamum was also the first city of Asia to support the imperial cult, the worship of the Roman Emperor. So Jesus says to this church, *These things says He who has the sharp two-edged sword: I know your works, and you dwell, where Satan's throne is. And you hold fast to My name, and did not deny My faith even in the days in which Antipas My faithful martyr was killed among you, where Satan dwells.*

Here citizens were required to worship the emperor; to refuse was to invite the charge of treason. Many of us associate the phrase *where Satan's throne is* with the prominence of Pergamum as the center of the imperial cult. There was a large medical center in Pergamum named after the serpent god Asclepius, and the city was well known for her college of medical priests. These things help us to see why Pergamum was called the place *Satan's throne is* and *where Satan dwells*. Pergamum had a large library containing 200,000 volumes. Like other cities, this city was a place of pagan religion, immorality, philosophy, and education.

After a sustained period of persecution , the Roman Empire reversed its stand and finally accepted Christianity. Under persecution, the church thrived and spread rapidly, but under the smile of official acceptance, the faith lost its vitality and vision. Under the patronage of the Emperor Constantine, Christianity was popularized. Superficial religion was substituted for reality, and ceremony replaced personal experience with God. Large numbers of pagans were baptized without ever having a personal relationship with Christ.

Jesus is characterized as having a *sharp, two-edged sword*. The sword here is a symbol of the Word of God that is used to denounce false teachings the church permitted. The Word of God is still the standard by which church teachings are to be measured. Teachings that do not measure up to this standard are to be rejected.

Observe things of which our Lord approves. First, the church at Pergamum was true to our Lord's name. His name stands for everything He is. To be true to His name means to recognize that Jesus is the Son of God, that we must worship God only, and that we must approach God through Him (Jn 14:6; 1 Tim 2:5). The reference to Antipas; (tradition holds was put inside a brass ox and roasted to death) implies our Lord's special approval of the faith in Him that characterized the people in this church in a time of great trial.

Jesus now points to two items He strongly condemns: **The first thing He condemns is idolatry and sexual immorality. These are connected together with very strong significance.**

IDOLATRY AND IMMORALITY

There is one lesson the Jews have learned in 4,000 years of History: ***GOD HATES IDOLS!***

The Northern Kingdom of Israel was destroyed in 722 BC by the Assyrians because of Idolatry. The Southern Kingdom of Judah was destroyed in 586 by the Babylonians because of Idolatry. The Book of Hosea over, and over equates idolatry with whoredom, as do other passages of Scripture. In the Old Testament Israel is the Wife of YHWH. Ho 2:2-13 says:

Plead with your mother, plead: for she is not my wife, neither am I her husband let her therefore put away her whoredoms out of her sight, and her adulteries from between her breasts; Lest I strip her naked, and set her as in the day that she was born, and make her as a wilderness, and set her like a dry land, and slay her with thirst. And I will not have mercy upon her children; for they be the children of whoredoms. For their mother has played the harlot: she that conceived them hath done shamefully: for she said, I will go after my lovers, that give me my bread and my water, my wool and my flax, mine oil and my drink. Therefore, behold, I will hedge up your way with thorns, and make a wall, that she shall not find her paths. And she shall follow after her lovers, but she shall not overtake them; and she shall seek them, but shall not find them: then shall she say, I will go and return to my first husband; for then was it better with me than now. For she did not know that I gave her corn, and wine, and oil, and multiplied her silver and gold, which they prepared for Baal. Therefore will I return, and take away my corn in the time thereof, and my wine in the season thereof, and will recover my wool and my flax given to cover her nakedness. And now will I discover her lewdness in the sight of her lovers, and none shall deliver her out of mine hand. I will also cause all her mirth to cease, her feast days, her new moons, and her sabbaths, and all her solemn feasts. And I will destroy her vines and her fig trees, whereof she hath said, These are my rewards that my lovers have given me: and I will make them a forest, and the beasts of the field shall eat them. And I will visit upon her the days of Baalim, wherein she burned incense to them, and she decked herself with her earrings and her jewels, and she went after her lovers, and forgot me, says the Lord. (KJV)

Examples from other Scripture which define Idolatry as Adultery are Jud 2:17, 8:27; I Chr 5:25; Ps 106:36-39; Ez 6:9, 20:30,23: and 23:30-35 where he warns Judah of following the example of her Sister, Israel into the whoredom of idolatry and suffering the consequences.

In the New Testament the word translated in English by *Fornication*, is the Greek word **Porneia,** which refers to any kind of sex outside of marriage, between one man and one woman. It is associated both with idolatry and separate from it.

Why do I make such an issue here? You will see usually in Revelation that *Idolatry* and *fornication* and connected with *and* which may be also translated as *even*. And it is followed by the phrase, *Eating Things Offered To Idols* which indicates true Idol Worship, a belief that the idols supply needs, both physical and spiritual. We will see later, in Revelation, that Israel will accept the Antichrist as the Christ, but when his Image is placed in the Holy of Holies in Jerusalem, The Spiritual Blinders will be removed from their eyes, and a revelation that Jesus is the Messiah will take place. So *Fornication* has an important meaning in the context of the Book of Revelation.

Why is Balaam is mentioned ? In Num 22-25 Balaam is called up by Balak who wants Balaam to come and curse the invading Israelites. Each time he opens his mouth he blesses them. So in 31:16 it talks about the council of Balaam which caused the people to sin. In the Apparently what he told the king was something like, *your daughters are beautiful, send them among the men of Israel will love them, and the ladies can lead them into worshipping Idols, and Their God The God* *of Israel will kill them for you.* Ch 25 states the Israelites *began to commit whoredom with the daughters of Moab, and ate and drank to other Gods,* resulting in the death of 24,000 in Israel.

During the Pergamum period, images of saints were placed in increasing numbers of churches. These images were said to be in the churches to *remind people to worship God,* but there always has been a danger that the presence of such images will cause people to worship them or the saints they represent rather than God. Nothing must ever detract from Him as the object of our worship.

The second thing Jesus condemns is holding to *the teaching of the Nicolaitans* (v. 15). Both physical appetite and spiritual discernment appear to be undisciplined in this church, which exists in a time of spiritual laxity.

In verse 16, Jesus warns people in Pergamum to repent of these things He has condemned. If they do not repent, *He will come to them suddenly and fight against them with the sword of His mouth. Jesus still gives this entire warning to us today when we do things of which He disapproves.* How dreadful it would be to have the Savior of the church become its Destroyer. The key to restored spiritual balance is genuine repentance.

During this period of History, the one meaning of the word, *Nicolaitans,* people conquerors, became true. In the New Testament Elder (**Presbuteros**), Bishop (**Episkopos**} and Pastor/ Shepherd (**Poimen**) are the same person. See Acts 20:17-38, Paul Calls the *Elders* from Ephesus and reminds them they are to *feed the flock of God—shepherd/pastor, over which God has made Overseers/Bishops.* I Pet 5:1-4 Uses the same terminology to describe the Elders, and calls himself, an Elder. In the 2nd Century Bishops were put above Elders, In the 3rd Century, The Bishop of Rome was becoming the unofficial Head of he Church, since it was the center of the Empire,

In the 4th Century, The Bishop of Rome was called by some, *The Successor of Peter.* In the 5th Century Bishops of large cities became Archbishops-Rulers Over Bishops. In the 5th Century The Emperor Valentinian VI made The Bishop of Rome The Head of the Western Church. About 600 Gregory proclaimed himself Pope, and taught the doctrine of Papal Infallibility; When the Pope Speaks *Ex Cathedra,* in behalf of the church, he is in *infallible.* In addition, The teaching that only The Church could interpret Scripture started and continued throughout time until the Protestant Reformation in 1517 challenged all these teachings, although they continue in some areas of *the church.*

Two things are promised to the Overcomer: Hidden Manna and a White Stone. The Hidden Manna is the spiritual food one receives as he or she partakes in fellowship with Christ, and the White Stone seems to have indicated acquittal in contrast to a Black Stone which would indicate condemnation that one on trial received as the verdict of the judicial tribunal. The Overcomer is justified, Declared *Not Guilty* by faith in Christ, and The Righteousness of Jesus Christ is credited to the Account of the Overcomer, so His or Her page in the Book of Life in Heaven reads, *Righteous!*

THE FOUR CHURCHES HERE AT THE TIME OF THE RAPTURE 2:18-3:22

It will be obvious as we study here certain beliefs of current churches will be mentioned. But the entire passage makes it clear, that although the teaching of some is contrary to Scripture, that, **in the first three of the four**, **there are true believers who have a relationship with Jesus Christ** in spite of the things being taught. In the fourth one, Jesus is knocking at individual's doors trying to get in.

THE LETTER TO THE CHURCH OF THYATIRA

2:18-29-AD600 On into the Great Tribulation, Thyatira means Unweary of Sacrifices

Thyatira, was an inland city that had a long military history. Thyatira was located in a rich agricultural area, and it was important as an industrial center. This city was famous for purple dye, and it was supported by a purple cloth industry that was manufactured under the control of well-organized trade guilds. Thyatira was not a religious or political center, and it was not a strong supporter of emperor worship. Lydia, *from the city of Thyatira, a seller of purple goods* (Acts 16:14) was converted under Paul's ministry in Philippi.

The opening of this letter, gives three further characteristics of our Lord. First, this is the **only** place in the book of Revelation where Jesus is called **THE SON OF GOD**, *with eyes like a flame of fire, and His feet like fine brass.* Why? Because the teaching of church of this period is not holding Him in His proper place., but substituting the preeminence of others over Jesus.

Peter is put as the Foundation of the Church. Mt 16:15-19 Peter had said, *You are The Christ, The Son of The Living God.* Jesus responded, *...Flesh and blood have not revealed **this** to you, but my Father Who is in heaven, and I say that you are Peter, and upon **this rock** I will build my church and the gates of Hades will not prevail against it, And I will give to you the keys of the Kingdom of Heaven, and whatsoever you bind on earth **shall have been** bound in heaven, and whatsoever you loose on earth **shall have been** loosed in heaven.*

Peter is the translation given to **Petros** which means a *Stone.* In the New Testament, you do not throw a Rock, but a Stone. If something is moveable it is a **Petros**, even if it weights 10 tons...

if it is movable it is **Petros**. *Petra*, *Rock*, is the Bedrock of the mountain. It is not movable. So Peter is a stone, but the Rock is Peter's statement given to him by God, **You are The Christ, The Son of the Living God.** As Paul states in I Corinthians 3:11, **For other foundation can no one lay than that which is laid, which is Jesus Christ.!**

You don't read of the Apostles in the Book of Acts telling people, *I forgive your sins.* They pointed them to receive Jesus and He provides forgiveness of sins.

I am trying not to get too technical in this book, but The translation given above, *whatsoever you bind on earth shall have been bound in heaven, and whatsoever you loose on earth shall have been loosed in heaven* is not seen in translations. It is a rare example of a Greek Construction known as a *Periphrastic Future Perfect*. An event in the future will bind and loose, and you will be able to continuously bind and loose because it will have already been done in heaven. The event of the future is the Cross, where everything needed was accomplished, so you, Peter, as a representative of my people, will be an agent to distribute what has already been done. Just like the feeding of the 5,000, Jesus produced the bread, the disciples distributed it. As I tell pastors when I teach around the world, *We are not in production (we can't save anyone)...but in distribution of what Jesus does as He empowers us*

Our Lord singles out four things of which He approves in the church at Thyatira: *Your works, love, service, faith* and *your works* then adds *and the last to be more than the first.* Jesus specifically mentions *works* twice. Although this is an area of approval, the implication is that the church is depending too much on works. Penance, works, are substituted for Repentance in Scripture. Forgiveness must be earned. As we noted earlier, we are not forgiven by works; we could never earn forgiveness, nor salvation.

The prominence of the risen Christ, which had so characterized the apostolic church, gave way to the prominence of the mother of Jesus. She tended to be held on a level with God, and her role as man's mediator with God became prominent in the teaching of the medieval church. The icons, relics, and human doctrines that crept into the church were symptoms of spiritual idolatry. The church no longer resembled the joyful force of believers recorded in Acts

. The Scriptures make it clear, *There one God and one Mediator between God and men, it is the man Christ Jesus!* .(I Tim 2:5) The repetition of the phrase, while doing *penance for sins* is *Hail Mary* as if *Hail* is some kind of a word meaning Praise. It is NOT. It is the Greek word, **chaire** which is simply *Greetings*. It is used to begin letters, or when meeting someone. Mary was a godly woman, but in what is called, *The Magnificat*, Mary states, *And my soul has rejoiced in God* *my Savior* (Lk. 1:47), She admitted her need of a Savior. The Bible makes it clear she had other Children, Lk 2:7 indicates Jesus was her *Firstborn* Son, Mt 1:25 indicates Joseph *was not knowing (have sexual relationship) her until after Jesus was born.* See also Mt 12:46, 13:55, Mk 3:31, Jn 2:12, 7:3, 5, I Cor. 9:5, Gal. 1:19.

The word means *Brothers*, not cousins, nor Josephs from a previous marriage. Notice in Jn 7, *His brothers did not believe in Him.* Suppose, your older brother, a carpenter, suddenly announced *I'm The Son of God, The Messiah who has been promised.* You would probably say, *You're Crazy!! In Mk 3:21,* when the presence of Jesus was drawing a crowd around a house where he was, his family said, *He is beside himself!* The same charge was brought against Paul in Ac 26:24, 2Co 5:13). Jn 7:5 Says, *neither did his brother believe in him.* But after His resurrection, He made a special appearance to James, His Brother, (I Cor. 15:7) and, if you read the Book of Acts you will discover Jesus Brother, James, Author of the Book of James, is considered the Head of the Church in Jerusalem, not Peter.

The idea of *Patron Saints* continued to grow during this period. This concept comes from Greek Mythology. Go to Athens and visit the Parthenon, which was build in honor of the Goddess Athena, The Protectress of Athens and other cities.

The power of the Priest, to change bread and wine into the literal body and blood of Christ became dominant. As indicated earlier; if you read the New Testament, you not find the office of a priest in the church mentioned; because the New Testament teaches every believer is a priest and has access to God through Jesus Christ. You don't need to go through a priest to have your sins forgiven or approach God. You find positions of Apostles Prophets, Evangelists, Pastors and Teachers and other helping ministries distinguished, but never a priest.

During this period the Church started teaching that extrabiblical (not Bible) literature was as authoritative as the Bible, and Tradition surpassed the Bible in authority. This church thus began to demonstrate characteristics of tolerance for much that was neither biblical nor helpful to the spiritual life of believers. These characteristics will exist throughout the Church Age and on into the Great Tribulation.

Now the same issue, Idolatry, that started in Pergamum continues in Thyatira Jezebel married Ahab, Israel's king, and led him into Idolatry, Baal worship, and thus the nation. Whoever this, *so called Prophetess* is at this time, it is obvious that she is *the Jezebel of that hour,* since she leads the people of Thyatira into *fornication, eating things offered to Ido*ls.

I see the reference to Jezebel, during this time in church history, as the the Church, itself leading into the worship of idols. Jesus Calls on this church to *Repent.* I think both the Protestant Reformation, and the later Charismatic Movement in the church gave this opportunity.

THERE IS A DIVISION AMONG THE CHILDREN OF JEZEBEL AND THE REST OF THE CHURCH IN THYATIRA:

Behold, I will cast her into a bed, and them that commit adultery with her into great tribulation, except they repent of their deeds. I will kill her children with death; and all the churches shall know that I am he which searches the reins and hearts: and I will give unto every one of you according to your works. But unto you I say, and unto the rest in Thyatira, as many as have not this doctrine, and which have not known the depths of Satan, as they speak; I will put upon you none other burden. But that which ye have already hold fast till I come

. Those who have become her children—who have accepted her wicked doctrines—will be thrown into *Great Tribulation.* But those who do not have the teaching of idolatry, and, therefore *have not known the depths of Satan* are told to *Hold that which you have until I come!* So one group will be thrown into Great Tribulation, but the rest, obviously will not. We will see how this fits into what is explained later in Revelation.

The Overcomers, those who persist until the end, are promised a share in Christ's rule over the nations. They are also promised *the morning star.* Jesus calls Himself, *The Bright and Morning Star* in 22:16. So it refers to a close relationship with Jesus, Himself, and thus sharing in His victory for eternity.

THE LETTER TO THE CHURCH IN SARDIS

3:1–6-AD 1517 and on into The Great Tribulation Sardis, Sardis means Prince of Joy.

The city of Sardis was built on a hill over one thousand feet above the surrounding plain. Citizens here had a strong sense of security because they believed their city was too strong to be conquered by an enemy. Sardis was considered to be a wealthy city and was known for jewelry, textiles, and dye. A temple dedicated to the goddess Artemis was located here, making it a strong pagan religious center. Moreover, the city lay on an important trade route down the Hermus valley. Sardis was less powerful under Roman rule than she had been previously.

To the church in Sardis *these things says He who has the seven Spirits of God and the seven stars: 'I know your works, that you have a name that you are alive, but you are dead* He possesses the seven spirits of God and the seven stars. As we saw , the stars represent messengers or leaders of the seven churches. It is He, Himself, who anoints the Messengers of His church with the

Holy Spirit. There is great need in every church for Him to bring his hands together in a new way, with a fresh empowering of the Holy Spirit as the time of his return draws near.

This church had a good reputation before people. Indeed, it may have been a model of organization and good programming, really being alive, but a church's reputation before humans is not what counts most! What counts most is what our Lord thinks of us. He says, *you are dead.* and in the next verse, *I have not found any of your works complete before My God!* Many churches that were born in a great move of the Spirit of God are now only social welfare agencies. It is good to help people materially, but it is far more important for a person be saved—to know Christ personally. Notice the five commands Jesus gives to His church:

1. *Keep becoming watchful!,...*In other words, Stay Awake! Cyrus defeated this *Unconquerable City,* by having a single soldier climb up between the rocks at night, enter the city, and open the gate for Cyrus' armies. The Song of Solomon reminds us, *It is the little foxes that spoil the vine, for our vines have tender grapes.* Satan will not tempt us through a huge sin to start; he will work on little things. But as I heard years ago, *Give Satan your finger and he will grab your hand, give him your hand and he will grab your arm, give him your arm and he will pull in.*

2. *Strengthen the things that remain which are about to die!* Why does this church start with 1517? This is the beginning of the Protestant Reformation, when the theme was, *Sola Scriptora , Scripture Only!* After the Dark Ages of Christianity, when the Word of God had been replaced by the things mentioned earlier in this chapter, The Bible, with its truth was again being proclaimed and lived. Many organizations, born believing the Word of God, no longer believe it. While finishing my second Masters, I sat in a class in a Denominational Seminary, a Denomination that was born in Revival Fire, Believing the Bible, Seeing lives transformed by the power of God, I sat under a professor that no longer believed anything in the Bible. I asked him, *Why do you bother teaching this, you obviously, don't believe what it says?,* I received he only "B" I ever received as a graduate student. He said, concerning a view of the Bible, *You don't Understand this Theory.* My comment back, was, *I obviously do, that's why I reject it.*

3. *Remember therefore how you received and heard!* They received and heard through the proclamation of the Word of God, which they now reject.

4. *Hold firm!* To what they heard and believed, and he adds,

5. *Repent!* Repent means to change your mind, and let your actions follow. Get back to the

Word of God, and start believing it and proclaiming it for what it is: The Truth! Then comes the warning, *If, therefore, you do not stay awake, I will come upon you as a thief, and you will no not know at what hour I will come upon you!* Notice the double negative, *no not*, emphasizing not knowing. Why won't they know, Primarily because they no longer believe the Word of God that talks of His return and gives the signs of His return.

I stated on the back cover of this book, **Why all date setters for the return of the Lord have been wrong, and why they will always be wrong**. Jesus taught in Matthew that *only the Father knows, the day,* and that *He is coming as a thief and we will not know when.* And in Acts 1:6-7, When the Apostles asked Jesus, *Are you at this time restore the again the kingdom to Israel?*, He answered, **It is not for you to know the times (Chronos) or the seasons (Chairos) which the Father has put in His own hands.**

Now since Jesus said, **It is not for you to know,** That means, **It is not for you to know. You are Not going to figure it out by the Jewish Calendar, Eclipses of the Sun, or any other means.**

Let me explain **Chronos** and **Chairos:** A Lady has 9 months of **Chronos,** Then, WAAAA! That's the **Chairos.** In other words, **Its not for you to know how much time is going to pass nor the specific time!** Jesus said, **Let your loins be girded about and your lights burning; and yourselves like men expecting their lord!** *This will be discussed more later.* Paul reminded the Thessalonians he would not even discuss the **Chronos and Charos.**

You have a few names, even in Sardis, who have not defiled their garments, and they shall walk with Me in white, for they are worthy. As we stated previously, many of the Spirit-born churches of the Reformation have fallen away from biblical Christianity. Even so, there are some today in every Spirit-born church and denomination who are still preaching the gospel of Christ, and people are receiving Jesus Christ and being Born Again! The promises to the Overcomer: The promise repeated, *They will be dressed in white,* and *their names will remain forever in the Book of Life and be acknowledged before God and His angels.*

THE LETTER TO THE CHURCH AT PHILADELPHIA

3:7-13- Late1800's to The Rapture. Philadelphia means Brotherly Love

The city of Philadelphia was built by a king of Pergamum, Attalus Philadelphus, who named it after himself. It was a place of major earthquakes, and the city was destroyed twice in the first century AD. It was a center of pagan worship and was known as *Little Athens.* This indicates the philosophy, religion, and immorality of the large city of Athens were present in Philadelphia.

The characteristics by which our Lord reveals himself to this church, *He Who is Holy, He Who is True*. The message to Philadelphia is different than the previous three, and the one to follow. In his Truth and Holiness, Jesus has no warning, no correction, but only commendation and teaching a truth not previously presented. *He Who has the Key of David, He who opens and no man shuts, who shuts and no man opens..* The last phrase is a quote from Is 22:21-22 , and It was considered by Jewish scholars as a prophecy of the Messiah who would have the glory (throne) of and key to (authority of) the House of David.

Jesus tells them, *I have set before you an open door and no man can shut it.* There are several doors only He can open and close. There is the Open Door of intimacy with Him (3:20). There is the is the Open Door of Evangelism (I Cor. 16:9 And, in 4:1 there is an Open Door in Heaven. There will be several open and closed doors in Revelation which we will see as we go through the book. The Significance of the Open Door in 4:1 is especially significant to the Church at Philadelphia and all true Christians. We will discuss that one in connection with chapter 4:1.

Jesus commends this church for having *a little strength* Paul reminds us of His *Stake in the Flesh,* which made him weak, for which sought the Lord three times, to which God replied *My Grace is enough for you, for (my) power is made complete in (your) weakness!* Is 40:31 reminds us, *They who wait on the Lord will **exchange** their strength!* Talk about, *the Best Trade we ever receive— We give God our Little Strength and He gives us His Strength.* There are 8 different Hebrew words translated in our English Bibles as *Wait on the Lord.* The one used here deals with spending time in the presence of God. I have told pastors and Christians all over the world, *Don't be so busy working for God you don't take time alone with Him!* God's people of all eras have experienced spiritual victory by depending mainly on the strength that God gives them rather than on their own strength. We, like Paul, can echo *I can do all things in Christ who keeps on putting power into me* (Ph 4:13)

Jesus commends them, Firstly, for *Keeping His Word,* Secondly for *Not Denying His Name.* His Name stands for Who He Is. He commends them, Thirdly, for *Keeping the Word of His Endurance. Endurance*: The determination to serve Him regardless of what happens, or what circumstances are against you. He refers to those *of the Synagogue of Satan who say they are Jews and are not, but lie.* The same group is mentioned in the Letter to Smyrna. They may be the opposition they have endured. The Jews were the first persecutors of Christians.

Jesus goes on to say, *because you have kept my command to persevere, I will keep you out of that hour of testing, which shall come to test them who dwell on the earth.* That *Hour of Testing* is known as *The Great Tribulation*, which is the time of *The Wrath of God*. Notice, He does not say, *I will keep you out of the difficulty*, but says, *I will keep you out of* (**tereo ek**) *that hour*. **Hour is a time measurement**. Not necessarily a 60 minutes period, but a definite period of time with a beginning and end. Jesus, in His prayer between The Last Supper and Gethsemane, praying for His Apostles prayed, *I am not asking in order that you take them the out of* (**airo ek**) *the world, but in order that you keep them out of* (**tereo ek**) *the evil*. I will say more in connection with Chapter 4. The promises to the overcomer *I will make him a pillar in the temple of My God, and he shall go out no more. I will write on him the name of My God and the name of the city of My God, the New Jerusalem, which comes down out of heaven from My God. And I will write on him My new name*. Emphasizing the intimate presence of God with the overcomer throughout eternity

THE LETTER TO THE CHURCH IN LAODICEA

3:14–22-From the late 1800's into the Great Tribulation- means People Judgment

The city of Laodicea was named after the wife of King Antiochus II, Laodice. It was a wealthy business center. The city was famous for its medicines, an ear ointment, and an eye powder. Since Laodicea had no water supply, water from hot springs six miles south of the city was brought through aqueducts to serve community needs. By the time this water reached the city, it was lukewarm. Laodiceans could easily identify with the Lord's reaction to their lukewarm condition, for they knew how sickening lukewarm water could be to the thirsty. When the city suffered a destructive earthquake in AD 60, its leaders, speaking with one voice, refused assistance from Rome, replying: *I have grown rich and am in need of nothing*.

The first of the three characteristics John attributes to Jesus in is that He is *The Amen*. Amen means *true* or *truly*, and is used to finalize statements and prayers. He, Himself is the conclusion of everything God has to say, and as such, He is *The Faithful and True Witness* of Who and What God is. Paul, prays for the Christians , *That their hearts may be comforted, having been knit together in love and into* **Epignosos** (Personal Intimate Relationship Knowledge) *of the mystery of God,* **CHRIST!**,(the NIV says *namely Christ*) in whom are hidden all the treasures of the wisdom and knowledge (Co. 2:2-3)

In the New Testament, **gnosis** is the basic word for *knowledge*. **epignosis** is experimental knowledge. There is true or false **gnosis** of Jesus Christ, but **epignosis** is always *true knowledge* of Jesus Christ. The NIV makes a distinction between the two words only in I Cor 13:12, *Now I know* (**gnosis**) *in part; then I shall know fully* (**epignosis**)**.** Most transltions of the Bible to not make the distinction that should be made between the two words. He is also, *the beginning of the creation of God*. God created all things through Jesus, as we are told throughout the New Testament.

Jesus does not commend anything in the church in Laodicea. The word implies that ministers and spiritual leaders consider it more important to please the people than to please God. Observe especially a condition in verses 15–19 that Jesus condemns in the church at Laodicea. Church members were *neither cold nor hot* in their spiritual condition. *Cold* meant to be away from God but to be aware of the need to get right with Him. *Lukewarm* means being away from God without realizing it. He says, *I will vomit you out of my mouth*, in other words, *You make me sick to my stomach.*

After quoting the statement of the Laodiceans, *I am rich, and increased with goods, and have need of* nothing, Jesus indicate their spiritual condition: they are really, *Wretched* (afflicted). *and Miserable* (pitiable), *and poor, and blind, and* naked. Laodicean believers are counseled to *buy from Me* (The only one who can provide the following)

1. *gold refined by fire, that you may be rich* which refers to the spiritual wealth Christians receive through tests and trials of their faith. Jb 23:10 and 1 Pet 1:7 teach us that such tests and trials produce purity in God's people in the manner that gold is purified by fire.

2. *White Raiment, that you may be clothed and the shame of your nakedness doesn't appear.* Cleansed by the Blood of Christ and declared, Righteous!!!! (See Zech 3:1ff)

3. *Anoint your eyes with eye salve so you may see.* He adds, *Those I love I rebuke and discipline.* (Rather than his usual use of the verb form of **Agape** He uses the verb form of **Philos**.)' And adds, *Be zealous therefore and repent.* REPENT OF WHAT? Their dependence on good works, religious rituals, lack of Jesus in their lives:

I have taken my stand at the door and I am knocking shows us He is outside the door of the church in Laodicea. He is not in this church at all. This church represents many of the false churches of these last days—churches that claim to be Christian but have nothing to do with Jesus Christ. Their teachings come from human opinions—not from the Word of God! Many of them deny the deity of Jesus Christ. He is still knocking, for He wants all to be saved (2Pet 3:9)

If anyone hears my voice and opens the door, I will come in to him and eat with him, and he with me. This is a spiritual feast that will satisfy the longing of every seeking heart. God feasts on men and women's love and fellowship.

The Bible is primarily the story of God seeking people (Lk 19:10). In Gen 3:9 God called to the man, *Where are you?* In John 4, as Jesus approached the woman of Samaria, He asked her to give him a drink. He was not seeking the water in the well. He was seeking a response that indicated her spiritual love and fellowship. This explains why Jesus did not want to eat when His disciples came back with food. This is why He said, *I have food to eat that you do not know about*; She had opened her heart to Him. **He wants your love and fellowship in the same way**. This spiritual love relationship is a feast for us and for Him too! PLEASE REPEAT THE FOLLOWING:

GOD LOVES ME AS IF I'M THE ONLY PERSON HE EVER HAD TO LOVE!

I AM AS IMPORTANT TO GOD AS ANY PERSON WHO HAS EVER LIVED!

GOD WANTS AN INTIMATE RELATIONSHIP WITH ME!

IF I WOULD HAVE BEEN THE ONLY PERSON WHO HAD EVER SINNED JESUS WOULD HAVE DIED JUST FOR ME

He also wants fellowship every person on earth. It's our responsibility to let others know of His love. You may not know a lot of Scriptures, but you have a personal testimony of what God has done for you. When Paul stood before Kings, in Acts, He gave his testimony. It is a fact that over ninety percent of everyone who meets Jesus Christ and is saved, happens because a friend invited them to church.

CHAPTER 4-5
After These Things

In the outline Jesus, Himself, gave for the book, part IV deals with ***The things which will take place after these things,*** (**Meta Tauta**) Part IV of this outline thus describes the things that must occur after ***the things John had seen*** and the ***things that are.*** Chapters 2 and 3 describe the Church Age, the things that follow are after the Church Age.

John says, ***After These Things,*** *I looked and behold a door was open in heaven, and the first voice which I had heard as a trumpet (the same voice that said in ch 1, I am alpha Omega, etc.) was speaking with me saying Come Up Here and I will show you things necessary to happen* ***After These Things.***

The fact that the it starts and ends with **Meta Tauta** makes it clear, they are to happen after the things recorded in chapters 2 and 3—after Ephesus, Smyrna, Pergamum, Thyatira, Sardis, Philadelphia and Laodicea. You cannot find the word, *Church* in the Book of Revelation from here until after the story is ended, and a warning is given to The church to be ready for His Coming in Chapter 22. It is also important that it includes the Greek word, **dei,** (Must, It is Necessary). The things in the rest of the book *Have To Happen* to conclude God's Story:
CHAPTER 66

When John hears the command to *Come Up Here!* Even though He is already *In the Spirit* in ch 1, He immediately *became in the spirit* and saw the Throne of God. We will get back to the discussion of chapter 4 later.

This is a Picture of the Rapture of the Church. In addition, to the verse beginning and ending with **Meta Tauta,** and the word, *Church* not being in Revelation again until the story is over, consider the following many evidences that there is The Rapture of the Church, and, it takes place at this point in Revelation.

UNIQUENESS OF THE GREAT TRIBULATION

If you have not previously studied biblical prophecy, you may not be familiar with this term.

Looking ahead to events that will take place after the church has been caught away, we see that the wicked—individuals, nations, and the collective, worldwide institutions and associations of ungodly people—will face the wrath of God. As this time of collective reckoning comes, it is referred to commonly as *The Day of The Lord*, But, Also, as *the great day of the wrath of God* (6:17) and as *the great tribulation* (7:14). The focus here is on the consummation of God's redemptive program as it concerns those who have rejected His grace and attempted to hinder His work on earth, CHAPTER 66

Seen in the light of the previous paragraph, the Great Tribulation does not concern the victorious church. The church will not experience God's wrath as it is revealed in the Great Tribulation (I Th 1:10, *Jesus has rescued us from the wrath to come,* and 5:9, *God has not appointed us to wrath...,* .Some say, *Why should the church of the last days be spared physical and mental suffering, or even martyrdom?* Of course, Christians have endured tribulation throughout the church's history. The Bible does indicate that hardships and tribulation (Ac 14:22, KJV) are the lot of believers in this world (2 Ti 3:10–13; Jn 16:33), but this type of tribulation does not represent the wrath of God. Only in the context of the end time is the accumulated wrath of God poured out. It is described as *the wine of God's wrath, poured full strength into the cup of his anger* (14:10). In the Great Tribulation, therefore, *the wrath of God is finished* (15:1).

Obviously, no other judgment in history since the Flood will touch so many people, and no other means of punishment has been described in Scripture as *the great day of God's wrath* (6:17). The Great Tribulation is therefore unique in history in terms of its nature, purpose, and scope. Many Christians today are suffering terribly, and many more will undoubtedly suffer before Jesus comes; however, this suffering is not to be compared with The Great Tribulation.

There is more to The Great Tribulation than Judgment of the ungodly. Jeremiah talks about that day, saying, *Alas! for that day is great, so that none is like it: it is even the time of Jacob's trouble; but he shall be saved out of it.* (30:7). Revelation makes it clear that **The Great Tribulation will also result in Israel recognizing Jesus Christ as their Messiah**

THE SEVENTY SEVENS: DANIEL 9

Daniel, concerned and praying about the captivity of Israel by The Babylonians, says in verse 1-2 that Jeremiah indicated the *Desolation of Jerusalem would last 70 years.* (Jer 25:11; 29:10). Why the desolation? The immediate cause of desolation, of course, was the sin of God's people, especially Idolatry, who rejected His Word, messengers, and initial judgment

(2 Chr 36:15–21). The longer-term cause, however, was the people's rejections of God's system of honoring the *sabbatical year*.

In Lev 25:1-4, 26:33-46 The people were instructed to *give the Land a Sabbath every seven years. They were not to plant, nor harvest.* They were told *If they didn't do this they would be removed from the land so it could rest and enjoy its Sabbaths.* And 2 Chr 36:21states clearly the 70 years are *To fulfill the word of the Lord by the mouth of Jeremiah, until the land had enjoyed her sabbaths: for as long as she lay desolate she kept sabbaths, to fulfil seventy years.* Since Israel had failed to give the land its Sabbath years for a period of 490 years, the people owed the land seventy years of rest.

So, Daniel was thinking about this initial 70 times 7, a 490-year period in which they had not obeyed God's Law of the Sabbath regarding the land. As he prayed in 9:1–19. One of the greatest prayers in the Bible, The period of judgment had nearly run its course. Restoration was now in view as the prophet pleaded for his people. At this point, Gabriel came to tell him about another 490-year period which concerned Israel's future. Verses 24-27. Unfortunately, The Older translations say *Seventy Weeks* in verse 25, which has caused all kinds of strange interpretations of this chapter. . The NIV accurately translates it **70 7's.** Daniel's thinking had been on the previous 70 7's when the Sabbath of the Land had been ignored. Now, Gabriel says, **70 7's are determined for your people and your Holy City.** There have been a particular 490 years in the past and a particular 490 years ahead, for Your People, The Jews, and Your Holy City, Jerusalem. All bible Prophecy centers around Jerusalem and the Jewish People. Read Zech 12-14, where it describes *all nations being against Jerusalem.*

Gabriel states that in the coming 70 7's 6 things are Decreed for The Jews and Jerusalem:

TO:

1. **FINISH THE TRANSGRESSION**

2. **MAKE AN END OF SINS**

3. **MAKE RECONCILIATION FOR INIQUITY**

4. **BRING IN EVERLASTING RIGHTEOUSNESS**

5. **SEAL UP THE VISION AND PROPHECY**

6. **ANOINT THE MOST HOLY PLACE**

All but number 3 take place in Revelation, **CHAPTER 66**. Remember: this prophecy is directed to Israel, not the church. These six elements include God's entire redemptive purpose for Israel.

Then in verses 25 and 26, Gabriel explains this time period with its special order of *sevens* in more detail. First, note how many *sevens* stand between the decree to restore and rebuild Jerusalem and the coming of the Anointed One. The Anointed One, *Messiah* in Hebrew, *Christ* in Greek. There are a total of sixty-nine *sevens-483* years. Amid all the facts that seem to be crowded into these verses, we see that

From the command to restore and rebuild Jerusalem (Neh. ch1-2) *unto Messiah, the, Ruler comes would be 7 7's and 62 7's*, thus 69 7's. Scholars have calculated that 483 years after the decree to rebuild Jerusalem, Jesus rode into Jerusalem on Palm Sunday proclaiming Himself, by this act, as Messiah to Jerusalem, *with the people crying Hosanna, (Please save us, or Save us now)* recognizing Him as Messiah. *(Zech 9:9 and Mt 21:4-11).*

The 7 7's, are the 49 years it took to rebuild Jerusalem during *times of trouble*. The 62 7's are the following 434 years, equaling 69 7's, 483 years, as above.

AFTER the 483 years, *the Messiah would be cut, but not for Himself.* He died for us.

Then, ***The People of The Ruler Who Will Come will destroy the City***. That took place in AD 70, approximately 40 years after Christ's Death and Resurrection. *The people who destroyed the city were from* **Rome**, Western Civilization, ***So The Ruler Who Will Come will be from Western Civilization***. Following that, He, The Ruler who shall come, *will confirm a covenant with many for one 'seven. In the middle of the seven he will put an end to sacrifice and offering. And at the temple he will set up an abomination that causes desolation, until the end that is decreed is poured out on him.*

NOTICE: THERE IS A GAP OF TIME BETWEEN THE DEATH OF CHRIST AND THE APPEARANCE OF THE RULER WHO WILL COME, SINCE JERUSALEM WAS NOT DESTROYED UNTIL 40 YEARS AFTER CHRIST'S DEATH, AND THE RULER IS TO COME AFTER THAT EVENT SOMETIME IN THE FUTURE.

We live in The Gap between the 69th 7 and the final 7. The *He* referred to is the one who is called *Antichrist,* and we shall focus on him especially in chapters 11-19. Daniel here notes that this one will make a contract with Israel for a period of *one seven*, that is, seven years. Halfway through this seven however, he will *cause the sacrifice and offering to end, and will set up the abomination of desolation.* The only place the Jews can offer sacrifices is the Temple in Jerusalem. So the temple must be built by the middle of the 7 years so he can stop the sacrifices and offerings. Israel will accept the Anti (Instead of) Christ as the Messiah, make a 7 years agreement with him concerning their Temple, it will be rebuilt, and in the middle of the 7 years, he will stop the sacrifices, and, we will see later, *sit in the temple of God showing himself that he is God*, and the spiritual blinders will be removed from Israel, and they will know Jesus Is Their Messiah. Idols are an abomination to God, and we are told about the Image of The Antichrist later. The image will be placed in the Temple at some point in the middle of the seven years, and that is when the blinders will be removed from their eyes. This **FINAL 7** is all still future and is described in parts of Daniel and in **CHAPTER 66.**

Jer 31:31–40 and Rom, chapters 9–11, point out that (1) God selected the people of Israel, (2) they are temporarily blinded, and (3) they will be restored. This restoration, will take place in the final *three and one half years of the seven-year period*.

THESE SEVEN YEARS ARE FOR ISRAEL—NOT THE CHURCH!

PASSAGE OF TIME IN THE SEVENTY SEVENS OF DANIEL 9:24–27				
Decree to Restore Jerusalem	First Coming of Christ	Time Gap	Rapture of the Church &The Day of The Lord	Revelation 19:11ff Armageddon
7 Sevens (7x7 years) |——49 years———| Nehemiah Ch 1-2	62 sevens (62x7 years) |— 434 years ——|		The Antichrist Covenant |———3½ years———| |——1,260 Days———|	Time, times and ½ time The Abomination of Desolation |———3½ years———|
|————————-483 years———————-|			|———————————-7 years————————————|	

THE RAPTURE OF THE CHURCH AND THE GREAT TRIBULATION

There are claims made that no one ever heard of a Rapture of the church prior to 1830. After Augustine, his concept of Revelation, A Spiritual Allegory, was held by the majority of the church. Prophecy was not under consideration. Councils were more concerned about other teachings. The Reformers were more concerned about the Authority of Scripture and

Justification by Faith. But once the Scriptures were again studied as they should be, then scholars began looking at prophecy.

Even prior to the Reformation, Pseudo-Ephraim, somewhere between 4th and 7th Century wrote about the church being removed prior to the Tribulation, and that Jesus was returning after the Tribulation. The following authors: Philip Doddridge, 1738; John Gill, 1748, used *Rapture* ,and indicated it could happen at any time, and would remove the Christians prior to the tribulation, and was separate from Christ returning as King of Kings and Lord of Lords. Others authors, who taught the removal of the Christians was prior to the Tribulation were James Macknight, 1763 and Thomas Scott, 1792. Peter Jurieu, 1687 taught there would be a **secret** coming of Christ to rapture the Christians and return to heaven prior to coming at Armageddon in his book, *Approaching Deliverance of The Church.*

I do not believe the Rapture will be secret. I believe it will be on of the most visible and noisy events in all of history as dead are raised, bodies changed, millions caught up. I am convinced it will be fully known what happened. I am also convinced that, because it will be so well know, that the Holy Spirit will use it throughout The Great Tribulation to draw people to Jesus.

I have been asked, *How can you say THE SECOND COMING takes place with the rapture of the church happening and then Jesus not coming to rule until 7 years later at Armageddon, that's two not one?* The Phrase, *THE SECOND COMING* is not a Scriptural Phrase. It is a statement of theologians. The only statement where *second* is used is in He 9:28, *Christ was once offered to bear the sins of many; and unto them that look for him shall he appear the second time without sin unto salvation.* That is the Rapture, and for those living at the end of the Great Tribulation who have received Jesus and not died.

SCRIPTURES SHOW THE RAPTURE IS PRIOR TO THE GREAT TRIBULATION

Church

Again, the word *church* is used seven times, and the word *churches* twelve times in the first three chapters of the book of Revelation. After John is caught up in 4:1 neither word is used again until the warning to churches after the story is ended. (22:16).

The Statements to Thyatira

Those who practice the doctrine of Jezebel, Idolatry, would be *thrown into Great Tribulation*. But to those who do not practice it, He says, *Hold Firm till I Come!* Obviously not in The Great Tribulation.

The Promise to The Church of Philadelphia

As was noted in Letter to the Church, He will keep them *Tereo ek* out of that **hour**. He does not say He will keep them out of harm, but out of the **hour.** Noah was kept out of the water, but he went through the hour/time.

The Christians are seen in Heaven in Chapter 5, and The Great Tribulation begins in chapter 6.

The Order of Events in1 Thessalonians *4:13–5:11*

Paul does not want them to misunderstand what will happen to *those who sleep in Jesus. Sleep* was the idiom of the day in the Gentile World for *death.* We might say, *She has gone to be with The Lord,* or *She has passed away.* It is made clear in 2 Co 5, that when a Christian leaves this life he or she is *Present With The Lord,* and Jesus said, *Whosoever lives and believes in me will never die!* Death is separation: *Physical Death:* The soul/spirit separates from the body. *Spiritual Death:* The Person is separated from God. *Eternal Death:* Eternal Separation from God in The Lake of Fire.

***If you die physically, while you are dead spiritually, you are dead eternally.* But when the Christian eyes close in death, they open in the presence of God-No separation, with Him now, with Him then.**

God breathed into man's nostrils the breath of life and man became a living soul:

The real you is a *Soul,* you live in a tent called the *body,* and you have a *Spirit.*

He tells us, *For if we believe that Jesus died and rose again, even so God will bring with Him those who have fallen asleep in Jesus.* So, when Jesus comes at the Rapture, those who are with Jesus now as Soul/Spirit will come back with Him, and their bodies will be raised and joined together with their Soul/Spirit. Jesus died for the *whole person, body, soul, spirit.*

To strengthen the assurance about those who have died, coming with Jesus, he adds, *For this we are saying to you by the Word of The Lord, that we who are living, who are remaining into the coming* (**parousia**) *of the Lord shall in no way (double negative.. **no not**) precede those who have fallen asleep.*

Because The Lord, Himself, with a shout of command, with voice of the archangel, with the trumpet of God, will descend from heaven and the dead in Christ will rise first, then we who are living and remaining shall be caught up with them in clouds into a meeting of the Lord in (the) air, and thus we shall be forever with the Lord. Therefore comfort one another with these words.

The Thessalonian letters are Paul's first two letters. It is apparent when he wrote these He expected the Lord to come in his lifetime. When you get to his last letters, Philippians, and

Second Timothy from Death Row, He declares, *For I am in a strait betwixt two, having a desire to depart, and to be with Christ; which is much rather better;*(Bad English, Good Greek) *Nevertheless to remain in the flesh is more needful for you.* (Ph 1:23-24) He expects to *depart and be with Christ,* and, *I am now ready to be offered, and the time of my departure is at hand. I have fought a good fight, I have finished my course, I have kept the faith...*(2 Ti 4:6-8)

We must remember the, *Rule of Prophetic Perspective* explained earlier. The prophets saw events not time gaps. Paul mentions two other things that happen. *The Voice of the Archangel, and The Trumpet of God.*

We will see that Michael, The Archangel, comes on the scene in the middle of the seven years to fight for Israel (Ch 12 and Dn. 12), and *The Trumpet of God*...This is not one of the trumpets of the Angels later in the book. The seven angels who sound trumpets are heralding the opening of the 7 sealed book. The *First Trumpet of God* sounded at Mt Sinai (Ex. 19:13; 20:18, He. 5:19) to assemble Israel as God's people, and the *Last Trumpet of God* will sound to reassemble Israel. Is. 27:12-13 speaks of *The Great Trumpet* being blown to *regather Israel. The Last Trumpet* (I Co. 15:51-58) is not the trumpet of the seventh angel. *It is the trumpet of God!* So Paul has been describing three major events The Rapture of the Church, The Conversion of Israel to Jesus, and the resulting attempt of Satan/Antichrist to destroy those Jews who Believe in Jesus. The last two happening between **The *parousia*** and **The *epiphaneia* of The *parousia*** (See the discussion of *words* following the second paragraph below)

It is a shame that there is a Chapter Division here. This is a letter, and the same thought continues. He goes on to demonstrate that the next event is the *The Day of The Lord. Concerning the times and seasons* (**Chronos** and **Chairos**: passages of time and appointed times) *you have no need that I write to you,* Why? *We know perfectly* **The Day of The Lord is coming** as a **Thief in the night**. **The Day of the Lord is The Great Tribulation.**

As I pointed out in the Letter to Sardis, Jesus made it clear to the apostles, in Acts, that *It is* **not for you to know** the **Chronos** nor the **Chairos** of the future events: So Paul will not uselessly discuss what is **not for us to know**. He goes on to explain that those who do not know Jesus the events will come upon them when *They say peace and safety, sudden destruction will come upon them as travail upon a woman with child and they shall not escape.* After describing the difference between the Christian and the non Christian, he adds, *God has not appointed us to wrath, but to obtain salvation by our Lord Jesus Christ, Who died for us, that, whether we wake or sleep, we should live together with Him. The Great Tribulation* is the time of *The Wrath of God*...Paul says We are not appointed to that!

Meanings of Words That Relate to Jesus' Coming

It has been customary for those who believe the rapture of the church will take place before the Great Tribulation to call the Rapture the **parousia**, a word that has come into English from Greek. In Greek, **parousia** means *a personal arrival or coming*.

In the New Testament it is used to refer to the coming of various persons (1 Co 16:17). When **parousia** is used of Jesus' coming in the future, it is never used alone to describe His return at the conclusion of the Tribulation period as King of kings and Lord of lords. However, it is used alone to describe His coming for the church at the Rapture.

The *Rapture* and the *Second Coming/Revelation* of our Lord are separated by a period of seven years—the *seventieth seven* of Daniel's prophecy. During this time the church will be with the Lord. This entire seven-year period is technically referred to as the **parousia.** Thus the **parousia** begins with the Rapture and ends with Jesus' return at the Battle of Armageddon (19:2). In the Greek New Testament, **parousia** is used in 1 Th 2:19, 3:13, 4:15, and 5:23 in connection with the Rapture.

While the word *rapture* is not used in the Bible, the concept is. The word *rapture* comes from the Latin word **repare,** which means to *snatch up with force*. The Greek word **harpadzo** in 1 Th 4:17 means the same thing. It is translated *caught up*.

2 Th 2:8 calls Jesus' coming at Armageddon the *Brightness of His Coming* (**epiphaneia** of His **parousia.**) In this case, **parousia** is used with another word to explain what part of the **parousia** is in view. Peter uses a similar word **ephanes** in Ac 2:20, where It is translated as *glorious, awesome, notable,* depending on which translation. It is obvious Peter is referring to the same event as that noted in 2 Th 2:8: the coming of Jesus at Armageddon. Literally, **epiphaneia** means *brightness* or *splendor*. It is used of Jesus' appearance as a man on earth in 2 Ti 1:10, of the Rapture when Christians will see Jesus in His brilliance, and of His coming at Armageddon when the world will see Him in His brilliance.

In some literature there is a discussion of the word I translated above as a *meeting* (**apantesis),** claiming the only other place the word is used in the New Testament is in Acts 28, 15 where when Paul landed in Italy, the Brothers came for a meeting with Paul, and they add, not in scripture, they went *immediately* (assumed) to Rome, so it means a meeting and you accompany someone to their destination immediately. It is also used in Matthew 25:6 with the wise and foolish virgins. But. the verb form of the word is used throughout the New Testament to refer to any kind of a meeting between people, as it is throughout the Common Greek of the day. The New Testament is not written in Classical Greek, but Common Greek. I call it *Street Greek*

The teaching of II Thessalonians 2 (quotes are from this chapter unless another book is named.)

Paul had outlined the order of events in I Th They knew The **parousia** would come first, then the *Day of the Lord*. He starts by saying, *Now we beseech you, Brothers, by the* **parousia** *of our Lord Jesus Christ, and by our gathering together unto Him, that you stop being shaken in mind, or be troubled neither by spirit, nor by word, nor by a letter as if from us, that the Day of the Lord is* here. (original text is not *The Day of Christ* as in KJV) The church was being persecuted, and it is obvious there were those telling them, *This is the Day of the Lord,* and someone had sent a letter and signed Paul's Name to it saying the same thing. From what Paul had taught, this meant to them they had missed the **Parousia., The Rapture!** One author made a statement, that *they could not have considered it the Day of the Lord because the things happening in Revelation were not happening.* But, The Book of Revelation had not yet been written, and they had little idea of the events of The Day of The Lord. As a matter of fact, Christians who have been persecuted even in modern times, having the Book of Revelation, have thought they were in *The Great Tribulation, The Day of the Lord.*

Paul reminds them, that *The Day of The Lord will not come until the Apostasy*, (or *The Apostate Women*), comes first. *Apostasy* refers to departure from the faith—false Christianity. (it is never used of physical departure) It refers to a great, worldwide religious system that is called the great prostitute in Rev. 17:1. This religious system will exercise tremendous power in the last days and *The Man of Sin is Revealed, the Son of Destruction, who opposes and exalts himself above all that is called God, or that is worshipped; so that he as God sits in the temple of God showing himself that he is God.* The words indicate, The Apostasy will come first and the The Antichrist will make a *sudden appearance* **(apokalupto)** no one will know who he is until. suddenly. he comes on the scene. Paul is telling them, **The fact that you do not see the Man of Sin means you have not missed the parousia.** The church is in heaven in Chapter 5 of Revelation and the Man of Sin makes his appearance in Chapter 6.

As we will see, Satan gives this man *His Throne, His Power and Great Authority,* (Ch 13:2) (He will accept what Satan offered Jesus), He will be *Energized by Satan with signs and lying wonders deceiving the unbelievers.* In addition, *God will send strong delusion to believe The Lie.* WHY? *That they all might be judged who believed not the truth, but had pleasure in unrighteousness.*

Notice the things said about this difficult time under the *Man of Sin.* First, there is something holding him from appearing, and the one hindering him will be taken out of the way and he will be revealed. Many writers believe the Holy Spirit will be removed, BUT

The whole Bible makes it clear there is nowhere where God is not. *in Him we live, and move and have out being.* Psalm 139 indicates *there is nowhere we can go without God being there, even among the stars or in Sheol.* The 144,000 of Israel are sealed. The seal of God is the Holy Spirit. People will be saved during the Great Tribulation, and the only way anyone can be saved is being drawn by the Holy Spirit. The Last Message in the Bible states, *The Spirit and The Bride say come...* Jesus said, *you are the salt of the earth!* Salt is antiseptic. It is the **Holy Spirit in the Church,** holding back the Man of Sin. And *The Lord will consume him with the Spirit of His mouth and destroy him with the Brightness of His coming* **(epiphaneia of His parousia),** Armageddon*!*

Only two events are said to come as a *Thief in the Night*

I Th 5:1 and 2 Pe 3:10 state, *The Day of The Lord will come as A Thief in the night.* Jesus indicates in Mt 24:43 that His coming at the **parousia** will be as a **Thief**, and in Rev 16:15 Jesus Says, *Behold, I come as a Thief,* and in 3:3, He warns the church of Sardis, *If you do not watch, I will come upon you as a Thief, and you will no not* (Double Negative) *know what hour I will come upon you.*

If the **parousia** would be *Mid-Tribulation* it would be exactly 3 ½ years after the Antichrist signs the seven year covenant with Israel, and the date would be know. If *Post-Tribulation*, at the *End of The Tribulation, The End of the Age, Armageddon,* it would be exactly 7 years after the covenant is signed. Why are the Armies gathered to Armageddon? Because they know exactly the day when Jesus is returning as King of Kings and Lord of Lords.

Discussion of Three End-time Questions

Matthew 24:1–25:13

After Jesus and His disciples came from the temple to the Mount of Olives, the disciples called attention to the temple's beauty and magnificence. Jesus responded by noting the entire structure would be totally destroyed. The disciples were troubled by this word and asked three specific questions: *(1) When will the temple be destroyed? (2) What will be the sign of Your parousia? (3) What will be the sign of the end of the age?* Matthew does not record Jesus' answer to the first question, but Luke records it in in Luke 21:20–21

When you see Jerusalem surrounded by armies, then know that the its desolation is near. Then let them which are in Judaea flee to the mountains; and let them which are in the midst of it depart out; and don't let those that are in the countries enter it . For these be the days of vengeance, that all things which are written may be fulfilled. But woe unto them that are pregnant, and to them who are nursing babies, in those days! for there shall be great distress in the land, and wrath upon this people. And they shall fall by the edge of the sword, and shall be led away captive into all nations:

and Jerusalem shall be trodden down of the Gentiles, until **the times of the Gentiles** be fulfilled. (Rev 11:2 states that the *Gentiles will tread the Holy City under foot for 42 months —3 ½ years. at the time of the events in 11*)

A question I ask teaching Bible College/Seminary students around the world, is: Both Matthew and Luke show the Temptation of Jesus: **1.** Both list the first one as Turning the Stones into Bread. **2.** Matthew shows the second one as Throwing Himself from the Highest Wall of the Temple, whereas Luke shows the second one as, Satan showing Jesus all the Kingdoms of the World, and offering to give them to Jesus, If He will bow down and worship Satan. **3.**Matthew shows the third one as bowing to Satan, and Luke shows the third one as Throwing Himself off the wall. **Which one is the correct Order? Why?**

Luke is showing Jesus as The Last Adam, who did not fail where the First Parents Failed. Eve *saw the tree was good for food, pleasant to the eyes, and a tree to be desired to make one wise.* Satan had told her, *You will be like God, knowing good and evil.* This fits the statement in I John 2:16, *For all that is in the world, The Lust of the Flesh, The Lust of the Eyes and the Pride of Life is not of the father but of the world,* This is the same order Luke presents for the Temptation of Jesus.

Anyone who has studied Matthew seriously knows that, frequently, Matthew uses a Topical Arrangement of his material rather than a Chronological Arrangement. His two chapters, on 8-9, include some Miracles that happened at different times in Jesus ministry. Matthew is the Gospel to The Jews. Showing how Jesus fulfilled prophecy, and that He is the King of the Jews. So the *Climax* of the Temptations is shown as *the one which would be the greatest for the one born to be King. I'll give you all these Kingdoms. You can have them now Jesus. All you have to do is bow down and worship me!*

The Apostles had asked Jesus in the order, obviously, that they understood the end times: **1.** *Jerusalem destroyed,* **2.** *The parousia,* **3.** *the end of the age.* Matthew, with his emphasis on the Jews, deals with the last half of the Tribulation first, because that is when the prophecies about Israel accepting Jesus will take place, and the *time of Jacobs Trouble,* which we discussed earlier, will reach its fiercest. **This is why it is necessary to study CHAPTER 66, which puts things in correct perspective.**

Question 3 relates to *the sign of the end of the age.* The *end of the age* will come at Armageddon when Jesus comes back as King of kings and Lord of lords. Paul uses the phrase, **The Age of This Kosmos** (Eph 2.2) as referring to the present age.

Matthew, next, gives us a preview of the experience of God's people throughout history on earth toward the end of the age. He speaks of Wars, Earthquakes, Famine, Disease, and calls them *the Beginning of Birth Pains*. He talks about False Prophets and False Christs deceiving many, iniquity overflowing and the love decreasing. He talks about enduring until *The End*.

Notice, among other things, that worldwide proclamation of the gospel is to occur *before the end comes*. Not before the **parousia.** 14:6-7 Prior to a description of many of the things that will take place after Ch 14, including *Armageddon, The End of The Age*, An Angel flies through Heaven Proclaiming the Gospel to the whole world. (6-7) That is the final preaching of the Gospel. It takes place just prior to *The End of The Age*.

There are several things which indicate Matthew primarily has Jews in mind, who as we will see later, will receive Jesus as their Messiah. He mentions they will be *hated of all nations*. (see Zech. Ch 12-14)

15–25 speak of the last three and one-half years of the Great Tribulation." (v. 15). Jesus refers to the prophecy in Daniel 9:27, saying *When you see the abomination of desolation. As spoken of by Daniel The Prophet, stand in the Holy Place, let them who be in Jerusalem flee...* That is the Holy of Holies in the Temple in Jerusalem and that will take place in the middle of the final seven years. We will see more details of the final three and one-half-year period later on in our study. Jesus also, said, *Pray that your flight be neither in the winter nor on the Sabbath Day,* which would only refer to Jews because they could only go so far on the Sabbath Day. (We will see more about fleeing from Jerusalem when we discuss Chapter 12)

He warns about the danger of responding to false Christs at any time, now or during the Great Tribulation. This warning indicates that when Jesus comes, those who are following false Christs will be like vultures gathered around and feeding on a dead carcass. The use of the word *lightning* here refers to the **epiphaneia** of Jesus'**parousia.** As we will see later in our discussion of Ch 12, the nation of Israel will not have to hunt for Jesus following the Battle of Armageddon. He will go where His people are and reveal himself to them.

He, then, describe the end of the age.. Here our Lord says He will send His angels to, *gather His elect . . . from one end of heaven to the other. The elect* here in heaven represent another piece of evidence that the church will not go through the Great Tribulation.

There is, next, a transition explaining the certainty of these prophecies, comparing them to the budding of a fig tree to fulfillment of signs that announce the approach of Jesus' coming. The fig tree's budding shows that summer is near, and the signs of the times presented in this discourse indicate that Jesus' coming is near also. A reminder that, according to Daniel 9, All prophecy centers around Jerusalem and the Jewish People. Isaiah 5:1-7 Indicate Israel and its people are the vineyard of God. The Fig Tree Is Planted in the Midst of the Vineyard:

In Luke 13: 6-9 Jesus spoke a parable: *A certain man had a fig tree planted in his vineyard; and he came and sought fruit on it, and found none. Then he said to the dresser of his vineyard, Behold, these three years I come seeking fruit on this fig tree, and find none: cut it down; why let it cumber the ground? And he answering said unto him, Lord, let it alone this year also, till I shall dig about it, and dung it: And if it bear fruit, well: and if not, then after that you will cut it down.*

The Gospel of John is centered on Jesus Trips to Jerusalem during the Feast Days over a three year period. It was during the last one that Jesus declared Himself as Messiah, and was rejected by the capital. In connection with these events He wept over Jerusalem, and later cursed the Fig Tree, even though it was not time for figs. It was not time for the Jewish eyes, as a people, to be opened. That will take place in **CHAPTER 66.**

Bible translators frequently are not interested in Bible Prophecy as such, and sometimes pick out the wrong meaning of a word. Many people have come up with different ideas because of the translation, ***this generation.*** Some, take it to mean all prophecy will be fulfilled 40 years later in the destruction of Jerusalem. Some have taken it to be the *generation Who Saw The Fig Tree, Jerusalem, Bud* during the 6 day war in 1967 when Israel won back the Old City, and have set dates for the coming of Jesus, which, of course, did not happen.

But, the primary meaning of the Greek word translated *generation,* **genea,** has to do with *those descending from a common ancestor,* **race.** Jesus is simply saying, ***This race will not pass away until all these things be fulfilled.*** **The Jewish Race, descended from Abraham, Isaac and Jacob will still be when these things are fulfilled** in **CHAPTER 66.**

We must not separate what follows from the last phrase of v. 34, about *all these things being fulfilled.* V. 36 adds, *But of that day and hour knows no man, no, not the angels of heaven, but my Father only.* The closing events of **CHAPTER 66, begin with the *parousia*, The Rapture of the Church. Jesus now gives His description of the *parousia*, with the emphasis of it happening without warning, and no one knowing when it will happen.**

37–39-The *coming,* **parousia,** *of the son of Man will be just like the days of Noah. For as in those days before the flood they were eating and drinking, marrying and giving in marriage, until the day Noah entered into the ark, and they did not know until the flood came and took them all away; so will the coming,* **parousia,** *of the Son of Man be. (NASB)*

In other words, **it will be business as usual,** when the rapture takes place. There will not be,

business as usual during The Great Tribulation: Just in the first half of the seven years, as we will study later, peace will be taken from the earth, there will be worldwide famine, and , one quarter of the earth's population killed. That's not **business as usual.** And, the last half of the seven years is worse. So comparison with the days of Noah shows the Lord's **parousia** will take place suddenly and without warning. By contrast, when Jesus comes to earth at the Battle of Armageddon at the end of the age, every eye will see Him. He will not come then as a thief. In fact, the armies of the world will know He is coming, and they will make war with Him. In the parable of the ten virgins (25:1–13), Jesus teaches about His sudden appearing at the beginning of the **parousia.**

The next phrase has caused a controversy: *Then there will be two men in the field; one will be taken and one will be left. Two women will be grinding at the mill; one will be taken and one will be left. (NASB)*

I have heard the following argument from some good brothers who believe the church is going through the Great Tribulation: *How can you say the word, **taken,** in verse 39 to means the people were taken away to destruction by he flood, and the same word, **taken,** in verses 40 and 41 mean taken into heaven at the Rapture?* Their idea is that the one **taken,** is the Christian, who is taken by the authorities and killed once the Antichrist comes on the scene.

The difference is in the Original Greek Text. The word translated, **taken,** in verse 39 is the verb **airo.** It is used in John 15:1, where Jesus states *I am the true vine, and My Father is the vinedresser. Every branch in Me that does not bear fruit,* **He takes away.** The word translated, **taken,** twice in verse 40 is the word, **paralambano.** It is used in Jn 14:2: *I go to prepare a place for you. If I go and prepare a place for you, I will come again and* **receive you to Myself**, *that where I am, there you may be also.* **paralambano** means to **Receive Alongside Of.**

As stated above, translators are not usually students of prophecy. These verses show a perfect picture of the Rapture of The Church. Luke 17 uses the same Greek terminology as Matthew describing the **parousia** being without warning, and adds, in addition to the *eating and drinking of Noah's day,* adds *Likewise also as it was in the* **days of Lot**; *they did eat, they drank, they bought, they sold, they planted, they built; But the same day that Lot went out of Sodom it rained fire and brimstone from heaven, and destroyed them all. Even thus shall it be in the day when the Son of man is revealed.* Remember the Angel was to destroy the entire area and while he was leading Lot out of Sodom, he told Lot to *flee into the mountains.* Lot was afraid to go into the mountains, so he requested the Angel not destroy a small city, and let Lot and his family go there. The angel answered, *Behold, I grant you this request also, not to overthrow the town of which you* *have spoken. Hurry, escape there, **for I cannot do anything until you arrive there. (19:22)** 2 Pet 4:6-9 reminds us that Lot was delivered before the destruction of Sodom and Gomorrah . Jesus said it will be the same as the days of Noah, as the days of Lot,* The Godly delivered before judgment.

Jesus ends the teaching by indicating, *If the owner of a house would know what time the thief was coming, he would be sure to watch, and goes on to say,* **In such an hour as you think not the Son of Man comes;** *and He follows this with the Parable of the Wise and Foolish Virgins which indicates His coming while they were sleeping. (See Appendix D outline of Matthew 24-25)*

THE SCENE IN HEAVEN, CHAPTER 4-5

The first thing John saw was a Throne was laid (firmly fixed, established). Revelation is the Book of the Throne, *thronos*. The word occurs 45 times in **CHAPTER 66,** 12 times here. In the midst of all the events to follow, God is still on the Throne. Obviously, this is a picture of the Father. God is called *invisible* (Col. 1:15; I Tim. 1:17; He. 11:27), Jesus said *God is Spirit* (Jn 4.24). So in John's description, His *appearance is like a jasper* (Diamond like—brilliance, purity), *like a sardine stone* (blood red-judgment and redemption—the first severe judgment of The Great Tribulation is a rider on a red horse). The Glory of God, indescribable. Around the throne *the Rainbow,* which indicates the Promises of God, both blessing and judgment are about to happen, and *24 elders on thrones, dressed in white, with crowns of gold on their heads.*

In Old Testament times the many priests were divided into twenty-four different orders, each order having a representative. When these representatives came together, they represented all the priesthood. Some believe these elders are angels. They usually believe the church will go through the Great Tribulation. *Nowhere in the Bible are angels called elders.* However, in Acts 20:17–28, I Pe 5:1ff. we see examples of those who are called elders, and they are not angels.

The twenty-four elders are sitting on Thrones, dressed in white *raiment,* (outer clothing such as robes) and have crowns of gold on their heads. The crown is the **stephanos,** *The Victors Crown* given to winners in games like the Olympics, and to Conquerors. When Jesus comes back later as *King of Kings and Lord of Lords,* he has **diadema** (English word, *diadem*) *The Kingly Crown.* (Actually plural in Ch. 19)

Who do the twenty-four elders of Revelation 4:4 represent? Some believe they represent only the church. They believe no Israelite has any part in this group because at this point Israel as a nation will not yet have accepted Jesus Christ as Savior. These scholars often use Daniel 12:2

to show the righteous people of the Old Testament will not be resurrected until just before or just after the Battle of Armageddon. I do not agree that such a conclusion can be based on this verse. Some men and women of God in the Old Testament were not Israelites (Noah, for example). According to the argument that no Israelite is represented by the twenty-four elders, Noah should be resurrected when the church is raptured, but not King David? Not Isaiah? This argument is not, therefore, valid.

The twenty-four here represents all the righteous people of the Old Testament and all the righteous people of the New Testament. Why? As we read Hebrews 11, we see it is the story of God's Old Testament heroes of faith. Some of these heroes were Israelites; some were not. Verses 39 and 40 indicate *the righteous of the Old Testament are made perfect or complete together with New Testament believers, the church.* The New Jerusalem, the home of the bride of Christ, in 21:12–14 lists in the foundation the names of the 12 apostles and in the gates are the names of the 12 Tribes of Israel. A comparison of these Scriptures indicates the righteous of the Old Testament are represented together with the righteous of the New Testament in the New Jerusalem by twenty-four representatives: twelve tribes and twelve apostles.

John sees *lightings and thunderings and voices: and there were seven torches of fire burning before the throne, which are the seven Spirits of God.* This is a strong picture of coming judgment from God.

Four *living ones* are described, and four *living ones* are also pointed out to us in Ezekiel 1. As one reads both of these passages, he or she may see the description in Ezekiel differs from that in Revelation. However, the use of the words *lion, ox, man,* and *eagle* in each description indicate what is pictured is the same in each of the two passages.

At the point of this prophecy, Ezekiel is in his thirtieth year, the year he is to begin his priesthood. God wants to let this young priest and future prophet know through a vision of *four living ones* that God still rules in the affairs of people. He Sees the king of wild animals, the *Lion,* the king of domesticated animals, the *Ox,* The king of birds, The *Eagle* and the king God placed over creation, *Man.* Above the created things, There is a platform of *the terrible crystal* (Ice). On top of the ice a throne and Ezekiel sees a man on a throne who has fire going up and down his body. This One is surrounded by dazzling light, and the glory that surrounds Him is like a rainbow on a rainy day. The rainbow signifies all of God's promises will be summed up in a man, while the fire shows this Man will purify and judge. It reminds the young Priest, who is to be a Prophet, That God is still over His Creation. Ezekiel tells us this **is the likeness of the Glory of the Lord.** God's glory represents everything He is: His nature, power, and character. Everything one can say about God can be summed up by the word *glory.* Heb.1:3 says Jesus is

The Brightness of God's Glory and the Express Image of His person. James 2:1 says, *My brothers do not have the Faith of our* **Lord Jesus Christ, The Glory**, *with respect of persons.* (Greek Text)

Remember the title of this book? It is *The Revelation of Jesus Christ* 1:1). There is the possibility that, since Ezekiel's vision was a vision of God's glory, and Jesus is God's glory, these *four living ones* represent characteristics of Jesus Christ in both Ezekiel and Revelation. This representation is not new; some of the early church writers of the second century had the same opinion. They believed the four Gospels pictured characteristics of the life of Jesus, which are indicated by the lion, ox, man, and eagle. One of these characteristics of Him is emphasized in each of the four Gospels.

The Lion Matthew To The Jews, Presents Jesus As The King of Israel

The Ox Mark To The Romans, Action, the Suffering Servant of God

The Man: Luke To The Greeks, The Perfect Man, The Last Adam Who Didn't Fail

The Eagle John To The Christians, The God Man, Who Gives Life To The Full

This chapter ends with the Living ones praising God, with the Elders falling down before God worshiping Him and throwing their crowns before Him, Why should they? **You are worthy O Lord, to receive glory and honor and power: for you have created all things, and for your pleasure they are and were created.**

THE SEVEN SEALED SCROLL

5:1-4 begins with John seeing a Scroll written on the inside and on the backside, and sealed with seven seals in God's right hand. So when the scroll is rolled up and sealed, what is written on the front would be on the inside, and what is written on the back would be on the outside. And *I saw a strong angel proclaiming with a loud voice, Who is worthy to open the book, and to loose the seals thereof? And no man in heaven, nor in earth, neither under the earth, was able to open the book, neither to look thereon. And I wept much, because no man was found worthy to open and to read the book, neither to look thereon.* (**book and scroll will be used interchangeably because various translations use one or the other) Why would John cry because no one could open the scroll?** Remember He is *in The Spirit.*

Also, Remember, the Bible is its own best interpreter. In the 26 pictures of Jesus given in Chapter one, it was pointed out that the primary picture of Jesus in the book of revelation is the **Go'el,** which is the Hebrew word used in the Old Testament, and is translated as *kinsman* *redeemer* or *nearest relative*. Its use is associated with the ownership of property and how property was passed on from one generation to another. Property during this period of time was protected by certain legal statutes. In the event one mortgaged his property and later could not redeem it, his **Go'el** could redeem it for him.

Lev 25:8–55 gives these details of property ownership for the people of Israel, including conditions of sale and terms of redeeming one's rights of ownership. This scriptural setting also includes terms of indenture—that is, the conditions under which poor persons might contract to work for others for given periods of time.

In the story of Ruth in the Bible we have the practical application of the **Go'el** principle in what Boaz did when he married Ruth (Ruth 3:9–12; 4:1–12). He redeemed, or bought back, Ruth's property for her. The terms of these property transactions were written on the inside of scrolls and stated what had to be done to redeem the property (Jer 32:11). The scroll was signed on the back with the names of the witnesses and the name of the **Go'el**. It was rolled up and sealed so the details of the agreement were on the inside and the names of the witnesses and the **Go'el** on the outside. In the event a person lost his property and could not redeem it, only his **Go'el** could open the seals and see what had to be done to redeem the property.

Heb. 2:6b-9 says: *What is man that you think of him or the son of man that you care for him? You made him for a little while lower than the angels. You crowned him with glory and honor You put all things under his feet. For when he put all things under subjection to him , he left nothing that is not subjected to him. But now we do not yet see all things under his control, but we see Jesus, who was made for a short time lower than the angels on account of the suffering of death, crowned with glory and honor so that by God's grace he would taste death in behalf of everyone.*

God made man in His image, gave him honor by putting him over all creation. Man lost it, gave into Satan's temptations, and, as a result, Jesus called Satan, *the ruler of the kosmos, the structured society,* (Jn 12:31; 14:30; 16:11), this and the curse was placed on creation and death, pain, suffering, misery, war, hatred, prejudice and all sin came into the world.

John knew that until someone could open the scroll to see what had to happen to take back what Adam lost, Satan would continue as a roaring lion, and sin, pain, misery, war, hatred, prejudice, and suffering would also continue. John knew that people could never be freed from the curse of sin and that God's kingdom would never come on earth unless someone could not only open this scroll, but could do what had to be done to take it back. So He Cried.

One of the Elders said to john: **Stop crying, look, The Lion of the tribe of Judah, The root/descendent (Hridza) of David, has overcome to open the book and its seals. (Hridza:** *Root, shoot, branch offspring, descendent,* the word is used all these different ways). Jesus is the *root*, the creator, who gave life to David, and He is also the *offspring*, the descendent of David.

Instead of a *lion*, John saw in the *in midst of the throne, and the four living ones and the elders, a lamb having been killed, having seven horns and seven eyes which are the seven spirits of God having been sent forth into all the earth.* Obviously, Thus Christ, God's Son and our **Go'el**, proceeds to lake the scroll out of the Father's hand. No one else can or ever could have done so or even dared to try.

When He had taken the book, The Great Praise begins: First, each one of the four living ones and twenty-four elders is praising Him with a harp, and each has a bowl of *incense/the prayers of saints* Musical instruments are frequently used to praise God in the Psalms. The prayers can possibly be summed up as , *Your kingdom come*, as in Matthew 6:10. And they are offered to Jesus, *for there is one God and one mediator between God and man, The Man, Christ Jesus!*

The Praise consists of them singing *a new song: You are worthy to take the book, and to open the seals thereof: for you were killed, and have redeemed us to God by your blood out of every tribe and tongue, and people, and nation; And have made us unto our God kings and priests: and we shall reign on the earth.* The Redeemed of all ages past are now physically in God's presence.

In Revelation, Christ is first mentioned as a Lamb in 5:6. Earlier, John the Baptist and Peter referred to Christ as a lamb. John the Baptist said that Jesus was *the Lamb of God, who takes away the sin of the world!* (Jn1:29). Referring to our spiritual redemption, Peter indicated we are saved by *the precious blood of Christ, like that of a lamb without blemish or spot* (1 Pet 1:19). Boaz indeed redeemed Ruth's property, but Christ has redeemed, spiritually and eternally, those who believe in Him. *Remember always that you are ransomed from the effects of sin by the blood of Christ the slain lamb! Without the shedding of blood there is no forgiveness of sins* (Heb 9:22).

Jesus poured out His entire sinless life for you, me, and all other people, including those who have not yet heard about it. *Remember also that to have our sins forgiven does not remove us from temptation to sin again.* Christ, however, overcame all temptation to sin (Lk 4:1–12), lives in us (Gal 2:20), and can enable us through our faith in Him, and the power of the Holy Spirit within to overcome all temptations (1 Cor 10:13). Paul, in Rom 6, instructs us to *know you are dead to sin, Log it down in your book, I am dead to sin, yield to The Holy Spirit.* What a great day of praise that is going to be for those who know Jesus Christ! From what is happening in our world, it appears this day will soon come. We must tell people about Jesus, for the time is drawing near when He is coming to take us to be with Him forever.

Then *myriads times myriads* (biggest number in Greek language) of angels join the praise adding, *Worthy is the Lamb that was killed to receive power, and riches, and wisdom, and strength, and honor, and glory, and blessing.* Then, *every created thing which is in heaven, and on the earth, and under the earth, and such as are in the sea, and all that are in them, I heard saying, Blessing, and honor, and glory, and power, be unto him that sits upon the throne, and unto the Lamb for ever and ever.* What an awesome moment.

All of Creation is praising God. Why? Because the Lamb has the book, he is now going to open it and do the things necessary to give man back his inheritance, to complete the events of **CHAPTER 66.**

CHAPTER 6
The Opening of the First Six Seals

Seal 1: As The Lamb opens the first seal of the seven-sealed scroll. one of the four living creatures says **Go!**. It is a command because *go* shows more clearly that nothing can move without permission from Heaven. It is a command to the rider on the white horse who holds a bow. As pointed out in the study of II Thes.2, The Day of The Lord begins with the appearance of the Man of Sin, The Antichrist. Moreover, the rider is given a *victor's crown* (**stephanos**), and he goes forward *as a conqueror and to conquer.* The crown has to be *given* to him.

. The primary meaning and usage of the preposition, **anti,** is *instead of,* The Antichrist is going to be the man the world and Israel accept as their Christ instead of the true Christ. For Israel to accept him as Messiah, he must be Jewish and A descendent of David. When Jesus comes back in Ch. 19, He too will be on a white horse; here in Revelation 6:2 the white horse rider is an imitation. Third, Jesus will have the **diadems** or *kingly crowns* on His head: crowns don't have to be *given* to Him. He is King of Kings. Fourth, the bow is a military weapon indicating he will have military power. Only the Antichrist needs that. The only weapon we will see Jesus need, is **the two edged sword of His mouth. He speaks and its done!**

Zech Ch 12–14 emphasize both God's judgment of the nations and His restoration of Israel. Jer 30:7 calls it *the time of Jacob's trouble* (KJV), while Dan 12:1 indicates it will be the *greatest time of trouble in history.* The Great Tribulation is the time of the wrath of God. We will see this as we go on through the book of Revelation. As we have endeavored to point out and as 1 Thes 5:9 clearly states, *Christians are not appointed to suffer wrath.*

The Antichrist is called by many names in the Bible *The Antichrist (1 Jn 2:18), The little horn (Dan 7:8, 23–26), King of fierce appearance (Dan 8:23) The prince that shall come (Dan 9:26–27, The worthless shepherd (Zech 11:15–17), The man of lawlessness (2 Thes 2:1–12), The son of destruction (2 Thes 2:3). The Wild Beast (Rev. 13). In addition, from Daniel, He will be: A Boastful speaker (7:8), A Military man (8:24) A Successful businessman (8:24) who will cause business to prosper*

(8:24), A Master of intrigue and deception (8:25), A Proud person (Daniel 8:25), A Man who seduces with flattery (11:32) One who magnifies himself above God (11:36), One who with gold, silver and precious stones honors the God of Forces or Fortresses, and a God unknown to his fathers. (11:38). 11:37 says, He will not regard the God of his Fathers,(Daniel only uses this phrase for Jews) nor the desire of women. This has caused some to claim he will be homosexual. That is not the meaning of this verse. Every Jewish girl was hoping and praying, strongly desiring, to be the mother of the coming Messiah. So it is an idiom for the Messiah, Jesus. He will not honor Jesus. (see Appendix C on Dan Ch 8 and 11 which show several principles of prophecy and these characteristics of the Antichrist.)

There are also verses like Is. 14:4, where he is pictured as King of Babylon, and Is. 10:5-6, 30:27-37, where he is pictured as The Assyrian, Daniel 8, where he is pictured as a Syrian. Whoever happens to be Israel's enemy is sometimes used by the prophets to project forward to the Antichrist. But we have shown previously, **He must be Jewish, and be from Western Civilization.** We will discuss the Antichrist further in connection with Revelation 13 and 17. For a time he will probably bring peace and straighten out the world's economy. **These events taking place will affect the entire world.**

Seal 2: As the second seal is opened, and the command given, **Go!** a fiery red horse emerges. He is ridden by one who carries a large sword. This rider has power to take peace from the earth. His emergence symbolizes war that will follow. (Possibly Ez Ch 38-39)

Seal 3: When He had opened the third seal, a living one said, **Go!** And a black horse whose rider carries a pair of scales went forth. And I heard a voice in the midst of the four beasts say, A measure of wheat for a **denarius**, and three measures of barley for a **denarius** and see you do not hurt the oil and the wine. A measure is about a quart, and is considered enough food for one adult for one day. A **denarius** is an adult's wage for one day. If you have to have wheat, you can feed only one person for a day's wage. If you are content with Barley, you can feed three persons on a day's wage. This is a huge worldwide famine. In the wake of war, as masses of people are diverted from food production to fighting, famine frequently follows. However, with the world's rapidly increasing population, the inability of the world's people to produce enough to feed themselves will doubtless make this matter worse.

Why is it said, Do not hurt the oil and the wine? Oil and Wine are considered luxuries.. A Rolls Royce in the driveway will not do you much good when you can't get food for your family. People will sell their souls for luxuries, at this time they will have to try to sell luxuries for food. They do not understand what Jesus meant when He told the woman of Samaria, Everyone who *drinks this water will thirst, again, but whoever drinks of the water that I will give him will never be thirsty again, for the water that I will give him will be in him a spring of water springing up into eternal life. (Jn 4:13–14).* Jesus was explaining that **satisfaction does not come from the outside in, but from the inside out**.

Seal 4. After the fourth seal is broken, and a living one says, *Go!* a pale (*chloros*-yellow green) horse emerges ridden by one called *Death* who is followed closely by *Hades.* Here Death and Hades are personified; that is, they are referred to as persons. Personification is common in the Old Testament. For example, in Proverbs wisdom is treated as if it were a woman (1:20 + many others). Hades always follows death for the non-Christian. A fourth part of the earths population will be killed *with sword, and with hunger, and with death, and with the wild animals of the earth.* What if your pet puppy or cat suddenly become wild?

Seal 5. Under the fifth seal John sees a host of martyrs. The martyrs of past history would have been resurrected at the Rapture. These are those who accept Jesus Christ during the first half of the Great Tribulation period and who will be killed because of their faith in God. They will be *under the altar* because God will consider their deaths as a sacrifice. Notice, they cry out to God for vengeance, *white robes are given to them,* and they are told, *rest yet for a little season, until their fellowservants also and their brethren, that were about to be killed as they were, should be fulfilled.* (for Greek students, **mello,** which you learned early in Greek usually means *about to ,*but frequently simply means *going to.*-See discussion by A. T. Robertson, *The Grammar of the Greek New Testament in the Light of Historical Research*). Here, *about to* fits the context and connects of the rest of the evens of **CHAPTER 66**

Seal 6 This is a good time for the reader to read chapter 11:2-13 about the 2 witnesses who witness for 3 ½ years, There is a lot of debate about which 3:1/2 years of the Tribulation are in mind. I am convinced that, up until now, people have believed the 2 witnesses were responsible for the things that have been happening to this point. But, after we see and hear what takes place during this seal no one would ever believe later that 2 people were causing these problems. Why are they not brought up until the 11th Chapter? I will discuss that later.

One of the greatest, most dramatic, pictures of the entire Bible is presented here. Some of the descriptions are *similes* or comparisons that use the words *as or like* to make the word pictures more vivid. The other descriptions make use of direct, literal language. In rapid order John sees a mighty earthquake, something, maybe, like an eclipse, causing the sun to become black, but a much longer period than a simple eclipse, a strange change in the moon in which it appears to earth dwellers to be blood red (which might be the result of volcanic ash or dust in the atmosphere brought about by the earthquake).

In addition, he sees many meteorites, fall to the earth, **THEN** *the heaven departed as a scroll when it is rolled together; and every mountain and island were moved out of their places.* If you look up outside today, depending on where you are in the world, you see darkness, stars, moon, or clear, cloudy, stormy skies. The sky above *suddenly disappears* even as the mountains and islands of the earth are moved from their places. What is the result of the *sky being rolled up like a scroll when its rolled together*? **Men see straight through to the throne of God**, and, *the kings of the earth, and the great men, and the rich men, and the chief captains, and the mighty men, and every slave and every free man, hid themselves in the dens and in the rocks of the mountains; And said to the mountains and rocks, Fall on us, and hide us from the face of him who sits on the throne, and from the wrath of the Lamb: For the great day of his wrath has come (simple past tense) and who shall be able to stand?.* Fear grips the hearts of all people as they realize this is a time unlike any other in human history. People have seen the wrath of nature on occasion, and they have felt the wrath of humanity at times. However, with the sky removed, they now are able to see directly to God's throne, and they realize what they have been experiencing, and will continue to experience is *The Wrath of the God of the Universe.* The events in Revelation will not be explainable by natural causes.

THIS EVENT TAKES US THE MIDST OF THE SEVEN WHEN THE ANTICHRIST BREAKS THE COVENANT AND CAUSES

THE SACRIFICES TO CEASE

THE MIDDLE OF *THE GREAT TRIBULATION,*

THE MIDDLE THE DAY OF THE LORD,

WE ARE GOING TO SEE A LOT OF THINGS THAT HAPPEN AT THE MIDDLE OF THE GREAT TRIBULATION PERIOD. LITERATURE IS NOT LIKE A SPLIT MOTION PICTURE SCREEN THAT CAN SHOW THEM ALL HAPPENING AT ONCE, LITERATURE HAS TO RECORD THE EVENTS SEPARATELY

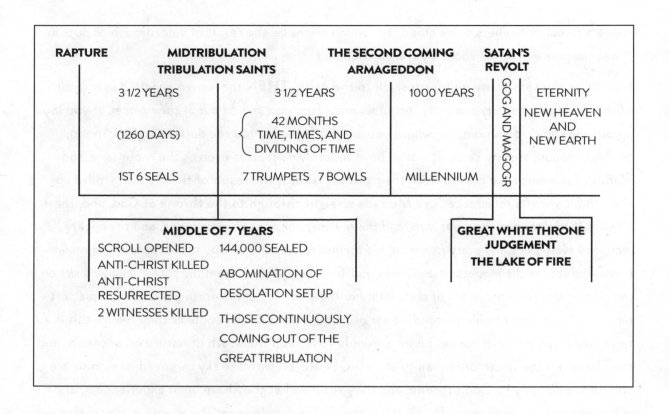

RAPTURE	MIDTRIBULATION	THE SECOND COMING	SATAN'S	
	TRIBULATION SAINTS	ARMAGEDDON	REVOLT	
3 1/2 YEARS	3 1/2 YEARS	1000 YEARS		ETERNITY
(1260 DAYS)	42 MONTHS TIME, TIMES, AND DIVIDING OF TIME		GOG AND MAGOGR	NEW HEAVEN AND NEW EARTH
1ST 6 SEALS	7 TRUMPETS 7 BOWLS	MILLENNIUM		

MIDDLE OF 7 YEARS

SCROLL OPENED	144,000 SEALED
ANTI-CHRIST KILLED	ABOMINATION OF DESOLATION SET UP
ANTI-CHRIST RESURRECTED	
2 WITNESSES KILLED	THOSE CONTINUOUSLY COMING OUT OF THE GREAT TRIBULATION

GREAT WHITE THRONE JUDGEMENT THE LAKE OF FIRE

CHAPTER 7
The First Parenthetical Enlargement

THE 144,000 OF ISRAEL AND THE WHITE ROBED MULTITUDE

After this, Instead of the Seventh Seal being opened, The Parenthetical Enlargement discusses two major events.

First John sees *four angels standing on the four corners of the earth, holding the four winds of the earth, that the wind should not blow on the earth, nor on the sea, nor against any tree.* Obviously they are holding back winds of judgment. For, the text goes on to indicate, these four angels those *to whom it was given to hurt the earth and the sea, Saying, Hurt not the earth, neither the sea, nor the trees, till we have sealed the servants of our God in their foreheads.* The protection provided by the seal is mentioned under the sounding of the 5th Trumpet in Ch 9.

I saw another angel ascending from the east, having the seal of the living God: The New Testament makes it clear, over and over, that the *seal of God* is *The Holy Spirit.* And, that *Jesus is the One who gives the Holy Spirit.* As, indicated earlier, this is one of the 26 pictures of Jesus in the Book. We, are told, *there were sealed one-hundred-forty-four-thousand of all the tribes of the children of Israel.* There is no basis, as some claim, that these are evangelists; we will see later, in Ch 12, that believing Jews have to flee from the Antichrist.

THE ORIGINAL TRIBES OF ISRAEL WERE:

REUBEN	JUDAH	GAD	ZEBULUN
SIMEON	DAN	ASHER	JOSEPH
LEVI	NAPTHLI	ISSACHAR	BENJAMIN

TWO OTHERS WERE ADDED IN GEN 48: EPHARAIM AND MANASSEH.

Jacob told Joseph, *I have given you one portion above your brothers.* The 2 portions were given to Joseph's sons, Ephraim and Manasseh. So Joseph does not have a separate portion. *So there are now 13 Tribes.* This elevated Joseph to Firstborn (IChr 5:1) However God Chose Levi as His Portion rather than the firstborn of every family.(Num 3:11-13) *So now the number is back down to 12 Tribes, and neither Joseph nor Levi have their own portion.*

But, here, 12,000 of 12 tribes are mentioned, but Levi is substituted for Dan, and Joseph is substituted for Ephraim. Some, good Christian Brothers I highly respect, feel they must find the church somewhere during The Great Tribulation. So, some, try to Claim this is Spiritual Israel-The Church. The church is not Spiritual Israel. Or because the names are not in order, and Dan and Ephraim are left out, try to say this must be the Church and Israel. If either of these are true, then language makes no sense whatsoever. Remember the rule from Chapter one of this book, *When the Obvious Sense, makes the Best Sense, Any Other Sense is Nonsense.* It states clearly, from the 12 twelve tribes of Israel. **Then why are Dan and Ephraim not mentioned?**

Consider The following points from Romans 9–11

1. Not all of Abraham's children will inherit the promises God gave Abraham; these promises must be inherited by faith (9:6–9).

2. God chose Israel on the basis of His will—not the people's works (9:10–18).

3. The majority of Israelites have fallen from God because of unbelief (9:27–33).

4. The only way anyone can be saved, Jew or Gentile, is by faith in Jesus Christ (10:6–13).

5. Believing Gentiles have been grafted into the root of a cultivated olive tree (11:11–24).

6. The spiritual blindness of Israel will be removed when the fullness of the Gentiles has come in (11:25).

7. 11:26 says, *all Israel shall be saved.*

However when you look at the entire argument, remember it states, in 9:6 states, *They are not all Israel which are of Israel.* So The conclusion of the argument in Romans is,, *All Israel who will be saved equals the Remnant Who will Receive Jesus Christ.* As we study Revelation it will be obvious that the majority of the Jews in the world will recognize Jesus as their Messiah to begin the last half of The Great Tribulation. Twelve is the *Number of Completion in Revelation.* James addresses his book to the *12 tribes,* the common expression for the Jews.

Then why are Dan and Ephraim not mentioned?

Earlier in this book, I spoke of *Spiritual Fornication/Idolatry* in connection with The Seven Churches. In the context of this book, Idolatry has such an important place. Dan was the first tribe to go into idolatry (Jud 18:30–31). Later, when the kingdom of Israel was divided following the death of Solomon, Jeroboam, the king of the Northern Kingdom, established two official centers of idolatry for his people: One was located in Dan, and the other was located in Bethel, a city in the land of Ephraim. Hosea renamed **Bethel (House of God) Bethaven (House of Emptyness)** (10:5) because of the Idols.

A reminder, The number one lesson that the Jews have learned in 4,000 years of history is, **God Hates Idols.** Looking ahead to the Antichrist's rule, we see he will attempt to lead Israel once again to forsake God and worship an idol made in his own image. He will forbid lawful worship and require all people to worship him and his image. This is the *abomination of desolation* Daniel mentions (9:27) and to which Jesus refers (Matthew 24:15). This latest expression of idolatry, like all others before it, will bring about the judgment of God on the Antichrist and his kingdom. So the omission of Dan and Ephraim, *in the context of Revelation*, are directly related to God's feelings about idolatry, and the fact that it will be the Image of the Antichrist being placed in the temple, that will result in the spiritual blinders being removed from the Jews. Ezekiel indicates these 2 tribes will have a portion in the Millennium.

THE GREAT MULTITUDE IN WHITE ROBES

John now sees *a great multitude, which no man could number, of all nations, and tribes, and people, and tongues, stood before the throne, and before the Lamb, clothed with white robes, and palms in their hands And cried with a loud voice, saying, Salvation to our God which sits upon the throne, and unto the Lamb. And all the angels stood round about the throne, and about the elders and the four beasts, and fell before the throne on their faces, and worshipped God, Saying, Amen: Blessing, and glory, and wisdom, and thanksgiving, and honor, and power, and might, be unto our God for ever and ever. Amen.*

What is the difference between this group and the Elders we who appeared in Ch.4

There are only 24 Elders, an uncountable number with the White Robes

The Elders sit on thrones, those with White Robes stand.

The Elders have Victors Crowns on their heads, the White Robed Multitude do not.

The Elders have harps and bowls of incense, only harps are held by the Multitude

Something else, The multitude praising God, in Ch 5, Raptured Saints, are called *Kings and Priests and are to reign on the earth*, It is said of the White Robed Multitude, *They will serve God day and night.* God will *dwell among them*, They will *hunger no more, thirst no more, neither will the sun light on them, nor any heat.* These are things that happen to people during the Great Tribulation. It goes on to say *God shall wipe away all tears from their eyes.* The have, obviously been going through an extremely difficult time.

John learns from one of the elders that the great multitude of people in white robes are *those who are **continuously coming** (Present Participle) **out of** The Great Tribulation., and have washed their robes and made them white in the blood of the Lamb*

The use of the Present Participle indicates people will be saved all during the Great Tribulation. Some have interpreted these will all be martyrs. Certainly some will be, but there will be natural causes of death, plus the plagues of the tribulation. They will be there because they *have washed their robes and made them white in the blood of the Lamb.* They will be in white robes like the martyrs under the 5th Seal. There will be a resurrection of those saved at the end, but, like saints who die now, *to be absent from the body is to be present with the Lord.*

CHAPTER 8
The Book is Opened and the First 4
of the 7 Trumpets Sound

Seal 7 With the opening of the seventh and final seal, the seven-sealed scroll is now entirely open Strangely, however, nothing takes place. Instead, there is silence in heaven for about half an hour. Why? This silence may emphasize the desire of all created beings in heaven to find out what remains inside the seven-sealed scroll. All these beings are probably wondering how people are going to receive their inheritance, how this age is going to be completed, and how all things are going to be put in their proper places.

John now sees seven trumpets given to *the seven angels who stand before God*. They are about to Herald the opening of the 7 Sealed Scroll. However, before these angels begin to sound their trumpets, another angel comes on the scene. He is given incense to offer with the prayers of the righteous on the golden altar before the throne. John observes as the smoke of the incense ascends with the prayers of the righteous into God's presence.

This other angel in verse is another picture of the person and ministry of the Lord Jesus Christ in the book of Revelation. In the Old Testament the golden censer was used to offer incense within the *Most Holy Place* on the Day of Atonement *only by The High Priest.*(Lev 16:12–13). The theme of The Book of Hebrews is that *Jesus is our Great High Priest.* In addition, the prayers of the saints are given to this other angel in to offer up to God with the incense. This portrays the ministry of Jesus who is the *one mediator between God and men* (1 Tim 2:5), interceding for them and presenting their petitions to God. Incense carries with it the thought of a pleasing smell to God. The sweetness of the odor of the burning incense rising as an offering to God indicating the spiritual pleasure God receives from this offering of incense and prayers.

Now, the angel fills the censer with fire from the altar and hurls it to the earth. At once, peals of thunder, rumblings, flashes of lightning, and an earthquake follow. It is not difficult to see a connection between the prayers of the righteous, such as those cries to God, *Your Kingdom*

Come, Your will be done on earth as it is in heaven, and the prayers of Martyrs that call for judgment of the wicked, and the onset of judgment that follows as the trumpets are sounded.

Trumpets are used in the Old Testament for *war, proclaiming great festivals, announcements of royalty, manifestations of God's Mighty Power, The overthrow of the ungodly, laying the foundation and dedication of the temple.* All these things take place in Revelation also.

Trumpet 1 As the first angel sounded his trumpet, hail and fire mixed with blood were hurled on the earth. One third of the earth was burned, as well as one third of all trees and all the green grass. A judgment such as this will tend to produce not only fear but also a grave effect on earth's ability to produce oxygen. The process of photosynthesis, the earth's ability to produce life-giving oxygen, depends on trees and green plant life.

Trumpet 2 At the second trumpet blast, a huge burning mountain was thrown into the sea. It caused one third of all the sea to turn to blood, one third of all marine life to die, and one third of all ships to be destroyed.

Trumpet 3 The third angel's trumpet sound brought a giant Meteorite to the earth. This Meteorite , called *Abysinth,* poisons one third of the fresh waters on earth, and many people died because of the poison water.

Trumpet 4 The fourth trumpet sound brought a bad effect on the sun, moon, and the stars so that their light was withheld from earth one third of the time. This judgment will obviously reach beyond planet earth to the solar system and the universe. Some scholars have raised an interesting question. Jesus, said, speaking of the The Tribulation in Mt 24:22 *unless those days be shortened there would be no flesh saved, but for the elect's sake those days will be shortened.* Its exactly 7 years, how can it be shortened. Their idea is that this *not shining for a third* may mean the rotation of the earth speeds up by a third, a 16 hour day. Just out of curiosity I asked two Physicists *would be the effect if that happened?* One said, *not much, the increased speed of rotation would increase gravity so you would feel a little heavier.* The other one said, because of that, *the gravitational pull would increase the effect of your by body weight from 2 to 4 times. That means if you weigh 150 pounds to walk or move would seem like you weighed from 300 to 600 pound.* Just a thought to ponder. *The main thing it is saying:* **there will be a designated time when this all ends**.

John hears an eagle call out in a loud voice as it flies in midair, **Woe, woe, woe (Οὐαὶ οὐαὶ οὐαὶ**— *an adjective expressing extreme displeasure and calling for retributive pain*) to those who dwell on the earth, at the sound of the other trumpets that the three angels are about to blow.

CHAPTER 9
The 5TH and 6TH Trumpets Sound

Trumpet 5 When the fifth trumpet sounded, John saw a *star that had fallen out of heaven to the earth. And to Him was given the key to the shaft of the Abyss.* We have seen in Ch 1 that *stars* can refer to *angels*, depending on the context. This one had fallen, previously, out of heaven, and is referred to as *Him*, Jesus said He *saw Satan fall like lightning from heaven*"(Lk 10:18). In addition, the fact this fallen star is given authority symbolized by the key to the shaft of the Abyss makes it obvious that fallen star is Satan.

In Lk 8:30-31, The Legion of Demons requests Jesus to *not command them to go into the abyss but to let them go into the hogs.* This, along with 2 Pet 2:4 and Jude 6, demonstrates there are fallen angels, demons, confined in the Abyss, while others are allowed to roam on the earth.

As the Abyss is opened John saw smoke rise from the pit, and out of the smoke a demonic army emerged on the earth. In Luke 8:32–33 demons possessed pigs, but here demons seem to possess locusts. These locusts have power like that of scorpions of the earth, and they have a specific mission: to torture people five months. The pain they cause will bring agony to all those who do not have the seal of God on their foreheads. In those days people will seek death in order to escape their agony, *but death will flee from them.*

The description of these demonic locusts and their numbers is awesome. Their leader is said to be *The Angel of the Abyss* (v. 11). His name, **Abaddon** in Hebrew and **Apollyon** in Greek, means *destruction and destroyer,* and in the wake of this infernal army there is only pain and the desire for death. This judgment is the *first woe;* consequently, *two* more fearful *woes* await the people of the earth.

Trumpet 6 describes the sounding of the sixth trumpet. As the scene unfolds, John hears a voice coming from the horns of the golden altar. This voice commands the sixth trumpet angel to *release the four angels who are bound at the Euphrates River.* The *Euphrates river* is considered to be the dividing line between the east and the west. It is used that way in preparation for Armageddon in 16:12. Earlier, four angels were holding back the winds of judgment. Those angels were not bound, but here the angels are bound. Angels who are in bondage are fallen angels. They are released for *an hour, and a day, and a month and a year to kill the third part of men.* The *idiom* does not refer to the length of time, Year, plus month plus day plus hour. It means there is an appointed time when this is going to begin.

There is a teaching that we can change God's appointed times by our efforts...No; as this scripture says it is already set. They lead a great army; and *The number of the armies of the horsemen was two hundred million.* Only China can field an army of two hundred million. In prophecy armies are depicted as horses and horsemen, (Ez 38:15; 39:20; Rev 19:14, 18, 21.) Both the horses and riders are frightening; *in the vision the horses and those who sat on them: the riders had breastplates the color of fire and of hyacinth (dark red or dark blue) and of brimstone; and the heads of the horses are like the heads of lions; and out of their mouths proceed fire and smoke and brimstone. A third of mankind was killed by these three plagues, by the fire and the smoke and the brimstone which proceeded out of their mouths. For the power of the horses is in their mouths and in their tails; for their tails are like serpents and have heads, and with them they do harm.* John is writing what he saw, in the language available to him; Obviously a great mechanized army is being pictured. Dan 11:44 refers to the movement of armies from the Orient against the Antichrist that try to stop him, but he destroys them (see Joel 2:1-11).

Yet, even in the face of this awful judgment, John observes the balance of earth's people are so entrapped by sin that they neither repent nor amend their ways. They continue to *worship demons* and *idols*, and continued to practice *murders, sorceries* (***pharmachon)*** *witchcraft, drugs.* (Those who practiced *witchcraft* frequently used drugs, but, even more relevant in our day is *drugs), fornication* (***porneia), thefts.*** Notice the first two, *worshiping demons and idols.* The two go hand in hand. (1Co 10:19-21)

CHAPTER 10
The Mighty Angel with the Scroll

The picture of Jesus as our **Go'el**, our *Kinsman Redeemer*, our *Nearest Relative*, now reaches a dramatic climax.

*And I saw another mighty angel come down from heaven, clothed with a cloud: and **a rainbow** was upon his head, and his **face was as it were the sun**, and his feet as pillars of fire:* John's description of God sitting on the throne, in 4:3, included **a rainbow** around the throne. Ezekiel's vision of the **likeness of the glory of the Lord** *(1:28)* included *seeing a man sitting on a throne...and it had brightness round about. As the **appearance of the bow that is in the cloud in the day of rain**, so was the appearance of the brightness round about.* **The rainbow is a symbol of God keeping his promises.**

Compare Daniel's vision, *Then I lifted up my eyes, and looked, and behold a certain man **clothed in linen**, whose **loins were girded with fine gol**d of Uphaz: His body also was like the beryl, and his **face as the appearance of lightning**, and his **eyes as lamps of fire**, and his arms and his **feet like in colour to polished brass**, and the voice of his words like the **voice of a multitud**e.(10:5-6)* with John's initial vision of Jesus in Ch 1, *in the midst of the seven candlesticks one like unto the Son of man, **clothed with a garment down to the foot**, and **girt about the paps with a golden girdle.** His head and his hairs were white like wool, as white as snow; and his **eyes were as a flame of fire**; And his **feet like unto fine brass**, as if they burned in a furnace; and his **voice as the sound of many waters**.*

It is obvious, comparing these passages, that the *mighty angel* in this chapter is Jesus. He is God and Man. As man he is our **Go'el**, *our nearest relative, our kinsman redeemer. And he had in his hand a little book open: and he set his right foot upon the sea, and his left foot on the earth.* Because of the size of this Angel, big enough to put one foot on the sea and the other on the dry land, it is described as a *little book in His right hand.*

And cried with a loud voice, as when a lion roars...And the angel which I saw stand upon the sea and upon the earth lifted up his hand to heaven, And swore by him who lives for ever and ever, who cre-

ated heaven, and the things that therein are, and the earth, and the things that therein are, and the sea, and the things which are therein, that there should be time no longer: But in the days of the voice of the seventh angel, when he shall begin to sound, the mystery of God should be finished, as he has declared to his servants the prophets. (the 7th angel does not sound until 11:15.

The Lion of Judah is Roaring!

The entire announcement by our *Go'el* is called a *proleptic statement*. A *proleptic statement* is a statement about the future as if what it states had already happened. Isaiah 9:6 is an example of a proleptic statement. It speaks as if Jesus is born about 750 years before His birth. The statement here is the announcement of the end.

As our **Go'el, he has already paid the bill with His blood, to redeem the property, Now He is going to take action, so He says, THERE IS NO MORE TIME! No more time for Satan, No more time for Idols, No more time for Sin, No more time for Death, No more time for Pain and Misery and suffering, No more time for The Curse.....**

I'M TAKING IT BACK!!!
WE WIN BECAUSE JESUS WINS!!

THE REST OF THE BOOK OF REVELATION IS WHAT IS REVEALED IN THE 7 SEALED BOOK. IT ENLARGES ON CERTAIN ASPECTS THAT HAVE BEEN MENTIONED PREVIOUSLY IN REVELATION , AND DESCRIBES THE EVENTS THAT HAVE TO HAPPEN TO TAKE MAN'S INHERITANCE BACK AND TO COMPLETE THE PLAN OF GOD

John observed that when the mighty angel took his stance on earth and sea and shouted, seven thunders spoke. What this message was is unknown, for the prophet was forbidden to record it We do know that the end of all things is in view and that the flow of events will move quickly forward to completion.

JOHN'S COMMISSION TO PROPHESY

John hears a voice from heaven that instructs him to take the scroll from the hand of the angel. In obedience, he approaches the angel and asks for the little scroll. The angel gives it to the prophet and instructs him: *Take and eat it; it will make your stomach bitter, but in your mouth it will be sweet as honey.* John does as he is told and finds the angel had described quite accurately what would happen. The little scroll tasted as sweet as honey, but it gave John a sour stomach.

Ezekiel records an experience similar to that of John in chapters 2 and 3 of his prophecy. There, Ezekiel was handed a scroll on which were written words of lament and warning and woe. He was told to eat the scroll, which he found sweet as honey in his mouth Immediately afterward, the prophet was told to go to the house of Israel and speak God's words to His people, which were words of judgment coming. This activity represents Ezekiel's prophetic commission. This explanation fits the context here.

John is to absorb the prophetic message completely. In doing so, he will find it produces mixed feelings in him. The knowledge that God is going to complete His plan for this world by restoring things in it according to His desire produces a sweet experience of joy in all believers. On the other hand, the knowledge that those without Christ—including loved ones—will face eternal damnation is a bitter fact for all believers to digest. Certainly this sobering fact ought to give every believer sufficient motivation to do everything possible to win the lost wherever they may be.

John is told, *You must again prophesy before many peoples and nations and languages and kings* (v. 11). While John is at the end of his life, his statement anticipates the impact this prophecy, as well as his Gospel and Letters, will have as they, together with the rest of the inspired Word of God, are proclaimed in the whole world . The Gospel of John is the most published single book in History.

CHAPTER 11

Measuring the Temple, the Two Witnesses and the Sounding of the 7TH Trumpet

The first thing disclosed from the open book concerns the Temple, Jerusalem, and the Jewish people:

And there was given me a reed like unto a rod: and the angel stood, saying, Rise, and measure the temple of God, and the altar, and those who are worshiping in it. . But the court which is outside the temple leave out, and don't measure it; for it is given unto the Gentiles: and the holy city they will tread under foot forty and two months.

Measuring a city means more than finding out its dimensions. Its use elsewhere in Scripture indicates measuring is *setting a city apart either to save or destroy it.* Since John is told to *measure the temple of God and the altar, and those who are worshiping there.* He is indicating, as we will see in Ch 12, the preservation of the true Jewish worshippers, the remnant of Israel, discussed earlier, who will not bow to the image of the Antichrist and will receive Jesus as their Messiah. however, *he is to exclude the outer court that has been given to the Gentiles.*

The temple itself (the Holy Place and the Most Holy Place) was surrounded by three courts. The first or nearest to the temple, the Court of the Priests, contained the altar of burnt offering and the great laver. It was restricted to priests alone. Next to this was the Court of the Israelites, which was separated into two parts: one for men and the other for women. The people of Israel who were ceremonially clean could assemble for worship in these areas. Outside these inner courts lay the Court of the Gentiles, which was open to all interested people—Jews and Gentiles. In the present case we see a contrast: The outer court and the Holy City are not preserved.

I remind you again, Jesus said, *Jerusalem shall be trodden down by the Gentile until The Time of The Gentiles be fulfilled.* At this point, it is stated that, *The Holy City they will tread under foot forty and two months.* So, there is a 3 ½ years period left in *The Time of The Gentiles* after the event concerning the 2 witness is over.

This is a good time for you to reread the discussion of Daniel 9, *The 70- 7's*

The Two Witnesses

Two powerful witnesses will prophesy for 1,260 days, 3 ½ years, of the Tribulation period. They will be *clothed in sackcloth,* which is a symbol of both mourning and repentance in the Old Testament. Both will take place under their ministry. They are referred to as *the two olive trees and the two lampstands that stand before the Lord of the earth.* Joshua the high priest and Zerubbabel the political ruler were raised up to rebuild the temple in Zechariah's time. Where the temple had stood was now a *great mountain* of rubble, blocking their vision, blocking their mission of rebuilding the temple, look like an impossible task.. (Zech 4)

So, God gives Zechariah a vision of *A golden menorah, with its 7 lamps burning brightly, above it a golden bowl with seven lips above it dripping oil into the lamps so they can keep burning, and two olive trees, one on each side, with pipes going into the bowl.* The angel speaking with Zechariah asked him if *he knew what these are?* He answered, No!, and the angel said, *This is the word of the Lord to Zerubbabel:* **Not by might, nor by power, but by my Spirit, says the Lord of hosts.** He explained that *great mountain would become a plain by* **Grace**.

Any effective ministry is only by a Gift of Grace and the Energizing by the Holy Spirit. That is how Paul describes his ministry in Eph 3:1-8. As Zerubbabel and Joshua were the *anointed ones* in that time, these two are the *anointed ones* for 1260 days. Similarly, these two end-time witnesses will execute their prophetic office through the power of the Holy Spirit.

In addition to anointed prophetic ministry, these two have a broad range of power. They have divine protection against assaults from enemies, power over natural elements, including the ability to prevent rain, and power to afflict the earth with every kind of plague as often as they want.

Why do the circumstances of the two witness occupy the first lengthy discussion inside the 7 sealed book? It is under the 6th Seal that the people of the world understand that what is happening is the *Great Day of God's Wrath*. Why didn't they know previously? This is explained here. After the revelation of the 6th seal, people would never believe two men were causing all this calamity. The fact that so many people turn to the Lord during the first half of the Tribulation is evidence of the two witnesses' ministry. They will have the same power concerning blood, plagues, and rain that Moses and Elijah had. (Ex, Ch 7-11, I Kg 17:1-7)

Some try insist they are Enoch and Elijah, *because its appointed unto man once to die.* And they didn't die, so they must come back and get killed. But if the Rapture takes place today, millions of Christians will never experience physical death, so, then, why should they have to? *If you* start with a wrong premise, you end up with a wrong conclusion. Others insist the two are Moses and Elijah since they will have ministries like those of the earlier prophets, Moses and Elijah appeared with Jesus on the Mount of Transfiguration. However Moses and Elijah stood on the mount with Jesus because He fulfilled the Law (represented by Moses) and the Prophets (represented by Elijah), which is indicated by the fact that they disappeared, and Jesus was left alone, and God said, *This is My Beloved Son, Hear Him!*

Mal 4:5 says Elijah will come *before the great and awesome day of the Lord comes.* The Apostles asked Jesus about this in Mt 17:10, *His disciples asked Him, Why then do the scribes say that Elijah must come first? And He answered and said, Elijah **is coming** and will restore all things; but I say to you that Elijah **has already come**, and they did not recognize him, but did to him whatever they wished. So also the Son of Man is going to suffer at their hands. Then the disciples understood that He had spoken to them about John the Baptist.* **Elijah has come and will come.** How could John the Baptist fulfill this prophecy? The Bible does not teach reincarnation. Gabriel, speaking to Zecharias about John being born to Elizabeth in Lk 1:17 says, *he* (John) *shall go before him* (Jesus) *in the spirit and power of Elijah.* He is to be the Old Testament style prophet for that day. The two witnesses will be the Old Testament Style Prophets of that time, dealing with the whole world, but primarily Israel. They will not be someone from the Old Testament.

As the prophets speak forth God's message, they will face opposition from the ungodly, but potential assassins will be completely powerless to hurt them. In fact, should they try, they will be immediately destroyed. We must remember the life of God's people is in His hands. We can serve God without fear, for He will keep us until our task is complete.

When they have finished their witness, the Beast that ascends from the Abyss will fight against them will overcome them and kill them. For the first time in Revelation we have a preview of the nature and power of the coming *Antichrist, the Beast of Revelation 13-19.*

The continuing description makes it even more clear that this event must refer to the first three and one half years climaxing with the 6th Seal. *Their dead bodies shall lie in the street of the great city, which spiritually is called Sodom and Egypt, where also our Lord was crucified..* Jerusalem is referred to as *Sodom* and *Egypt.* Sodom speaks of moral degradation, and Egypt symbolizes oppression, slavery, and idolatry, Jerusalem will be the political center of the World.

On their TV's IPAD's, phones, etc. The people of the world will see, etc. the bodies lying in the streets of Jerusalem *for three days and a half* , and this will prompt a worldwide celebration. WHY? *They that dwell upon the earth shall rejoice over them, and make merry, and shall send gifts* one to another; *because these two prophets tormented them that dwelt on the earth.* So it is obvious the people have not understood it is God doing all this. But, *after three days and an half the Spirit of life from God entered into them, and they stood upon their feet; and great fear fell upon those who were watching them. And they heard a great voice from heaven saying unto them, Come up here!. And they ascended up to heaven in a cloud; and their enemies watched them.* As their enemies look on, the prophets are translated to heaven. Before their enemies can return to their ungodly pursuits, however, the city is shaken by the tremors of a mighty earthquake that destroy one-tenth of the city. Survivors are terrified and *give glory to the God of heaven.* They, now, obviously, recognize God is doing this, but they still don't repent. Notice how this fits with the comments of the world regarding the 6th Seal. **The *second woe* has now passed, and *the third* is on its way**

Trumpet 7 now sounds:. *The kingdoms of this world are become the kingdoms of our Lord, and of his Christ; and he shall reign for ever and ever.* This is another *proleptic statement,* that is, it looks forward to the end of the conflict in chapter 19, speaking as if it were an accomplished fact. As the Elders worship God, there is a second *proleptic statement, We give You thanks, O Lord God Almighty, Who is , and was, and is to come; because You have taken to Yourself Your great power, and have reigned.* However, as we shall see, this final period involves an extended length of time during which *the nations are angry, the dead will be judged, You will give reward unto Your servants the prophets, and to the saints, and them that fear Your name, small and great and You will destroy them who destroy the earth.*

As this scene concludes, the focus shifts to God's temple in heaven that is opened, revealing the *ark of the covenant,* which is again, as was the measurement of the Temple in 11:1, a reminder that God will keep his covenants with Israel. (The real ark is somewhere in Jerusalem today).. **Remember, Revelation is a Picture Book**. The accompanying lightning, thunder, hailstorm, and earthquake both attend God's presence and signify His wrath as the revelation continues. **It's a shame a chapter division comes between this last vision and the next one , as the next vision is showing God's protection of *The Remnant of Israel.***

CHAPTER 12

The Woman, Her Son and the Dragon

John records the appearance of a great sign in heaven This sign that appears in heaven points to a reality on earth. John sees a, pregnant woman clothed with the sun, wearing a crown of twelve stars, and having the moon under her feet. She is in the agony of childbirth, nearly ready to deliver, while a great red dragon stands by waiting to devour her child as soon as he is born.

Remember, *the Bible is its own best interpreter.* The only other place in Scripture you find the description of the *Sun, Moon and Twelve Stars,* is in Genesis 37, where Joseph tells his brothers, *I have dreamed a dream more; and, behold, the sun and the moon and the eleven stars were bowing down to me. And he told it to his father, and to his brothers: and his father rebuked him, and said unto him, What is this dream you have dreamed?* Jacob interprets the dream accurately , *Shall I and your mother and your brothers indeed come to bow down ourselves to you to the earth?.* Every scholarly book I have read on Revelation, regardless of disagreement on other positions, states that this is Israel. Again, *When the Obvious Sense, makes the Best Sense, any other Sense, is Nonsense.*

In the Old Testament Israel is mentioned on occasion as a married woman, the wife of Jehovah (Is 54:1; Jer 3:1–14; Ho 2:14–23). In fact, Israel is the only group of God's people in Scripture that is referred to as a married woman. The church, by contrast, is referred to as a virgin (2 Cor 11:2), never as an expectant mother. Israel is also mentioned as a woman in travail (Is 26:7; 66:7; Mic 4:10; 5:3). Israel waited and waited expectantly for their Messiah, *the seed of the woman who was coming to crush the head of the serpent* (Gen.3:15) to come.

A second sign appears in heaven; *and behold a great red dragon, having seven heads and ten horns, and seven crowns upon his heads. And his tail drew the third part of the stars of heaven, and did cast them to the earth: and the dragon stood before the woman who was ready to be delivered, to devour her child as soon as it was born.* The Dragon is called, later in this picture, *the Old Serpent, the Devil, and Satan who deceives the whole world.* There is a possible hint here that when Satan fell a third part of the angels fell with him. I'm not sure you can push only one verse of scripture, *a third*, that far without other supporting Scriptures. We do know that angels are called, *ministering spirits* in Heb 1:14, and demons are commonly called, *unclean spirits* throughout the New Testament. Demons are obviously *fallen angels*. Some try to teach a preAdamic race are demons, but the Bible makes it clear Adam is the first man, and every scripture used to teach a preAdamic race is taken out of context, and disagrees with the whole Bible. (See my book, *The Most Often Asked Questions on Sunday Night Alive*) As mentioned previously, see Gen 5:1 *This is the book of the generations of Adam. In the day that God created man, in the likeness of God made he him; Male and female created he them; and blessed them, and called their name Adam, in the day when they were created.* (KJV best fits the context of the entire chapter) An obvious picture of how Satan tried to destroy Jesus as soon as he was born by inspiring Herod to kill all he babies under 2 years old.

In spite of Satan, *She gave birth to a son, a male, who is to rule all the nations with a rod of iron; and her child was caught up to God and to His throne.* Notice he is called a *Son*, a *Male*, and a *Child*. A *Son* is an heir who has reached the age of majority, to make decisions. A *Male*; Jesus was a man's man. One who could cause 12 men to leave their work behind and follow him, a man, who by himself could *overturn the tables of the moneychangers in the temple and drive the merchants out.* I have said publically, *He could play fullback for the Kansas City Chiefs and would score a touchdown every time.* A *Child*, totally human (of course also Totally divine-100 percent man and 100 percent God). Later, at Armageddon, the same description is given of him, *ruling all nations with a rod of iron.* Of course he has been *caught up* and is in heaven as Our Great High Priest.

We are now told, *The woman fled into the desert, where she has a place prepared of God, that they should feed her there a thousand two hundred and sixty days,* three and a half Biblical years. This event is so important, it is enlarged on later in this same chapter as taking place *for a **time, and times, and half a time**,* so I will discuss the details at that point.

The next description is of a *war in heaven,* **Michael** *and his angels waging war with the dragon. The dragon and his angels waged war, and they were not strong enough, and there was no longer a place found for them in heaven. And the great dragon* (Political Power) *was thrown down, the serpent* (sneaky, crafty) *of old who is called the devil* (Greek *diabolos*: slanderer, accuser) *and Satan* (Hebrew: adversary) *who deceives the whole world; he was thrown down to the earth, and his angels were thrown down with him.*

In Ch 12 of his book, **Daniel describes the same event recorded in this chapter,** *Now at that time* **Michael,** *the great prince who stands guard over the sons of your people, will arise. And there* will be a time of distress such as never occurred since there was a nation until that time; and at that time your people, everyone who is found written in the book, will be rescued (Dan 12:1 NASB). Daniel is told later it has to do with the *end of time*..

So Satan is cast down to earth permanently, and there is rejoicing in heaven saying, *Now the salvation, and the power, and the kingdom of our God and the authority of His Christ have come, for the accuser of our brethren has been thrown down, he who accuses them before our God day and night. And they overcame him because of the blood of the Lamb and because of the word of their testimony, and they did not love their life even when faced with death* (NASB).

Satan is the accuser. He keeps reminding Christians of our failures. God not only forgives, He forgets. You have no past...*if anyone be in Christ, he is a new creation, old things have passed away and all things have become new.* Just as an example, both Abraham and Sarah laughed when they were told She would have a child at 90, and when Sarah was asked, *Why did you laugh?* She said, *I didn't laugh,* She lied. Yet when the Holy Spirit inspires Hebrews eleven , He can not record the failures of faith....**We can go back and read them, but with God they no loner exist.** We overcome Satan's accusations *by the blood of the lamb and he word of their/our testimony.* The Blood has atoned (covered) our sins...we give our testimony of Faith in Christ, and we might have to overcome him by being killed because we reuse to back down on our testimony, as is happening to many Christians around the world today...always has, always will.

Now, the story of the Woman fleeing into the desert is enlarged upon as Satan tries to destroy the *woman who had brought forth the male. And to the woman were given two wings of a great eagle, that she might fly into the desert, into her place, where she is nourished for a* **time, and times, and half a time**, *from the face of the serpent.* I have heard some say that the 2 wings indicate *Israel will be preserved by an air lift.* But in Ex 19:4 speaking of the deliverance from Egypt, God says, *...I bare you on eagles wings....* They didn't have airplanes in 1450 BC. It simply means a *deliverance by God.* Dan 12:7 also indicates the events will be for a **time, times and a half a time,** when he shall have accomplished to scatter the power of the holy people that **all these things shall be accomplished.**

The next picture, as Satan is trying to destroy Israel, states *and the serpent cast out of his mouth water as a flood after the woman, that he might cause her to be carried away of the flood. And the earth helped the woman, and the earth opened her mouth, and swallowed up the flood which the dragon cast out of his mouth* demonstrates miraculous deliverance.

The place where the woman flees has been described twice as being *in the desert,* and once as a place *prepared by God.* Hosea says *God will lead Israel into the desert and deal tenderly with her there* (Hosea 2:14). So **the remnant of Israel, those who accept Jesus Christ, will flee into the desert for three and a half years, protected by Michael and he angels. Where will the remnant go in the desert?**

Micah 2:12 says, *I will surely assemble, O Jacob, all of you; I will surely gather the* **remnant** *of Israel; I will put them together as the sheep of* **Bozrah**, *as the flock in the midst of their fold: they shall make great noise by reason of the multitude of men.* Like I stated earlier, translators usually are not students of prophecy. In some translations the only place they don't translate **Bozrah** as *Bozrah* in the whole Bible is here., It was also called **Sela**, (*rock*), and **Mt Seir.** God said, *I have given* **Mt. Seir** *to Esau for a possession.* (Du 2:4) The modern name is **Petra. Petra** is in **Jordan. Why would an Arab country allow all these Jews to be in their country?**

C. M. Ward, whom I mentioned in the Acknowledgments, spoke years ago about Jacob having to run from his brother Esau who promised to kill him as soon as, Isaac, their father, died. Jacob ran for his life, and 20 years later he is returning to his own land. His brother Esau is coming with 400 men. He is not coming to say, *welcome home deceiver!* He is coming to fulfill his vow to kill Jacob. Jacob divides the people into two groups thinking if *Esau kills one group the other will escape.* But that night, God wrestles with Jacob, turns him into *Israel. When God changed Jacob, He changed Esau.* Instead of killing him, he fell on his neck and kissed him. He used this as a picture in this chapter of Revelation. I am firmly convinced from study of prophecy, that when the spiritual blinders fall of Israel they will fall off all the descendants of Abraham including the Arabs. It is also interesting that Dan 11:41 indicates the Antichrist will not control **Edom, Moab,** and **Ammon.** These three nations make up the modern country of **Jordan.**

Petra stands up like a large mountain range in the desert of Jordan. It was originally an Edomite settlement, but about 300 BC, Nabateans converted it into the amazing rock-cut city of Petra. To enter Petra one walks or rides on horseback through a narrow passage called the *sik*, which is about a mile long, with granite walls going up on each side hundreds of feet. *I went through it on a camel.* No large car could pass through this narrow passage, and since Petra is relatively inaccessible, this increases its isolation. Inside there is a twenty-two square mile area that is surrounded by sheer cliffs. Petra has temples, houses, and other living areas carved into the face of the rock. Some scholars estimate as many two and a half million people could be housed in Petra. It certainly is a *prepared place.* What is to stop the Antichrist from dropping a hydrogen bomb in the middle?....**Michael and his angels!**

Now, In 63:1 Isaiah asks, *Who is this coming from Edom, with dyed garments from* **Bozrah**? *that is glorious in his apparel, traveling in the greatness of his strength?* The one coming from **Bozrah** answers, *I that speak in righteousness, mighty to save.* Only one person can make that statement...**Jesus!** He is asked, *Why are you red in your apparel, your clothes like him that treads in the winefat?* **Jesus** answers, *I have trodden the winepress alone; and of the people there was none with me: for I will tread them in my anger, and trample them in my fury; and their blood shall be sprinkled upon my garments, and I will stain all my raiment. For the day of vengeance is in my heart, and the year of my redeemed is come.*

Both 14:19 and 19:15 of Revelation describe Armageddon as **trampling the Winepress of the Wrath of God.** So, here is Jesus, having trampled Winepress of the Wrath of God at Armageddon coming from *Bozrah.* **WHY?** Micah has said the **remnant** of Israel are in *Bozrah.* Now lets look at the rest of the quote from Micah:

The breaker is come up before them: they have broken up, and have passed through the gate, and are gone out by it: and their king shall pass before them, and the Lord on the head of them. So following Armageddon, Jesus will go to *Bozrah,* with his clothing still stained from the winepress of God's Wrath. He will reveal himself to the **remnant of Israel,** who there and *They shall look on him whom they have pierced.*(Zech 12:10) He is *The Breaker,* The one who cause them to break up camp, and He will lead them out through the *sic (gate)* across the desert of Judea, He will approach the Mount of Olives on the East of Jerusalem, and as Zech 14:3-4 indicates *the Mountain will cleave from east to west, and there will be a very great valley and half of the mountain shall move to the north and half to the south.* He will lead them through the valley and approach that Easter Gate, which the Arabs have sealed with steel and concrete, and put a cemetery outside, so *the Jewish Messiah, who is a Priest cannot walk through it without being defiled,* and, therefore cannot come through the gate. Why do they think He will come that way? Ezekiel 43:1-4 prophesies *And, behold, the glory of the God of Israel came from the way of the east: and **his** voice was like a noise of many waters: and the earth shined with **his** glory.... And the glory of the Lord came into the house by the way of the gate whose prospect is toward the east.* Jesus will lead the **remnant** through the Gate and into the Temple area. **And, if you know Jesus Christ you will have a seat on the 50 yard line watching it happen!**

There is a teaching that every Jew must return to Israel, and some, misuse a verse in Romans to teach that the *primary* purpose of the church is to preach to Jews and get them all back to Jerusalem. But notice the final passage of this chapter. The Devil cannot bother those who are in **Petra,** so *And the dragon was wroth with the woman, and went to make war with the remnant of her seed, which keep the commandments of God, and have the testimony of Jesus Christ.* The blinders will have been removed from the **remnant** who are in Israel, but there are more Jews in other cities of the world than there are in Jerusalem, and all of Israel. They, too, will have the blinders removed and become part of the **remnant,** so the enemy, who so hates Israel because God has chosen them will make war against them.

Note: All three designations are given for the last 3 ½ years of the Great Tribulation, *Time, Times and half, or the dividing, of time, 42 months, 1260 days.* The only designation given to the first 3 ½ years is *1260 days; 1260 days* is also used for the second half, indicating two equal periods, But use of *time, tines and half a time,* and *42 months* are only used of the last half of the seven year period by both Daniel and Revelation. The only designation of time for the two witnesses *is 1260 days.* A reminder: A Biblical Year is 360 days.

CHAPTER 13
Babylon

THE FINAL KINGDOM OF THIS WORLD, POLITICALLY, RELIGIOUSLY AND COMMERCIALLY IS CALLED BABYLON

Why Babylon? The original name was Babel and it was founded by Nimrod, who was said to be a *mighty hunter before the Lord*, in other words, *in your face God*. Then, God had told men to *fill the earth* but the people of earth said, *Come, let us build for ourselves a city, and a tower whose top will reach into heaven, and let us make for ourselves a name, otherwise we will be scattered abroad over the face of the whole earth. The Tower of Babel: Man's Organized Rebellion Against God.* Isaiah 14 begins by addressing, The King of Babylon and says, *How are you fallen from heaven, O Lucifer, son of the morning how are you cut down to the ground, you who weakened the nations! For you have said in your heart, I will ascend into heaven, I will exalt my throne above the stars of God: I will sit also upon the mount of the congregation, in the sides of the north: I will ascend above the heights of the clouds; I will be like the most High. Yet you will be brought down to hell, to the sides of the pit.*

IN CHAPTER 66, BABYLON IS MAN'S ORGANIZED REBELLION UNDER SATAN AGAINST GOD, OR, SIMPLY THE WORLD SYSTEM AGAINST GOD.

POLITICAL BABYLON

TEN NATION WORLD GOVERNMENT HEADED BY THE ANTICHRIST

RELIGIOUS BABYLON

WORLD RELIGION HEADED BY THE FALSE PROPHET

COMMERCIAL BABYLON

WORLD BUYING AND SELLING HEADED BY THE FALSE PROPHET

During the *Gulf War* with Iraq, people who hadn't studied prophecy until then started saying, *Babylon will be rebuilt and be world headquarters,* ignoring the fact that Is 13:19–22 indicates that once the city was destroyed, it would never again be inhabited . The whole context indicates it will never reach that place of importance again.

Another interesting sidelight about Babylon. It is a fact that Babylon originated the Horoscope. Look what Isaiah has to say about that to Babylon. *Stand now with your enchantments, and with the multitude of your sorceries, wherein you have labored from your youth; if so be you will be able to profit, if so be you may prevail. You are wearied in the multitude of your counselors. Let now the astrologers, the stargazers, the monthly prognosticators, stand up, and save you from these things that shall come upon you .Behold, they shall be as stubble; the fire shall burn them; they shall not deliver themselves from the power of the flame: there shall not be a coal to warm at, nor fire to sit before.* (Is 47:12-14)

I have been asked over the years, *What is your sign, or you a Leo, or what? What sign were you born under?* To which I have responded, *I was born again under the sign of the cross January 28, 1951.*

DANIEL CHAPTER 2 FROM BABYLON TO BABYLON

In verses 1-13, Nebuchadnezzar, The King of Babylon has a dream. He calls for his *magicians* (cast spells, enchanters), *Sorcerers* (who use magic and drugs), and *Astrologers* (Star gazers), and The Chaldeans, (The High Priests, able to make mysteries known) to tell him what he had dreamed. They responded by asking him what he had dreamed. The King responded that they must make the dream known to him, plus the interpretation He demands they tell him what he had dreamed and the interpretation, said if you cant tell me the dream you would speak *lying and corrupt words before me till the times change. Therefore tell me the dream, and I shall know that you can show me its interpretation.* They responded that no man could ever do what he asks, and *no one can show it to the king except the gods, whose dwelling is not with flesh.* So the King decreed that *all the wise men of Babylon should be destroyed.*

The Wise Men of Babylon included Daniel, who reported the command to Hannaniah, Michael and Azariah. These were the three other Youths (teen agers) who were taken from Israel to Babylon in Daniel Ch 1. Their names were those that glorified God. The first thing the heathen empire wanted to do, of course, was destroy their faith. So they changed their names to honor the Gods of Babylon. Sounds like many Universities today.

Daniel: God Is Judge..................changed to ... Belteshazzar....Bel's Prince

Haaniah: YHWH Is Gracious.......changed to ... Shadrach.........Inspiration of Rach

Mishael: Who Is What God Is ......changed to ... Meshach..........Who is what Shach is

Azariah: YHWH Helps................changed to ... Abednego........Seervant of Nebo

The four of them prayed, and then the mystery was revealed to Daniel in a vision of the night. Then Daniel blessed the God of heaven. Daniel answered and said: "Blessed be the name of God forever and ever, to whom belong wisdom and might. He changes times and seasons; he removes kings and sets up kings; he gives wisdom to the wise and knowledge to those who have understanding; he reveals deep and hidden things; he knows what is in the darkness, and the light dwells with him. To you, O God of my fathers, I give thanks and praise, for you have given me wisdom and might, and have now made known to me what we asked of you, for you have made known to us the king's matter. (ESV)

*So, Daniel went into Arioch, whom the king had appointed to destroy the wise men of Babylon. He went and said thus to him: Do not destroy the wise men of Babylon; bring me in before the king, and I will show the king the interpretation. When Daniel is brought before Nebuchadnezzar he makes it clear to him that there is a God in heaven who reveals mysteries, and he has made known to King Nebuchadnezzar **what will be in the latter days.***

STARTING WITH VERSE 4 OF THIS CHAPTER, THE CHALDEANS SPOKE TO THE KING IN ARAMAIC. THE LANGUAGE OF THE BOOK OF DANIEL STAYS IN ARAMAIC UNTIL THE END OF CHAPTER 7 BECAUSE IT OUTLINES THE TIMES OF THE GENTILES WHICH START AND END WITH BABYLON

DANIEL EXPLAINS THE DREAM

You saw, O king, and behold, a great image. This image, mighty and of exceeding brightness, stood before you, and its appearance was frightening. The head of this image was of fine gold, its chest and arms of silver, its middle and thighs of bronze, its legs of iron, its feet partly of iron and partly of clay. As you looked, a stone was cut out by no human hand, and it struck the image on its feet of iron and clay, and broke them in pieces. Then the iron, the clay, the bronze, the silver, and the gold, all together were broken in pieces, and became like the chaff of the summer threshing floors; and the wind carried them away, so that not a trace of them could be found. But the stone that struck the image became a great mountain and filled the whole earth. vs. 31-35 (ESV)

Notice the details. The Head was of Gold, The Chest and Arms were of Silver, The Middle and Thighs of Bronze, The Legs were of Iron and the Feet were part Iron and Part Clay. A stone cut out without hands hit the image in its feet and the entire image was carried away, and the

GOLD:
BABYLON; 625-539 BC

SILVER:
MEDO-PERSIA; 539-333 BC

BRONZE:
GREECE; 333-323 BC

IRON:
ROME; 45 BC

PART IRON/CLAY:
BABYLON

stone became a great mountain that filled the whole earth. We don't have to guess, what the image represents ..Daniel went on to Explain it.

You, O king, the king of kings, to whom the God of heaven has given the kingdom, the power, and the might, and the glory, and into whose hand he has given, wherever they dwell, the children of man, the beasts of the field, and the birds of the heavens, making you rule over them all—you are the head of gold. Another kingdom inferior to you shall arise after you, and yet a third kingdom of bronze, which shall rule over all the earth. And there shall be a fourth kingdom, strong as iron, because iron breaks to pieces and shatters all things. And like iron that crushes, it shall break and crush all these. And as you saw the feet and toes, partly of potter's clay and partly of iron, it shall be a divided king-

dom, but some of the firmness of iron shall be in it, just as you saw iron mixed with the soft clay. And as the toes of the feet were partly iron and partly clay, so the kingdom shall be partly strong and partly brittle. As you saw the iron mixed with soft clay, so they will mix with one another in marriage, but they will not hold together, just as iron does not mix with clay. And in the days of these kings the God of heaven will set up a kingdom that shall never be destroyed, nor shall the kingdom be left to another people. It shall break in pieces all these kingdoms and bring them to an end, and it shall stand forever, just as you saw that a stone was cut from a mountain by no human hand, and that it broke in pieces the iron, the bronze, the clay, the silver, and the gold. A great God has made known to the king **what shall be after this.** *The dream is certain, and its interpretation sure."* vs 37-45 (ESV)

On my power point presentation of revelation, the small stone hits the image in the feet, and it breaks away, scatters every direction, and the rock grows and fills the entire screen. This is what Nebuchadnezzar saw. The Head of Gold Is **Babylon.** The Last kingdom, represented by the ten toes, the ten nation confederacy under the Antichrist is Called **Babylon**. So This is the World System, The Organized rebellion Under Satan against God, what will be destroyed when The Stone hits the image in the feet at Armageddon. **Babylon to Babylon.**

These are the four empires that have had a great impact on the people of God, the first three with Israel, and of course, Rome with Jews and Christians; and goes on, with the iron continuing as part of the ten toes of the image until the setting up of the kingdom of our Lord Jesus Christ, when the rock destroys the image These empires were not *world* empires, but we have to remember, that in that day, to imply that what the king ruled over was <u>not the whole world</u> would have meant execution.

The *head of Gold* , *Babylon* would be succeeded by the *arms and breast Silver* Kingdom *Media and Persia*. (We will use the term *Medo-Persia* hereafter). Medo-Persia held control for a little over two hundred years. Then, it was succeeded by the *belly and thighs Bronze* Kingdom of *Greece*. Under young Alexander The Great, who at age 23 set out to conquer Western Civilization, and after conquering most of it died at age 33. His empire was divided among his four generals, however, The *Grecian* or *Hellenistic* influence was spread to a vast area from Europe to Persia and throughout the Middle East, including Egypt, and was predominant for a period of about three hundred years. Alexander carried the Greek Language and Platonic Philosophy with him.. Greek became the second language of most of Western Society, and parts of the Middle East, so that when it was time for the New Testament, people spoke their own language plus *Common Greek*, or as I call it, *Street Greek*, and Platonic Philosophy kept influencing false Christian teachers from time to time, and still does today. Alexander's primary teacher had been the philosopher Aristotle, who was, himself, a student of Plato.

Paul states in Gal.4:4, **When The Fullness of Time was Come, God sent forth His Son**.... God prepared the World for the coming of Jesus. First, as mentioned above, The universal language in which to write the New Testament. Then, A Ruler in Egypt, Ptolemy Philadelphius, about 200 years before Jesus was born, because there were so many Jews living in parts of Egypt, particularly, Alexandria, and knowing they had *Sacred* Scriptures which spoke of a coming king, and peace and many other things: appointed 70 scholars to translate those *Scriptures* into Greek. The Greek Translation is known as The Septuagint. It is abbreviated LXX, The Roman Numeral 70. Most of the quotes from the Old Testament, particularly in Paul's letters are from the LXX, not the Hebrew text.

Not only that, but the sacred name of God, YHWH in the Hebrew Old Testament, uses the Greek, **kurios**, *Lord* in the LXX and it is, of course, part of the phrase, *The Lord Jesus Christ.* The LXX was the bible of the Gentile New Testament Church. (See Appendix B on God's Name) The third factor, preparing the world, Was the Roman Empire that made it safe for a Roman Citizen, like Paul, to safely travel over western countries to spread the gospel.

The final piece was God moving on a heathen Emperor , to want a census of the Empire, so a tax was put on everyone in the Roman Empire. To pay the tax you had to return to the place of your ancestry, causing Mary and Joseph to Go to Bethlehem, so Jesus could be born in the place Micah had prophesied 700+ years previously. (Mi 5:2)

Then came The *legs of iron Rome* It had been forming for about 700 years and absorbed what the previous kingdoms had controlled and added greatly to these domains. Julius Caesar changed it from a republic to an Empire about 45, BC. The Roman Empire was divided into two parts: the Eastern and Western Empires. Rome, which was the capital of the western division, lasted until AD 476, but the eastern division of the empire with its capital at Constantinople stood until AD 1453. And while the empire as such died, a number of the nations of which it was composed continued to exist as independent nation-states.

Then, the final earthly government, that would arise, is pictured on the image by the *feet and toes part of iron and part of brittle clay.* Years ago, when the European Common Market was formed, many people who had not studied prophecy previously started to teach *this is the revived Roman Empire.* I tried to caution some of my friends: *If that were true, the feet and 10 toes would have to be all Iron.* Since the feet and toes are part *iron and clay,* this final entity will be composed partly of old Roman Empire countries and partly of countries not included in the old Roman Empire (the clay).

And it represents man's last attempt to rule on earth. For as Daniel says, *in the days of those kings the God of heaven will set up a kingdom that shall never be destroyed*, the stone, that falls at the end was *cut from a mountain by no human hand*. The crushing stone, which smashes the image in the feet, and becomes a great mountain that fills the earth, **prefigures Armageddon, the ending of Human Government, the finish of Babylon and Man's Rebellion Under Satan Against God, and the whole concluding parts of CHAPTER 66**

THE TWO WILD BEASTS

And The Dragon stood on the seashore, then I saw a beast coming out of the sea ,having ten horns, and seven heads, and on his horn wee ten diadems, and on his heads were blasphemous names. Satan stands on the shore and calls one up in his image. The only difference between them is, In Ch 12 the crowns are on the seven heads, here the crowns are on the horns. We will be told later, of the same description in Dan, 7, and Rev 17, that the 10 horns are 10 kings. The fact that the crowns are on the heads of Satan, shows he is the power behind the kings.

And the beast which I saw was like a leopard, and his feet were like those of a bear, and his mouth like the mouth of a lion. And the dragon gave him his power and his throne and great authority. There is only one other place in scripture where the *leopard*, the *bear* and the *lion are mentioned together;* **It is Daniel, Chapter 7:**

Daniel 7 begins, *in the first year of Belshazzar king of Babylon.* Two things are very important in this opening statement.

1. There are Liberals, who no longer believe the Bible, that said for many years, *there was never a King of Babylon named Belshazzar*, who is prominent in chapters 5 and 7. However, Archaeologists since have discovered documents that indicate Belshazzar served as Co-Regent with his father, Nabonidus, who had moved to the other palace in Tiema and Belshazzar stayed in Babylon. (Probably the earliest mention of him under Naboindus is cuneiform text 135 in a collection At The Archaeological Museum in Florence published in 1958, although he had been earlier mentioned in 1929). In, addition, when Daniel read the *handwriting on the wall* in Ch 5, Belshazzar proclaimed Daniel **third ruler** in the *Kingdom* supports what the archaeologists have stated. Belshazzar was already **second**.

2. Most of the books on Daniel, I read over the years, make Daniel 7 a rehash of The Image of Chapter 2, Babylon, Medo-Persia, Greece and Rome. However, verse 17 states plainly, *These great beasts, which are four, are four kings which* **shall arise** *out of the earth.* Belshazzar was the last ruler of Babylon , so the first beast in chapter 7 cannot be Babylon. As mentioned previously, *The Image showed the Time of The Gentiles, Babylon to Babylon, ending with the 10 toes of Iron and clay.* Here in this chapter, the final Kingdom is with ten kings, and we will see that immediately after that Kingdom, Jesus comes sets up His Kingdom for ever. The Image shows the entire Time of the Gentiles, but chapter 7 shows the final three main powers in western civilization being part of the 10 Kingdom Empire of the Antichrist The 10 horns are also mentioned in Rev 17:12, were Johns says , *the ten horns are ten kings which have received no kingdom as yet.* **So they were still future when John wrote.**

I saw in my vision by night, and, behold, the four winds of the heaven strove upon the great sea. And four great beasts came up from the sea, diverse one from another. The first was like a lion, and had eagle's wings: I beheld till the wings thereof were plucked, and it was lifted up from the earth, and made stand upon the feet as a man, and a man's heart was given to it. And behold another beast, a second, like to a bear, and it raised up itself on one side, and it had three ribs in the mouth of it between the teeth of it: and they said thus unto it, Arise, devour much flesh. After this I beheld, and lo another, like a leopard, which had upon the back of it four wings of a fowl; the beast had also four heads; and dominion was given to it. After this I saw in the night visions, and behold a fourth beast, dreadful and terrible, and strong exceedingly; and it had great iron teeth: it devoured and brake in pieces, and stamped the residue with the feet of it: and it was diverse from all the beasts that were before it; and it had ten horns.

It is significant that the beast comes out of the sea. Rev 17:15 indicates that the sea, in this context, from which this beast will come, refers to *the peoples of the earth.* It is interesting today that the strong nations in Western civilization are, as a result of people rising against Monarchies, Republics, and not governed by Kings. Even England, which has a Beautiful Monarchy, is governed by a Parliament.

I considered the horns, and, behold, there came up among them another little horn, before whom there were three of the first horns plucked up by the roots: and, behold, in this horn were eyes like the eyes of man, and a mouth speaking great things.... **So there will be 10 nation confederacy, but one person will come up who will take control of three of the nations, and through the 3 he will rule the 10 and through the 10 rule the world.** And the only 3 nations mentioned are the *Lion, Bear, Leopard, the same as Rev13.* Rev. 17:12-13 adds, *And the ten horns which you saw are ten* *kings, which have received no kingdom as yet; but receive power as kings one hour with the beast. These have one mind, and shall give their power and strength unto the beast.* The idiom indicates that once the Beast comes on the scene their authority as kings will appear for only an hour, after which he will have full control.

Notice the events next: *I beheld till the thrones were cast down, and the Ancient of days did sit, whose garment was white as snow, and the hair of his head like the pure wool: his throne was like the fiery flame, and his wheels as burning fire. A fiery stream issued and came forth from before him: thousand thousands ministered unto him, and ten thousand times ten thousand stood before him: the judgment was set, and the books were opened..... I beheld then because of the voice of the great words which the horn spoke: I beheld even till the beast was slain, and his body destroyed, and given to the burning flame. As concerning the rest of the beasts, they had their dominion taken away: yet their lives were prolonged for a season and time.* Here is a preliminary picture of the final events of this age. These events follow Armageddon in Rev 19. The beast is destroyed, but the nations of the world will go on into the millennium with Christ as Ruler. Only the armies are killed at Armageddon. Notice the next scene from Daniel:

*I saw in the night visions, and, behold, one like the **Son of man** came with the clouds of heaven, and came to the Ancient of days, and they brought him near before him. And there was given him dominion, and glory, and a kingdom, that all people, nations, and languages, should serve him: his dominion is an everlasting dominion, which shall not pass away, and his kingdom that which shall not be destroyed.* I was taught, as a young Chistian, *that when Jesus used this phrase he was teaching that he was human.* That is not the case. Those who heard him knew He was referencing this passage of Daniel, thus indicating He was The Messiah.

Daniel, now, inquires to know more about the 4th Beast, who *made war with the saints, and prevailed against them; Until the Ancient of days came, and judgment was given to the saints of the most High; and the time came for the saints to possessed the kingdom.* and is told:

The fourth beast shall be the fourth kingdom upon earth, which shall be diverse from all kingdoms, and shall devour the whole earth, and shall tread it down, and break it in pieces. And the ten horns out of this kingdom are ten kings that shall arise: and another shall rise after them; and he shall be diverse from the first, and he shall subdue three kings. And he shall speak great words against the most High, and shall wear out the saints of the most High, and think to change times and laws: and they shall be given into his hand until **a time and times and the dividing of time. Obviously the same as listed in Revelation time, times and a half a time, 1260 days, 42 months. 3 ½ Biblical years. (Reminder, A Biblical Year is 360 days.)**

Back now to Revelation: After describing he beast's arrival from the sea, John says: *And I saw one of his heads as it were wounded to death; and the wound of his death was healed: and all the world wondered after the beast.* The same Greek Verb, **sphadzo** (sacrificed, killed by violence, that is used of Jesus as a *lamb that had been slain* in Chapter 5, same tense both places, perfect, passive participle, means *it has been done*). The phrase means *he was killed.* And **he was resurrected**. Satan cannot resurrect the dead, only God can do that. Remember 2Th 2 said, *God will send strong delusion to believe the lie.* And as a result, Satanic worship reaches its pinnacle; as *all the world wondered after the beast. And they worshipped the dragon which gave power unto the beast: and they worshipped the beast, saying, Who is like unto the beast? who is able to make war with him?* **They will find out at Armageddon!!!!**

An interesting text in Ch 17 says: *The beast that thou saw was, and is not; and shall ascend out of the abyss, and go into perdition: and they that dwell on the earth shall wonder, whose names were not written in the book of life from the foundation of the world, when they behold the beast that was, and is not, and yet is....And there are seven kings: five are fallen, and one is, and the other is not yet come; and when he cometh, he must continue a short space. And the beast that was, and is not, even he is the eighth, and is of the seven, and goes into destruction.* (vs 8, 10-11)There have been all kinds of ideas and hypothesis about this passage. The term, *fallen,* implies more than just saying *they died.* It implies being removed, killed. If John is thinking of his own time, he is indicating that 5 emperors of Rome have died, there is one on the throne now, there is one more coming who will only be on the throne for a short time, but the beast, after a looooong time, antichrist is the eighth and is one of the seven. This has caused some to say when the antichrist is killed one of the Caesars will come and inhabit the body when he comes back to life. Thus, the Roman Empire will be revived. But again, the final kingdom is part iron and part clay. Not all from The Roman Empire. The bible does not teach reincarnation.

But, a simpler, contextual, meaning is that, initially the ten kingdom confederacy, like all other organizations, will have a Main Leader, one of the Kings in this case. There will be 7 different ones, At this point in the discussion 5 have fallen, one is, the 6th , The beast, who will be killed. We are not told how long he will be dead before his resurrection, At the time the beast is killed, immediately a 7th one will be appointed, (If the President of the United States is killed, immediately the Vice President is sworn in as President,) He continues for a short time. Why, because the because the beast will be resurrected, *he is the 8th , and is one of the 7*—The 6th one. Might be only 3 days and 3 nights...*He is the Imitation Christ, The Instead of Christ!*

*There was given to him a mouth speaking arrogant words and blasphemies, and authority to act for **forty-two months** was given to him. And he opened his mouth in blasphemies against God, to blaspheme His name and His tabernacle, that is, those who dwell in heaven. It was also given to him to make war with the saints and to overcome them, and authority over every tribe and people and tongue and nation was given to him. All who dwell on the earth will worship him, everyone whose name has not been written in the book of life of **the Lamb who has been slain from the foundation of the world***

The Book of Hebrews, (9:13) states, *It is not possible for the blood of bulls and goats to take away sin!* Then how could God forgive the sins in the Old Testament? God even shed blood to cover the nakedness of Adam and Eve with skins, Important people brought sacrifices, fathers brought an animal to have the blood shed for his families sins, The High Priest would enter the Holy of Holies on *Yom Kippur, The Day of Atonement*, with blood for his own sins and sins of the people, and God would forgive! How could he do that? *Jesus is the Lamb slain from the foundation of the world.* God planned to send Jesus before creation. God wanted people in His image to love.

As mentioned earlier, Love has to be by choice. You can buy a robot, put batteries in it, it will say, *I love you!*, but it can't. God knew we would all misuse our free will, as Isaiah said, *all we like sheep have gone astray, we have turned every one to his own way, but the Lord laid on Him the iniquity of us all.* When God shed blood for Adam and Eve, When Noah brought sacrifice for his sins, when the fathers brought one for their families, when the High Priest sacrificed,

GOD FORGAVE THE SIN AND PUT IT ON A MASTERCARD ACCOUNT AND 2000 YEARS AGO THE MASTER CAME AND PAID THE BILL, AND ESTABLISHED A GIFT CARD FOR WHOSOEVER WILL.

OUR RESPONSIBILITY IS TO DISTRIBUTE THE GIFT CARDS

Before introducing the Second Beast, John states, *If any man have an ear, let him hear. He that leads into captivity shall go into captivity: he that kills with the sword must be killed with the sword. Here is the endurance and the faith of the saints.* He is instructing the saints, those who will receive Jesus Christ under this tremendous difficulty, not to use the tactics of the those who are trying to destroy them. God will avenge, but you keep exercising your faith and enduring. Jesus had said about this time, *He who endures to the end shall be saved!*(Mt 24:13)

And I beheld another beast coming up out of the earth; and he had two horns like a **lamb,** *and he spoke as* **a dragon.** *Jesus is the Lamb, Satan is the Dragon,* so this one, who is called, *The False Prophet,* in 16:13; 19:20; 20:10, gives the appears like a The lamb, but his speech, the things he declares, the orders he give, is the speech of The Dragon. Thus he is leader of a religious system that appears to be Christian, but is really Satanic. We will see in Ch 17, where the religions system is pictured as *a Prostitute,* and is called, *The Mother of Prostitutes,* indicating the joining of other religions into this one with world wide control. Since I have for over 50 years taught chapter 17 immediately after this chapter, I will do so here also.

He exercises all the authority of the first beast in his presence, and causes the earth and those who dwell in it to worship the first beast, of whom the wound of his death was healed. The religious leader, The False Prophet, serves in the presence of the Antichrist, as Administrator carrying the Satanic agendas of the Antichrist. How does he cause those who live on the earth to worship the Antichrist? *He performs great* **signs,** *so that he even makes fire come down out of heaven to the earth in the presence of men. And he deceives those who dwell on the earth because of the* **signs** *which it was given him to perform in the presence of the beast.* Don't forget, people know technology, and these will be *signs* for which there is no scientific explanation. They are visible, powerful, and Satanic in origin. People will be overwhelmed by the *signs.* **A *sign* is a miracle pointing to a *spiritual truth.*** This is why John, in his gospel, calls the particular miracles he presents of Jesus *signs,* because, as he indicates they *point* to a purpose: *truly Jesus did many other signs in the presence of His disciples, which are not written in this book; but these are written that you may believe that Jesus is the Christ, the Son of God, and that believing you may have life in His name.* The life Jesus called, *Life to the full!* (Jn 20:30-31)

As the result of the signs he is able to convince *those who dwell on the earth to make an image to the beast who had the stroke of the sword and has come to life. And it was given to him to give a spirit (demon) to the image of the beast, so that the image of the beast would even speak and cause as many as do not worship the image of the beast to be killed.* (I, along with many others, translate the Greek **pneuma,** *wind, breath,* or *spirit,* in this context as *spirit.* Demons are frequently called unclean spirits in the New Testament, and we will read in ch 16 about *spirits of demons doing signs.*) And to carry out the command and death sentence, *And he causes all, the small and the great, and the rich and the poor, and the free men and the slaves, to be given a mark on their right hand or on their forehead, and he insures that no one will be able to buy or to sell, except the one who has the mark, either the name of the beast or the number of his name.* We do not know the name., nor the mark, which is made with an engraving or etching tool, on the skin, and with what is currently available, probably a microchip inserted into the skin. But, the number is given: **666.**

Bible students, over the years, have been very ingenious in coming up with **666** using various names, During WWII, They had Mussolini of Italy as him, Some had Henry Kissinger, US Secretary of State as him, Some have used *kaisar neron,* which is Greek for *Caesar Nero, but use Hebrew Characters which are actually used for numbers, K=100, S=60, R=200, O=6, N=50.* I don't go along with any of this type of thing. God's number in Revelation would be **7**, man's Number is **6. 777** The Holy Trinity: God, The Father, God, The Son, God The Holy Spirit. **666** The Satanic Trinity: Satan, The False God; The Antichrist, The False Christ; The False Prophet, The False Holy Spirit.

As the Holy Spirit points people to and draws people to Jesus , the False Prophet draws people to and points s people to the Antichrist and His image. The mark will be in the right hand or the forehead. In Scripture frequently, the right hand is the hand of action, and, the Bible also makes it clear that the real battle is in the Mind. So the Satanic forces will try to control both the actions and thinking of the people of the world.

People worry, unnecessarily, about anything they get with the number **666** on it. Before I did the live tv program I did it on radio for several years. A lady called in one day and said, *Pastor Westlake, I have a check with* **666** *on it and I'm afraid to cash it.* I said, *Send to me!* I went on to assure her she should go ahead and cash it. The **666** is connected with the worship of the Antichrist, and has no relevance other than at that time.. The False Prophet, through the Religious system, and by the authority of the antichrist, will be controlling the commerce. No buying or selling if you do not worship the image of the Antichrist. No person, family, state, or nation can conduct its financial or business affairs or receive credit in the world monetary system without being part of the Antichrist's system. As I travel to various parts of the world, I still find people who want *The American Dollars.* I was in Singapore teaching in March of this year, 2018, and observed the TV program, Asia's Got Talent. The Prize, one hundred thousand *American dollars* They won't be worth anything then.

CHAPTER 17

The Great Prostitute
The Religious System of the False Prophet

Come, I will show you the judgment of the great prostitute who is seated on many waters, with whom the kings of the earth have committed sexual immorality, and with the wine of whose sexual immorality the dwellers on earth have become drunk." And he carried me away in the Spirit into a wilderness, and I saw a woman sitting on a scarlet beast that was full of blasphemous names, and it had seven heads and ten horns. (ESV)

The woman is riding the beast with the ten horns.. It is the political power that carries the woman, thus gives authority to the woman to administrate. We are reminded, again, of the death and resurrection of the Beast, *The beast that you saw was, and is not; and shall ascend out of the bottomless pit, and go into perdition: and they that dwell on the earth shall wonder, whose names were not written in the book of life from the foundation of the world, when they behold the beast that was, and is not, and yet is.* We have already seen that the False Prophet *looks like a lamb but speaks like the dragon.* A Religious system that appears to be Christian, practicing sexual immorality (**porneia**=as we have studied religious adultery, idolatry) Let's read the description:

Please take note: There have been many great Christians in the Roman Catholic Church who have received Jesus Christ and have a personal relationship with Him. I have known many great Priests and Nuns over the past years, whom I greatly admire. I have quoted from Great Catholic Christians of the past in many of my sermons and College Classes, but this is clearly a picture of the Roman Catholic Church's final practice of Christianity. **The true Christians will have been raptured, so its, technically no longer a church.** V 9 says: *the seven heads are seven mountains on which the woman is seated,* Obviously, Rome. The same sins are listed here as were indicated in the warnings to the Churches of Pergamum and Thyatira, which were present, and added to in the Middle Ages, but here at a later period of time, **The last days, intensified during the final 3 ½ years.**

A case in point, I was invited years ago, while pastoring in Cape Girardeau, Missouri, to go to a Catholic High School and teach on the Baptism in The Holy Spirit and Speaking In Other Tongues. I always point out that *Believing in Jesus,* is much more than mental ascent that Jesus is The Son of God; that you must receive Him personally as Lord and Savior. So my *Battle Plan* was to emphasize that they needed to become real believers. There were several hundred students, priests and nuns in the auditorium and I So wrote on the board, *What does it mean to believe in Jesus Christ?* A young nun, who looked as if she was in her 20s, raised her hand and said, *It means to recognize you are a sinner, to ask God The Father to forgive your sins In Jesus Name, and to ask Jesus to come into your heart, and be born again by the Holy Spirit.* There went my *Battle Plan.* I have had the privilege of ministering in Catholic Churches over the years in the Kansas City area.

The woman was arrayed in purple and scarlet, and adorned with gold and jewels and pearls, (what *Christian* organization dresses and has riches like that?) *holding in her hand a golden cup full of abominations and the impurities of her sexual immorality.* (uses spiritual fornication/idols to *aid* worship, and even parades a loaf of bread through the city in a cart telling people to worship Jesus, for a priest has supposedly turned that loaf into the body of Jesus) And *on her forehead was written a name of mystery: Babylon the great, mother of prostitutes and of earth's abominations.* Several scholars have traced much of the practices of the same church to Babylon Mystery Religions..(see, for example, John Walvoord on *Revelation*)

The fact is, the religions of the world will join her, *she is the mother of prostitutes.* Just considering current times, what religious leader, in the whole world, could call a meeting of various religions together. At Pope Francis inauguration, March , 2013, religious leaders from all religions met together in Rome. To promote respect and unity. The direction of many *Christian* churches today is to reject the Bible standard and to substitute a host of other man-made option. This tendency will increase rapidly as the doctrine of demons finds its way into the false religious systems of this world . So all religions will compromise into the one. **Between writing this, and the final edit (Mar 2019) There was a similar meeting in Abu Dhabi primarily with the Pope and Sheik Ahmed el Tayyib, Grand Iman of Al-Azhar Mosque in Cairo along with many Christians Jews Muslims and many other religions. The Pope is the only religious leader in the world who could call such a meeting…. A forrunner of the coming False Prophet.** *The many waters she sits on in v.15: The waters that you saw, where the prostitute is seated, are peoples and multitudes and nations and languages.* The When Jesus declared , *I am the way the truth and the life, and no man comes to the father except by me,* He meant what He said!

And I saw the woman, drunk with the blood of the saints, the blood of the martyrs of Jesus. V.18 indicates *The woman...is the great city that has dominion over the kings of the earth.* Rome, physically, had dominion in John's day, but in addition, Roman Catholic Theology teaches that the Pope has temporal authority also, meaning over kings and governors, and if you read history you can see times of that conflict, and, If you read history, you can read about the Inquisitions of the Catholic Church, were non Catholics were murdered by the thousands in past. I sat in a meeting in the late 1950's and heard a Missionary to Columbia, South America, tell of *his pregnant wife being murdered by a mob led by Roman Catholic Priests.* **Again, please, I am talking about the system, not individuals.** I had religion, in non Catholic churches, before I met Jesus when I was 19. Religion can undermine what the bible teaches about true Christianity.

The Apostle Paul, describing his religious credentials before he met Jesus Christ in Ph 3, says, literally *I threw them to the dogs for the sake of Christ.* Then, Paul, one of the greatest scholars in history tries to explain the difference between having religious credentials and knowing Jesus, starts a sentence, *but, indeed, therefore, at least, even (**alla men oun ge kai**)* That doesn't make sense in any language in the history of the world. But Paul is so overwhelmed by the difference that's all he can say. I translate those words with one that expresses to me the difference when I met Jesus. **WOW!**

I love the statement I heard in the pulpit of our church by an ex Muslim who is now a Christian Pastor. *I studied the various religions and became a Christian because I discovered they were all religions except Christianity. Christianity is a relationship.*: I remind you again, Jesus said in 3:20, ***I have taken my stand at the door and I am knocking, and if anyone hears my voice and opens the door I will come into him and will feast with him and he will feast with me. If you don't know Him, you are missing real life..He's knocking! He paid your sin bill on the cross! He loves you! He created you to have an intimate relationship with Him.*** We will save verses 15 and following on the Prostitute till later.

CHAPTER 14
Parenthetical Enlargements
Showing the Major Closing Events of this Age

I mentioned in the discussion of Parenthetical Enlargements, that this shows things that will happen in the rest of the book to complete God's plan for this age. So these are preliminary announcements of the events that are described in more detail. Again, a movie screen could divide up and show everything at once, but literature has to progress a page at a time.

And I looked, and, lo, a Lamb stood on the mount Zion, and with him an hundred forty and four thousand, having his Father's name written in their foreheads. Obviously the same group sealed in chapter 7.

As discussed in connection with Ch 12, Jesus will go to **Bozra,** and reveal himself to the remnant of Israel who are there being preserved by Michael and His Angels from Satan and the Antichrist. He will lead them out of there and into Jerusalem through the Eastern Gate and the *Glory of God will fill the temple.* This will happen, as I pointed out, after Armageddon. Because that is the climax after everything else that has to happen it is presented first with some additional details.

The remnant are referred to both as the 144,000, 12 times 12 indicating completion, and the woman of chapter 12. They are standing on *The Mount Zion.* It is amazing to me that some authors on Revelation consider this to be in heaven. There are organizations, like the Mormons, who consider Mount Zion to be Salt Lake City, or Independence, Missouri. *The Mount Zion is, on earth and it is Jerusalem.* John is standing on earth and *I heard a voice from heaven, as the voice of many waters, and as the voice of a great thunder: and I heard the voice of harpers harping with their harps: And they sung as it were a new song before the throne, and before the four beasts, and the elders: and no man could learn that song but the hundred and forty and four thousand, which were redeemed from the earth/land.*

Again, to repeat, translators do not usually understand prophecy. In the Old Testament, the Hebrew word, *eretz* is used for the *earth*, but also *for the land of canaan*. This confusion is one of the things that caused the idea that Satan had a kingdom on earth prior to Genesis to produce the Gap Theory., which claims there were humans before Adam and Eve, and they are demons today. It was because the context of many of the scriptures, taken out of context to prove this theory, have to do with the land of Canaan, not the earth.

The Greek, word, for earth, *ge,* prounced *gay*, is used the same way in the New Testament. Joseph and Mary went into Egypt after Herod's decree, and when Herod died, God told Joseph in Mt 1:20-21 *Arise, and take the young child and his mother, and go into the land (ge) of Israel: for they are dead which sought the young child's life. And he arose, and took the young child and his mother, and came into the land (ge)of Israel.* Ac 7:3, speaks of Abraham going into the *land (ge) of Canaan* This fits with both Chs 7 and 12. The Israelites who knew Jesus prior to the rapture are in heaven, those who accepted Him during the last 3 ½ years are in this group standing on Mount Zion. He gives a farther description of them *These are they which were not defiled with women; for they are virgins. These are they which follow the Lamb wherever he goes. These were redeemed from among men, being the firstfruits unto God and to the Lamb. And in their mouth was found no deceit: for they are without fault before the throne of God.*

Remember the context of Revelation, not defiled with women, virgins, not fornication/idolatry *they follow the lamb wherever He goes*, they have followed him from *bozra,* *Firstfruits,* obviously from context from Israel. No *deceit,* contrasting them with Jacob, who was full of deceit, as He did Nathanael, *a true Israelite in whom is no deceit.* (Jn 1:47) Phillip, after meeting Jesus, went out to bring Nathanael to Jesus.

Jesus saw Nathanael coming toward him and exclaimed, Look, a true Israelite in whom there is no deceit! Nathanael asked him, How do you know me? Jesus replied, Before Philip called you, when you were under the fig tree, I saw you. What is significant about the fig tree? The custom was to meditate on Scripture under the shade of a fig tree. Just the fact that Jesus knew Nathanael was under the fig tree created belief, so *Nathanael answered him, Rabbi, you are the Son of God; you are the king of Israel!* But there is more to the story. *Jesus said to him, Because I told you that I saw you under the fig tree, do you believe? You will see greater things than these.* What greater things? The fact that Jesus had already referred to Jacob, He is telling Nathanael, *I not only know where you were, I know what Scriptures on which you were meditating:* Jacob running from Esau, had a dream about the ladder reaching between heaven and earth, and the angels going up and down on it, *He continued, Truly, truly I say to you, you will see heaven opened and the angels of God ascending and descending on the Son of Man.* He is telling Nathanael, **I am that ladder that you saw in the dream. I am the one through whom the blessings of heaven come down, and through whom you can reach up to God.**

The 1st angel, appears in this parenthetical enlargement; *I saw another angel fly in the midst of heaven, having the everlasting gospel to preach unto them that dwell on the earth, and to every nation, and kindred, and tongue, and people, Saying with a loud voice, Fear God, and give glory to him; for the hour of his judgment is come: and worship him that made heaven, and earth, and the sea, and the fountains of waters.* Remember, Jesus said in Mt 24, *this gospel must be preached in all the world, then shall the* **end** *come.* This is that event, giving people a final chance, to stop the false worship and worship the true God, before Armageddon.

The 2nd angel, flies saying, *Babylon is fallen, is fallen, that great city, because she made all nations drink of the wine of the wrath of her fornication. Religious Babylon* falls in ch 17, *Commercial Babylon* in 18, and *Political Babylon* in 19 at Armageddon. This is prefigured in Daniel. Please read Daniel 5. Belshazzar made a great feast, worshiping the false Gods, when, *In the same hour came forth fingers of a man's hand, and wrote over against the candlestick upon the plaster of the wall of the king's palace: and the king saw the part of the hand that wrote. Then the king's countenance was changed, and his thoughts troubled him, so that the joints of his loins were loosed, and his knees smote one against another.* No one could read it until Daniel came in. Daniel pointed out the words were, *mene, mene tekel, uphrasin* (Lit. *number, number weights and divisions*-the last word *upharsin* is *peres* with the addition of *u (and)* plus *in (plural ending)* , which Daniel interpreted to mean, *God has numbered your kingdom, and finished it...You are weighed in the balances, and are found wanting...Your kingdom is divided, and given to the Medes and Persians.* **Babylon fell that night!**

IMPOSSIBLE! How could the impregnable city of Babylon fall? The city had double walls, towers, and 8 double gates strong enough for Chariots to ride on top. There was no weapon in that day that could break into the walls. The river, Euphrates, ran through the city, along which were strong walls, gates down to the water. Where the river entered and left the city were iron bars hanging down into the water from the top of the gates, so no army could enter the city by the water gates. Isaiah, who wrote almost 200 years before Cyrus , (See *Isaiah*, by Dr. Stanley M. Horton), God speaking of Jerusalem being rebuilt, 44:26-45:6 (NASB), says:

It is I who says of Jerusalem, She shall be inhabited! And of the cities of Judah, They shall be built. And I will raise up her ruins again. It is I who says to the depth of the sea, Be dried up! And I will make your rivers dry. It is I who says of Cyrus, He is My shepherd! And he will perform all My desire.

And he declares of Jerusalem, She will be built, And of the temple, Your foundation will be laid. Thus says the Lord to Cyrus His anointed, Whom I have taken by the right hand, To subdue nations before him And to loose the loins of kings; To open doors before him so that gates will not be shut: I will go before you and make the rough places smooth; I will shatter the doors of bronze and cut through their iron bars. I will give you the treasures of darkness And hidden wealth of secret places, so that you may know that it is I, The Lord, the God of Israel, who calls you by your name. For the sake of Jacob My servant, And Israel My chosen one, I have also called you by your name; I have given you a title of honor though you have not known Me. I am the Lord, and there is no other; Besides Me there is no God. I will gird you, though you have not known Me; That men may know from the rising to the setting of the sun That there is no one besides Me. I am the Lord, and there is no other. God names Cyrus, mentions the sea being dried, the gates not shut, says he will give Cyrus the treasures of darkness, and wealth of secret places:

The following is from Herodotus, *The Father of History*, who wrote in the fifth century BC: After indicating that the Babylonians *had made provisions for many years, and therefore, were under no apprehensions about a siege;* writes: *Cyrus, Having stationed he bulk of his army near the passage of the river where it enters Babylon, and again having stationed another division beyond the city, where the river makes its exit, he gave order to his forces to enter the city as soon as they should see the river fordable, he marched away with the ineffective part of his army.....He diverted the river, by means of a canal, into the lake, which was before a swamp, he made the ancient channel fordable by the sinking of the river. When this took place, the Persians, who were appointed for that purpose close to the stream of the river, which had now subsided to about the middle of a man's thigh, entered Babylon by this passage. If, however, the Babylonians had been aware of it beforehand, or had known what Cyrus was about, the would not have suffered the Persians to enter the city, but would have utterly destroyed them; for having shut all the little gates that lead to the river, and mounting the walls that extend along the banks of the river, they would have caught them as in a net; whereas the Persians came upon them by surprise.* He goes on to indicate the last part of the city taken was the center and, *those, who inhabited the center knew nothing of the capture (for it happened to be a festival); but they were dancing at the time and enjoying themselves, till they received certain information of the truth. And thus Babylon was taken for the first time.* **God has a reason for everything in His Word; I can't help believe that the passage of Isaiah was shown to Cyrus, and thus had a strong influence on his decision he allowed the return to Jerusalem.**

The 3rd angel follows *saying with a loud voice,*

If anyone worships the beast and his image, and receives a mark on his forehead or on his hand, he also will drink of the wine of the wrath of God, which is mixed in full strength in the cup of His anger; and he will be tormented with fire and brimstone in the presence of the holy angels and in the presence of the Lamb. And the smoke of their torment goes up forever and ever; they have no rest day and night, those who worship the beast and his image, and whoever receives the mark of his name. Many teach, in this day, that Hell is either temporary, like a purgatory to purify you; or those in hell were burned up. Jesus taught it *is eternal fire* (Mk 9:42-48); that it was *prepared for the devil and his angels* (Mt 25:41). And He taught, very pointedly, that those who choose to follow Satan will be forever with him. The teaching in Revelation is very strong, here and later, that it is eternal. **As we read about their eternal punishment, we must pray that God will give us a new sense of urgency as we present Jesus Christ to a lost world.**

This is followed by a reference to the *Remnant of Israel* who have received Jesus Christ, *Here is the perseverance of the saints who keep the commandments of God and their faith in Jesus.* Then John says, *I heard a voice from heaven, saying, Write, Blessed are the dead who die in the Lord from now on! Yes, says the Spirit, so that they may rest from their labors, for their works follow with them* He is encouraging them to *not give in, the end is near, and if they are killed, it will result in rest* from the difficulties they have endured of the enemy trying to kill them, and of the Tribulation period itself. He points out that, *their works will follow them*; God remembers how they have served Him and been faithful to Him in spite of the circumstances, and He does reward *faithfulness.*

I remind pastors and other students, that *God's definition of success is Faithfulness.* I tell them that, in God's sight, I was just as *successful* when I pastored a church that had 13 people the first Sunday I was there as pastor, and the attendance was up because my mother was visiting, and I had to haul batteries and generators up and down ladders in a warehouse to survive financially; as I was pastoring a church averaging over 5,000, because *I was doing what God wanted me to do, where He wanted me to do it.* I firmly believe a Children's Sunday School teacher, who is faithful to do what God has given her to do will have just as big a reward as the Apostle Paul.

Paul, In Eph 3 reminds us that his ministry is a result of the *gift* and *grace* of God and is accomplished by the *effective energizing* of God's power. In ch 4 he teaches that every believer has received *graced, gifted by God.* Frequently when I am preaching or teaching, say in Kansas City, I like to have people say to each other, *You are gifted by God,* then, *you are God's gift to your Church,* then, *You are God's gift to your brothers and sisters in Christ,* then, *You are God's gift to the Kansas City area,* then, **Don't be an unopened gift!** I like to remind them that Jesus taught in John 14 he was going to send us *another one like himself, the Holy Spirit to live on the inside,* and then, He said, *the Father and I are coming with Him.* That is why He is Called, *The Spirit of God,*

The Spirit of God's Son, The Spirit of Christ, The Spirit that raised Christ from the dead, The Spirit of Truth, etc. I ask them to tell the one sitting next to them, **You are a power packed package.** As Paul says in Phi., *I can do all things in Christ Who keeps putting power into me.* I remind them, you don't need to know Scriptures backward and forward to reach the lost. When Paul stood before kings, in Acts, He gave His Testimony. YOU HAVE A TESTIMONY TO SHARE. You can tell people what God has done for you, and you can invite them to church. **Over 90 percent of anyone saved, anywhere in the world, is saved because *a friend invites them to church*.**

THE ANNOUNCEMENTS OF THE HARVEST AND THE WINEPRESS

The 7th Chapter referred to a *great multitude that no man could number out of every nation, tribe, people and tongue...clothed in white robes....*and John was told, *these are those* **continually coming out** *of The Great Tribulation, and have washed their robes and made them white in the blood of the lamb.* This will be a great number who have laid down their lives to rebel against the policies and rule of the Antichrist and the False Prophet along with their false religions system.

As was pointed out above, this is a parenthetical picture of a final resurrection of the righteous to come. *And I looked, and behold a white cloud, and upon the cloud one sat like unto a Son of man, having on his head a golden crown, and in his hand a sharp sickle. And another angel came out of the temple, crying with a loud voice to him that sat on the cloud, Thrust in thy sickle, and reap: for the time is come for you to reap; for the harvest of the earth is ripe. And he that sat on the cloud thrust in his sickle on the earth; and the earth was reaped.*

The crown here is the **stephanos,** the Gold Victors Crown, possibly an indication that those being harvested have overcome as He, Himself overcame, even though they have not yet been given crowns as the Elders wore in heaven.

Then, immediately connected is the preliminary picture of the harvest of the ungodly at the end of the age, Armageddon. *And another angel came out of the temple which is in heaven, he also having a sharp sickle. And another angel came out from the altar, which had power over fire; and cried with a loud cry to him that had the sharp sickle, saying, Thrust in your sharp sickle, and gather the clusters of the vine of the earth; for her grapes are fully ripe. And the angel thrust in his sickle into the earth, and gathered the vine of the earth, and cast it into the great winepress of the wrath of God. And the winepress was trodden without the city, and blood came out of the winepress, even unto the horse bridles, by the space of a thousand and six hundred furlongs* (175-200 miles). *Armageddon* means literally *the Mountain of Megiddo.* As you stand on this mountain, 55 miles north of Jerusalem, you have a view of the *Rift Valley,* the deepest depression on earth. It runs from Megiddo, South for about 3,700 miles into Southeastern Africa. The Dead Sea, the lowest place on earth, 1,412 feet below sea level, is in this valley. On my first trip to Israel, we had an atomic scientist with us who said, *this valley is one of the few places on earth that would hold all the armies of earth, and is formed in such a way that one nuclear bomb would spread through the whole valley and kill them all.* Of course, Our Lord doesn't need or use nuclear bombs. **All He has to do is to speak and its done.** A reminder, as we saw previously, while His clothing is stained from the winepress, He will go to *Petra* and reveal Himself to the Remnant of Israel.

CHAPTER 15

Preparation for the 7 Last Plagues of the Day of the Lord, the Great Tribulation

John now sees, *A Great and Marvelous Sign, seven angels having the seven last plagues; for in them is the wrath of God is completed.* John had seen two other *Great Signs*; The first was a pregnant women clothed with the sun, and twelve stars under her feet, and the second was a great red dragon. Here John saw seven angels who have the seven last plagues of the Tribulation. While the emphasis in this verse is on the word *last*, the number seven is important too. It speaks of completeness! In this case, it refers to the completeness and certainty of God's wrath against all unrighteousness. The judgments of God thus become more intense as the Tribulation moves toward its climax.

As the end is drawing near, many of the faithful remnant of Israel have been killed for their faith in Jesus Christ and others have died from natural causes, and as he had told them, *Blessed are the dead which die in the Lord from henceforth: Yes, says the Spirit, that they may rest from their labors; and their works do follow them.* Then, as now, *to be absent from the body is to be present with the Lord,* so they are rejoicing in the Presence of God; *I saw as it were a sea of glass mingled with fire: and them that had had been victorious over the beast, and over his image, and over his mark, and over the number of his name, stand on the sea of glass, having the harps of God.* As these victors stand beside the crystal sea, they sing a song of praise to God. The theme of their song is deliverance. As the people of Israel praised God for their deliverance from Egypt (Ex 15), so these ones redeemed out of the Tribulation from the hatred and hostility of the beast will sing a song of deliverance to God. *And they sing the song of Moses the servant of God, and the song of the Lamb, saying, Great and marvelous are your works, Lord God Almighty; just and true are your ways, King of saints. Who shall not fear you , O Lord, and glorify your name? for you only are holy: for all nations shall come and worship before you; for your righteous acts have been revealed.*

In their song, they are reminding us of who God is *Who will not fear, O Lord, and glorify your name?* While the nations do not glorify God nor fear Him in their sin-hardened hearts during the Tribulation, the day will come when they will both fear Him and acknowledge Him as Lord (14:7; Je 10:7). all nations worshiping God is a familiar theme of the prophets, and we see this borne out in the next statement: *For you alone are holy. All nations will come and worship you.* (Ps2:8-9; 24:1-10; 66:1-4; 72:8-11; 86:9; Is 2:17; 9:6-7; 66:18-23; Da 7:14; Zeph 2:11; Zech 14:9.) This statement does not mean everyone will be saved; It does mean that during, the Millennium, all nations will be required to go to Jerusalem to worship, but, obviously, when we see what happens when Satan is loosed after the Millennium, many will not have been true worshippers, *in spirit and in truth,* as Jesus defined true worship. The ultimate kingdom of God will include a family whose members are drawn from all nations. They will worship God and extol His righteous works. Even though there are others who have been killed for their faith, the emphasis here is on the Jewish remnant because *they sing the song of Moses the servant of God, and the song of the Lamb*

To continue the emphasis being on God fulfilling His promises to the Israelites, *And after that I looked, and, behold, the temple of the tabernacle of the testimony in heaven was opened: THEN, the seven angels came out of the temple, having the seven plagues, clothed in pure and white linen, and having their breasts girded with golden sashes. And one of the four living ones gave unto the seven angels seven golden bowls full of the wrath of God, who lives for ever and ever. And the temple was filled with smoke from the glory of God, and from his power; and no man was able to enter into the temple, until the seven plagues of the seven angels were finished.*

The only other place *Golden Bowls* are mentioned is in 5:8. There they were *full of incense which are the prayers of the saints.* Both the prayers of the Martyrs for retribution, and the prayers of saints all down through history, in accordance with Jesus instruction, *after this manner pray...* **Your Kingdom come, Your will be done on earth as it is in heaven....are now going to be fulfilled!!!!!**

CHAPTER 16

THE 7 BOWLS OF THE WRATH OF GOD

There is a striking parallel between the trumpet judgments and the present series of plagues. But while there is some similarity, one should not assume they are identical. While the trumpet series, in a sense, calls people to repentance, the bowl series represents the final wrath of God for this age. Compare some of these with the plagues on Egypt prior to the Exodus. Humanity was affected indirectly by the first four trumpets, but they are affected directly by the bowls at the outset of this latter series of judgments. These are called; ***The Seven Last Plagues because in them he Wrath Of God is finished***

John hears "*a loud voice from the temple* telling the seven angels, *Go and pour out on the earth the seven bowls of the wrath of God* (16:1). This voice is God's, or Christ's, for all others have been excluded from the temple until the seven angels have completed their mission.

1st Bowl The first angel pour out his bowl on the people who *had the mark of the beast, and upon those who worshipped his image.* Those who bear the mark of the beast during the Tribulation will now bear the marks of God's wrath. This plague will bring painful ulcers on all who are the beast's, probably where the mark is.. All people will have to make a decision and declare their loyalty for either Christ or Antichrist. (Compare this plague with that of the sixth Egyptian plague, in which humans and beasts suffered with festering boils, in Ex 9:9–11.)

2nd Bowl As the second bowl is outpoured, every living thing in the sea dies (v. 3). Like the 1st Egyptian plague (Ex 7:20–21) and the 2nd second trumpet the waters turn to blood. Under the 2nd trumpet it was a third of the waters, here it is all the large bodies of water . It is *like the blood of a dead man- coagulated/clotted blood.* This plague will have more far-reaching implications, for all sea life dies. All marine food resources are thus lost, and the sea becomes putrid and unfit for any use.

3rd Bowl The third angel pours out his bowl and, *all flowing waters and springs-the rivers and streams-fresh waters* are turned into blood. Water is a critical necessity for life and survival, and even in normal times shortages of water produce crises. But this plague will bring about a universal crisis. We see the panic in our day when water is polluted, the lines of people to buy bottled water where it is available. And John heard *the angel of the waters saying, Righteous are You, who are and who were, O Holy One, because You judged these things; for they poured out the blood of saints and prophets, and You have given them blood to drink. They deserve it.* The next phrase is best translated *And I heard from the altar, your judgments are true and righteous.* It is obviously a voice from the altar, although the word, voice, is not in the text. It does not imply, as some translations indicate, the altar, itself, is speaking.

God is spoken of as *righteous* both when He forgives sin and when he judges. God told Adam, *of the tree of the knowledge of good and evil, you will not eat of it: for in the day that you eat of it, you will certainly die.* (Gen 2:17) Adam and Eve did not die physically the day they ate, they were put out of the Garden, away from fellowship with God, they died *spiritually that day.* Physical death was pronounced that day, but came later for them. How can a Holy God overlook sin? How can a Holy God forgive the sinner? He can be *righteous* when He forgives? How can God declare I have never sinned, when I know I'm guilty?

I was frequently asked on the TV live Question and Answer Program I did for 24 years, *Explain The Trinity.* I answered, *I can't explain my wife, let alone The Trinity.* Jn 1:18 makes an unusual statement in the Greek text, *no one has seen God at any time, the unique God, The one existing in the bosom of the father, He has exegeted Him. Exegesis* means to fully reveal. It is used by Bible Students when we attempt to fully explain a Scripture. Jesus revealed fully who and what God is.

God has forever existed as God the Father, God the Son, and God the Holy Spirit. There was never a time when God was not Father, Son and Holy Spirit This verse said *He was continuously existing in the bosom of The Father.* That means when he was a helpless baby lying in a stone feeding trough, *He was existing in the bosom of The Father;* When he was a boy learning to be a carpenter, *He was existing in the bosom of The Father;* When He was performing miracles and teaching, *He was existing in the bosom of the Father;* When He prayed in Gethsemane while His Father put the sins of every person who ever lived or will live on Him, *He was existing in the Bosom of The Father;* When He was on the whipping post, *He was existing in the bosom of the Father;* When He was being nailed to the cross, being *wounded for our transgressions, and bruised for our iniquities, He was existing in the bosom of the Father;* When he was suffering on the cross, bearing the punishment for our sins, *He was existing in the bosom of the Father.*

There was never a time when God was not Father, Son and Holy Spirit. God gave me a wonderful wife, Jean, Whom I could tell every day for almost 60 years, *I love you forever,* and mean it. I miss her so much. But God The Father, God The Son, God, The Holy Spirit, having been together for ever and for ever and for ever, suddenly, God the Father, and Jesus, *ripped apart*!!!*eli, eli, lema sabachthani? My God my God, Why have you forsaken me?* (Mt 27;46, as prophesied in Ps 22:1) The crushing impact on both The Son and The Father, and the Holy Spirit to be torn apart!. WHY? *Because He loves you as if you are the only one He ever had to love!* **That is true for every person you meet. God wants, both you and them in eternity with Him.**

Jesus had to pay the full price for our sins. *He made Him who knew no sin to be sin on our behalf, so that we might become the righteousness of God in Him.* He had to die spiritually as well as physically. As I can't explain how God could be split apart. I can't explain how Jesus, 100 percent God and 100 percent man could be tempted, but He was. I can't explain how God the Son could become a helpless baby, but He did. I can't explain how God could put the sin of the whole world on His Son, but He did.

There are those who try to say that Jesus went into hell to be tormented for three days and three nights, but Jesus told the thief, *Today you will be with me in Paradise!* **Paradise is not Hell**. The spiritual death did not have to last long...just the fact...the impact was sufficient in the light of an eternity of being together. Jesus was able to say when the atonement for our sins was complete, *It is Finished.* **(tetelestai.)**

This is the Greek Perfect tense. If I say *I am here.* That is usually simply the present tense. But If I make the same statement, but have in mind, *I got up this morning, took a shower, got dressed, ate breakfast, got in my car, drove over here, and as a result of all that happening, I am here.* That is the Greek perfect tense. So, when Jesus said *IT IS FINISHED,* it goes all the way back from the determination of the Father for Jesus to come and die for our sins, through the promise to Eve, that her descendant would crush the serpents head, through all the animal sacrifices pointing to His death on the cross, through all the fallen history of man, through all the prophecies of what Jesus would accomplish to redeem fallen man, IT IS FINISHED!!!, *its accomplished!*

Then He could say, Father, *into your hands I commit my spirit!* He was no longer dead spiritually, Then He died physically. The physical resurrection was the proof that all He had taught is true, and that the full atonement for our sin was made when he said, **tetelestai!** The Father agreed, *it is finished,* and to demonstrate it, He ripped the veil of the Holy of Holies in two, indicating the full price had been paid for people's sins and there was now access into God's presence.

So to answer the question asked at the beginning of this discussion, How can a Holy God overlook, forgive sin. Immediately after saying *all have sinned and fall short of the glory of God,* Paul adds, that we *are justified by his grace as a gift, through the redemption that is in Christ Jesus, whom God put forward as a propitiation by his blood, to be received by faith. This was to show God's righteousness, because in his divine forbearance he had passed over former sins. It was to show his righteousness at the present time, so that he might be just and the justifier of the one who has faith in Jesus.* (Rom 3:23ff ESV) Understand that *just, justified, justifier* are all part of of the same word translated in your bible as *righteous.* So God is *righteous* when he declares you *righteous* because He punished His son in your place...your sin bill was canceled, you are a new creation, you are not guilty of ever having sinned. Romans teaches that God not only blotted out our past sins, but he took Christ's *righteousness* and put it down on your account. Your own *righteousness,* My own *righteousness,* would never be sufficient. Wouldn't it be nice if someone took a millionaires bank account and put all that money on your account! If you could see your page in God's book, if you know Jesus Christ, there is one word there, Righteous! (Rom, Ch 4-*imputed, reckoned* literally is *put down to your account*)

4ᵗʰ Bowl As the fourth bowl is emptied, God overrules the processes of nature, enabling the sun to afflict humanity. Now the sun is given power to scorch people with fire. Though seared by the intense heat, these hardened sinners refuse to repent and instead curse the name of God who has control over these plagues. The indication here is that followers of the universal beast cult recognize the omnipotence of God, but they refuse to repent and arrogantly curse Him instead. Whether the atmosphere is diffused or unusual solar activity occurs, people suffer severely because of this plague.

5ᵗʰ Bowl The fifth bowl plunges the kingdom of the beast into darkness like the Egyptian plague before the Exodus (Ex 10:21–23). People once again suffer terribly, but instead of turning to God they curse Him for their pains. We are not told why people are so anguished and gnaw their tongues in pain. Perhaps the darkness will bring excessive cold for which people are not prepared. Whatever it is, we may be sure that darkness not only intensifies the distress of the previous plagues but also adds terror all its own. It is more than an Eclipse!

6ᵗʰ Bowl, The sixth angel *poured out his bowl on the great river Euphrates, and its water was dried up, to prepare the way for the kings from the sun rising(east.).* As mentioned previously, The Euphrates, in Bible Prophecy, is consider the dividing line between East and West. And John saw *coming out of the mouth of the dragon and out of the mouth of the beast and out of the mouth of the false prophet, three unclean spirits like frogs.* (Here, the second beast is called the *False prophet* for the first time.) *they are spirits of demons working signs, which go out to the kings of the whole world, to gather them together for the war of the great day of The Almighty God.* Signs are again used to deceive gullible people. You would think, after all this time of God pouring out His Wrath, that people would stop believing the lies of the Antichrist and False Prophet, but apparently, the signs convince them otherwise. They had said when the Antichrist was res-urrected, *Who is like Him and who can make war with Him?* They, obviously still hold that opin-ion. They will soon find out

The next phrase should be in brackets (*Behold I am coming like a thief. Blessed is the who stays awake and keeps his clothing , so that he will not walk about naked and men see his shame*) As pointed out pre-viously, The only two events that *come as a thief,* are the **parousia/rapture,** and the **Day of the Lord.**

The Day of Armageddon will be well known. So he is giving this warning to those of us who read this prior to the start of that day. We are to look for his coming, live like He is coming, and try to have as many others ready for His Coming as we can. Vision of this 6ᵗʰ Bowl ends with, *he gathered them together into a place called in the Hebrew tongue Armageddon.*

7ᵗʰ Bowl When the seventh bowl is poured out, *there came a great voice out of the temple of heaven, from the throne, saying, It is done*. A proleptic statement indicates all is over. Again, not like a movie screen that can divide and show things taking place at the same time, litera-ture has to use different pages. The plagues have been poured out and everything, people, The Antichrist, The False Prophet, demons, Satan, himself, and this world, stands on the threshold of eternity. Notice how the pouring out of the seventh bowl compares with what happens at the opening of the 7ᵗʰ Seal and at the sounding of the 7ᵗʰ trumpet, but much more intense here; *there were voices, and thunders, and lightnings; and there was a great earthquake, such as was not since men were upon the earth, so mighty an earthquake, and so great. And the great city was divided into three parts, and the cities of the nations fell: and great Babylon came in remembrance before God, to give unto her the cup of the wine of the fierceness of his wrath. And every island fled away, and the mountains were not found..*

I can't help think of the flood in Noah's day, water vapor around the earth came pouring down like rain, *the fountains in the earth burst forth.* Thus giant earthquakes, and when God got rid of the water that had fallen, *he raised the mountains and lowered the oceans* which would result in more earthquakes. *You clothed the earth with floods of water, water that covered even the moun-tains At your command, the water fled; at the sound of your thunder, it hurried away .Mountains rose and valleys sank to the levels you decreed. Then you set a firm boundary for the seas, so they* ***would never again cover the eart****h.* (Ps 104:6-9)

Notice, the ending statement. God promised Noah He would never again cover the earth with water and put the rainbow in the sky to confirm. This earthquake is greater than any in history. The prophet also saw great hailstones weighing about 110 pounds each fall from the sky on people in this fearful plague. Imagine the damage to almost everything. Finally, notice that people do not repent under the torment of the seventh bowl. Instead, they curse God. There is no indication that people repent under any of the seven bowl judgments!

Some, as mentioned previously, have tried to equate the 7 seals, 7 trumpets and 7 bowls, as just a repetition of the same thing, only adding more details. However, just because there are similarities between some of them., that does not mean they are the same events. They are different, as indicated by the contexts. And the emphasis on the bowls is that they are the *Last of the Wrath of God*. I have arranged all 21 below.

Number	Seal	Trumpet	Bowl
1	White Horse Rider Bow but no arrows	Hail and fire hurled down on the earth	Painful sores on people with the Best's mark
2	Red Horses Rider takes place from the earth	Something like a mountain thrown into the sea	Death of every living thing in the sea
3	Black Horse Rider brings famine	Death of many from poison waters	Rivers and springs turned into blood
4	Personification of death and hades ¼ of people killed	Darkening of a third of the sun, moon, and stars	People scorched by fire from the sun
5	Godly martyrs under the altar	Locusts (demons) from the abyss	Beast's Kingdom is darkened
6	Sky rolled back every island and mountain moved	A demonic army of 200 million 1/3 of people die	Euphrates dried up to prepare the way for the kings of the East
7	7 sealed book open fire, thundering earthquake	Proleptic statement: Kingdoms of this world are now God and Christ's	God says, *It is Done!* Greatest earthquake 110 pound hail stones

The Destruction of Religious, Commercial, Political Babylon

The World System Under Satan Against God

The False religious system under the False Prophet has been riding The Beast. I am convinced, The political leaders, the kings, must of thought the religious system could control, and stop the plagues and the judgment of God, since it was leading the world in the worship of the beast, and beyond the beast to Satan. So the feeling seems to be, *Why do we need her? Why should we finance her? Lets just follow our leader, The Beast, without her being involved. She is of no use. She's gaining too much power with the people.*

The Destruction of Religious Babylon 17:16-19

And the ten horns which you saw upon the beast, these shall hate the prostitute , and shall make her desolate and naked, and shall eat her flesh, and burn her with fire. For God has put in their hearts to fulfill his will, and to agree, and give their kingdom unto the beast, until the words of God shall be fulfilled. And the woman which you saw is that great city, which reigns over the kings of the earth.

But, obviously, this system, as we have seen, and the city, control also the commerce of the world, so as a result of Religious Babylon being destroyed, Commercial Babylon is also destroyed, it is the great city, with its 7 hills, and the woman who sits on it.

The Destruction of Commercial Babylon. 18:1-24

I saw another angel coming down from heaven, having great authority, and the earth was illuminated with his glory. And he cried mightily with a loud voice, saying, Babylon the great is fallen, is fallen, and has become a dwelling place of demons, a prison for every foul spirit, and a cage for every unclean and hated bird! For all the nations have drunk of the wine of the wrath of her fornication, the kings of the earth have committed fornication with her, and the merchants of the earth have become rich through the abundance of her luxury.

Again, as pointed out earlier, The Ancient City of Babylon, as Isaiah said, *will never be rebuilt*, never reach that place of importance again. All prophecy centers around Jerusalem, but the religious center will be Rome, as is clearly indicated. Although the commercial system might be centered Rome, Brussels, London, Paris or New York, or any other major city, my impression is its Rome because of the descriptions that follow, and the fact that it was the religious system that controlled the buying and selling. *The whole system is Babylon!*

So whatever the city is, living in it must be like a madhouse. Notice how frequently *fornication* continues in Revelation; Remember the whole commercial system, the privilege of being able to buy or sell, is connected with the *worship of the Antichrist and his image/Spiritual Fornication*

I heard another voice from heaven, saying , Come out of her, my people, that ye be not partakers of her sins ,and that ye receive not of her plagues. For her sins have reached unto heaven, and God hath remembered her iniquities. Reward her even as she rewarded you, and double unto her double according to her works: in the cup which she hath filled fill to her double. How much she hath glorified herself, and lived deliciously, so much torment and sorrow give her: for she says in her heart, I sit a queen , and am no widow, and shall see no sorrow. Therefore shall her plagues come in one day, death, and mourning, and famine; and she shall be utterly burned with fire: for the Lord God Who judges her is strong.

In view of the coming judgment, a warning call is given: *Come out of her my people*, and the reasons are set forth. God's people are to get out of the doomed city lest they share in her sins and judgment. A similar call was given by Jeremiah: *Go out of the midst of her, my people! Let every one save his life from the fierce anger of the Lord!* (Je 51:45). There is a warning intrinsic in this to be careful not to be involved in the activities of the Antichrist's system of worship or commerce. The strong need to purchase the necessities of life need to be smothered , since to buy them requires acceptance of the worship of the Antichrist and his image.

The voice continues to speak from heaven, but now the theme changes. The angels of judgment are now ordered to inflict a just reward on this city. Babylon has shed the blood of saints and prophets, and she is about to receive in kind the reward for her own cruelty. Compared to the luxury she has enjoyed in arrogant self-confidence, the coming devastation represents a radical reversal of fortunes. Over a long period of time she grew to a rather sudden place of new fame, glory, and power with the Antichrist, but she will experience an abrupt end.

Reaction of world leaders to the collapse of the world's financial capital; *And the kings of the earth, who have committed fornication and lived deliciously with her , shall wail and grieve for her, when they shall see the smoke of her burning, Standing afar off for the fear of her torment, saying, Alas, alas, (ουαι ουαι the same words translated Woe, woe, woe in 8:13) that great city Babylon, that mighty city! for in one hour your judgment has come.*

Wail and Lament are very strong words expressing outward displays of emotion. They are unnerved to find the ultimate form of humanity's political, religious, social, and economic order has suffered such a sudden and irreversible fate. They *stand far off*. Of course these kings are not all ruling in that city. Most of them will be in other nations. Imagine them standing in their offices of royalty watching it in living color on their TV or satellite as their whole world is collapsing.

Not only the kings, but also the merchants *wail and mourn over her, because no one buys their merchandise (lit. cargos) any more.* Cargos of,

1. *Precious minerals: gold and silver,*

2. *Valuable stones precious stones and pearls.*

3. *Clothing: fine linen and purple and silk and scarlet,*

4. *Furniture and home decorations: every kind of citron wood and every article of ivory and every article made from very costly wood and bronze and iron and marble*

5. *Perfumes and Spices: and cinnamon and spice and incense and perfume and frankincense*

6. *Food and drink: wine and olive oil and fine flour and wheat 7. Livestock: cattle and sheep, and horses*

7. *Chariots,* and the **worst of all,**

8. *Human Trafficking: slaves and human lives.* **Their grief is caused not because of sympathy for the fate of proud Babylon but because her fate spells economic disaster for them.**

The collapse of Babylon's commercial system is the collapse of the entire materialistic, idolatrous world. People have already seen the destruction of the religious system, Everything they put their confidence is gone except the Antichrist himself, and he too will soon be gone.

There is nothing wrong with having nice *things,* as long as you hold them loosely. As Jesus said, *Life does not consist of the abundance of things a person has.* (Lk 12:15) What if Jesus told you, what he told the person commonly called, *the Rich Young Ruler; sell everything you have give to the poor take up your cross and follow me.* (Make sure its Jesus, not some evangelist or preacher)

He asked Jesus, *What good thing can I do to inherit eternal life?* Jesus answered, *if you will enter into life keep the commandments.* He responded, *Which ones?* Jesus quoted/paraphrased the last 6 of the 10. These have to do with our relationship with other people. The young man answered, *All these I have kept from my youth, what do I lack?* What he was lacking was obedience to the first 4 commandments that have to do with our relationship with God, Himself. To obey the first 4, he was to *sell what you have, give to the poor, and you will have treasure in heaven, take up the cross and follow me. He went away sorrowful, for he had great possessions.* His money was his God. (Mt 19:16ff, Mk 10:19ff, Lk 18:18ff)

I heard years ago about 2 young men watching a millionaire being buried in his Roles Royce, and one said, *Man, that's living!* No, its still dying!

Government leaders, merchants, and transportation magnates join in this dirge. And why should they not lament? Their *treasure is on earth where moth and rust corrupt and where thieves break through and steal.* They have lost everything, and now they face a far worse fate: the loss of their souls! Remember, *Where your treasure is, there will your heart be also!*

I feel compelled to refer to I Tim 6:5ff where Paul is warning him about false teachers including those who *suppose that godliness is a means of gain. But godliness actually is a means of great gain when accompanied by contentment. For we have brought nothing into the world, so we cannot take anything out of it either. If we have food and covering, with these we shall be content. But those who want to get rich fall into temptation and a snare and many foolish and harmful desires which plunge men into ruin and destruction. For the love of money is a root of all sorts of evil, and some by longing for it have wandered away from the faith and pierced themselves with many griefs. But flee from these things, you man of God, and pursue righteousness, godliness, faith, love, perseverance and gentleness. Fight the good fight of faith; take hold of the eternal life to which you were called....*(NASB)

So they see everything lost: *The merchants of these things, who became rich from her, will stand at a distance because of the fear of her torment, weeping and mourning, saying, Woe, woe, the great city, she who was clothed in fine linen and purple and scarlet, and adorned with gold and precious stones and pearls; for in one hour such great wealth has been laid waste! And every shipmaster and every passenger and sailor, and as many as make their living by the sea, stood at a distance, and were crying out as they saw the smoke of her burning, saying, What city is like the great city? And they threw dust on their heads and were crying out, weeping and mourning, saying, Woe, woe, the great city, in which all who had ships at sea became rich by her wealth, for in one hour she has been laid waste!*.

By contrast, however, the saints, apostles, and prophets in heaven are encouraged to *Rejoice over her, O heaven, and you saints and apostles and prophets, because God has pronounced judgment for you against her.* Then God gives a powerful illustration of the sudden total destruction of the city that until now controlled both worship and commerce., and thus the commerce itself.

Then a strong angel took up a stone like a great millstone and threw it into the sea, saying, So will Babylon, the great city, be thrown down with violence, and will not be found any longer. And the sound of harpists and musicians and flute-players and trumpeters will not be heard in you any longer; and no craftsman of any craft will be found in you any longer; and the sound of a mill will not be heard in you any longer; and the light of a lamp will not shine in you any longer; and the voice of the bridegroom and bride will not be heard in you any longer; for your merchants were the great men of the earth, because all the nations were deceived by your sorcery. And in her was found the blood of prophets and of saints and of all who have been slain on the earth (NASB).

John sees the portrayal of Babylon's destruction. A mighty angel picks up a large boulder and throws it into the sea, symbolizing the violent overthrow of the city. Babylon's fate will occur at the end of the Great Tribulation in an unprecedented time of destruction. As a result, there will be no further music and joy, building, industry, crafts, light, or marriage celebrations. The city will be dead: silent and dark.

Thus, with the destruction of Babylon, the way will be paved for the presentation of the main theme of the book of Revelation: the second coming of Christ. Remember, it is not wrong to have things, but it is wrong when they have us.

CHAPTER 19
The Theme of Chapter 66—
The Return of Christ

From this point on the tone in Revelation changes. From the horrors of the Great Tribulation the reader now moves to times of blessing. Chapter 19 ushers in the greatest event ever for humankind: the second coming of Christ. He came the first time as the baby laying in a stone feeding trough, to be crucified for our sins, and being mocked while hanging on the cross,

If you are the Son of God, come down from the cross. So also the chief priests, with the scribes and elders, mocked him, saying, He saved others; he cannot save himself. He is the King of Israel; let him come down now from the cross, and we will believe in him.(Mt 27:41-42)

He is coming down, and the whole world will believe him and *every knee will bow of things in heaven, and things on earth and things under the earth, and every tongue will confess that Jesus Christ is Lord to the glory of God the Father.* (Ph 2:10-11)

The Great Praise—The Hallelujah Chorus 1-6

The word **hallelujah** is used for the first time in the New Testament. It is a Hebrew word that means **praise the Lord!** Since the term is used four times in this chapter, as someone observed that *this is the New Testament hallelujah chorus.* God is to be praised for who He is as well as for what He has done. He reigns! Therefore humanity for the first time in their existence will be able to live in a perfect environment under conditions of perfect equity and justice.

*The 1ˢᵗ Hallelujah After these things I heard something like a loud voice of a great multitude in heaven, saying, **Hallelujah!*** They are praising for two main reasons, Firstly, *The Salvation and The Glory and The Power belong to our God;* Salvation is totally of God. Man cannot earn it, don't deserve it, its origin, action, and completion are all on God's initiation. All man can do is exercise Faith in Jesus Christ and Receive Him as Lord and Savior, and follow Him by the power of His Holy Spirit within. His alone is *The Glory and The Power.*

And they are praising Him secondly, *because His judgments are true and righteous; for He has judged the great prostitute who was corrupting the earth with her immorality, and He has avenged the blood of His bond-servants on her.*. This thanksgiving contrasts sharply with the wailing of leaders, merchants, and seafarers whose fortunes collapsed with the destruction of the beast's economic capital.

The 2nd Hallelujah *And a second time they said,* **Hallelujah!** *Her smoke rises up forever and ever. And the twenty-four elders and the four living ones fell down and worshiped God who sits on the throne saying,*

The 3rd Hallelujah: *Amen.* **Hallelujah!** A recognition that such a world system will never rise again. God has been longsuffering with people, even with ungodly nations. But these things will be nor more. From now on God will reign in Righteousness and Truth, and sin will be abolished. Our **Go'el, our nearest relative,** is about to take back man's inheritance lost in the Garden of Eden.

The 4th Hallelujah!

And a voice came from the throne, saying, Whose voice is giving instruction? In Heb 2:5ff, The Holy Spirit compares Jesus with Adam, using quotes from the 8th Ps, indicating Adam lost his position of *having all things under him,* and Jesus came to restore what Adam lost, *by tasting death for everyone,* and concludes the comparison He is not ashamed to call those he has led to salvation *brothers.*

I'm reminded, every time I read that passage, when our oldest daughter Linda was born at a small hospital in Bad Axe, Michigan, in the days where fathers were not allowed to get to touch the newborn, but had to only look at them through a glass window, I saw this *red, wrinkled, little girl with a patch of black hair,* and pointed her out to everyone nearby...*She's mine....She's a Westlake.* My Brother and Sister, you may sometimes be ashamed of yourself, you may feel at times you have failed God, You may listen to the accusations of the devil, but God looks at you, and, because of Jesus, and His love for you, says, *I'm not ashamed to call her mine! I'm not ashamed to call him mine!*

The discussion in Hebrews ends with a quote from Ps 22:22, Jesus Saying, *I will proclaim Your name to My brethren, In the midst of the church I will sing praise to you.* It is God the Son, our Savior and Redeemer leading His church *from the throne* in praise to The Father:

Give praise to our God, all you His bond-servants, you who fear Him, the small and the great. Then I heard something like the voice of a great multitude and like the sound of many waters and like the sound of mighty peals of thunder, saying,

Hallelujah! For the Lord our God, the Almighty, reigns.

The Wedding Supper of the Lamb-The Angel Messenger 7-10

The *Interpreting angel (messenger),* who was sent by God to show John the visions (1:1), now speaks again: *Let us rejoice and be glad and give the glory to Him, for the marriage of the Lamb has come and His bride has made herself ready. It was given to her to clothe herself in fine linen, bright and clean; for the fine linen is the righteous acts of the saints.* Why do I say this statement is from a different source than the *voice from the throne? We will see later this is the voice of a man, a prophet.* God the Father and God the Son are on the throne.

This type of change is common in *apocalyptic literature*, as is one who has been called by expositors *The interpreting Angel. The Interpreting Angel,* can clearly be seen in both Daniel and Zechariah. The vision of the He Goat and Ram in Dan 8 is explained by, *one standing by.* in 9:21 Gabriel explains the 70 7's to Daniel; throughout the first 6 chapters of Zech things are explained to him by an angel, the most quoted is the vision of the menorah and the bowl and the olive trees in Zec 4. The Angel had to explain the vision.

The change between voice, not explained, is seen in Daniel 10 when he sees a vision, obviously, of Jesus, falls on his face, hears his voice, then a hand touches him, sets him up on his knees, and speaks to him. Now it is obvious that the second one he hears is not Jesus, because this one declares he was in a battle and *Michael* came to help him. Jesus doesn't need Michaels help. He sees a second vision of Jesus, and after that, another angels speaks to him. Its very confusing. Some authors see three separate angels in that chapter, some see two, with no statement made that it is a different one speaking.

Paul reminds the Corinthians, *I am jealous for you with the jealousy of God himself. I promised you as a pure bride to one husband—Christ.* (NLT). It is interesting that the Greek word, **arrabon,** used in Ep 1,:...*after you believed you were sealed with the Holy Spirit of Promise, who is the **earnest** of our inheritance....*means a *down payment or a guarantee;* in Modern Greek it is the word use for an **engagement ring,** We, who know Jesus Christ, received the *engagement ring* when we asked Jesus Christ to come into our hearts and lives, and made a commitment of our lives to Him. **The wedding is soon to come.**

The word, *gamos,* is translated in most English translations as *marriage or wedding* in verse 7 and *marriage supper, marriage feast or wedding feast,* or *wedding banquet* in v9. This word is used twenty-two times in the New Testament, and all except Heb 13:4, refer primarily to the wedding banquet or feast. Then he said to me, *Write, Blessed are those who are invited to the marriage supper of the Lamb, And he said unto me, These are the true sayings of God.* The *Wedding Feast* is now ready to take place.

The wedding of that day consisted of several parts, or steps in order. First, the marriage contract was arranged by the parents of the couple seeking to be married. This was the engagement. Should this engagement be broken, it was necessary to obtain a legal divorce.

As Mt 1:18-25 indicates Mary, who was engaged to Joseph, was to give birth to Jesus, and before Joseph was instructed about the situation by Gabriel, *he was minded to put her away privately.* (with only 2 witnesses so as not to shame her publicly). Second, when the parents agreed that the couple was ready to be married, The Father of groom the told his son, *Go and get your Bride.* The groom then had to go to the home of the bride and take her to his home for the wedding. (This custom corresponds with Jesus' indication in Matthew 24:36 that the time of His return is under the Father's control. Thus, *when the Father says it is time*, the Son will come for His bride and take her to be at home with Him.) Third, there was a supper or banquet to which guests were invited. It was a time of great rejoicing. Examples of the wedding supper are found in Mt 22:1–14 and 25:1–13.

An interesting correlation, Jesus performed His first miracle at a wedding in Cana in Galilee (Jn 2:1ff). When Jesus turned the water into wine, and the director of the feast had tasted it, called the bridegroom and ended his comments by saying, *you have kept the best until now*

I have used this in my marriage ceremonies for years, reminding the couple getting married, *I know you're thinking, Lord you have kept the best until now.* But, if you remember that real **JOY** comes from daily putting **J**esus first, **O**ther second, **Y**ourself last, as you grow together, you will be able to say throughout your lives, *Lord you have kept the best until now.*

People will have been saved by receiving Jesus throughout the tribulation, even, probably, one day before Armageddon; many who have received Jesus Christ have never died, including the remnant of Israel, So, I am a firm believer that the banquet will take place after Armageddon, and take place in Jerusalem, the faithful of every age will be part of the Bride, and the guests will be the remaining inhabitants of the earth and the angels. (Remember the home of the Bride, New Jerusalem will have the names of the 12 apostles and the 12 tribes of Israel inscribed)

In conjunction with the wedding of the Lamb, the bride is said to have *made herself ready, and white robes are the righteous acts of the saints..* While the appropriate preparation for heaven is the new birth, which is altogether the work of God in Christ, there must be a human response. 1Jn 3:2–3, after reminding us because of God's love we are *children of God,* concludes by saying, *everyone who has this hope keeps purifying himself even as He is pure.,* and 2 Co 7:1 affirms this responsibility. Paul, In Eph 2:8-9 after indicating we are saved by grace in that magnificent passage, adds, in v 10, *For we are his workmanship, created in Christ Jesus unto good works, which God has before ordained that we should walk in them.*

Missouri is the *Show Me!* State. I think James, the Brother of Jesus and author of the book of James, must have had some influence with Missouri somewhere; His book may be summed up with, *You say you're a Christian, Show Me!* While we are not saved by our works, after we are saved, our works show a change has taken place in our lives.

Of course, like Paul in Philippians, on Death Row, reminds those who think they are perfect, fully grown, etc., that He, has *no yet obtained or have already become perfect.* (3:12ff) If you think God is finished growing you, ask your spouse, or, even better, your children, they'll let you know God isn't finished with you yet.

Jesus, as his last act with the apostles before going to Gethsemane, had a Passover Supper, saying, *This do in remembrance of me;* how fitting the new age should begin with the Supper. I'm sure many homemakers are thinking, *it will take a long time to get all that ready.* But this is the God who created a billion times a billion worlds just by speaking the word. A feast is no problem. Since it is by divine invitation, attendance at the wedding banquet is especially meaningful. That invitation is still open for those who do not know Jesus to Receive Him.

John's reaction to this whole vision, and the angel who lead him through these experiences, and the ones to follow, *I fell at his feet to worship him. And he said, Do not do this, because I am your fellow servant, and of your brothers that have the testimony of Jesus: Worship God; for the testimony of Jesus is the spirit of prophecy.* All prophecy is centered on Jesus. The Bible is a Book about Jesus Christ He walks on every page from *in the* beginning in Genesis, to the final *Amen* of Revelation.

ARMAGEDDON 11-21

This day has been anticipated throughout the Old and New Testaments promising judgment of the ungodly and blessings for the godly. 2Th 2:7ff, *And to you who are troubled rest with us, when the Lord Jesus shall be revealed from heaven with his mighty angels, In flaming fire taking* vengeance on them that know not God, and that obey not the gospel of our Lord Jesus Christ: Who shall be punished with everlasting destruction from the presence of the Lord, and from the glory of his power; We will see this at Armageddon and later at The Great White Throne.

The passage continues, *when he shall come to be glorified in his saints, and to be admired in all them that believe (because our testimony among you was believed) in that day).* Tit 3:11ff, says that, *having denied ungodliness and worldly lusts, Let us live sensibly, righteously and godly in this present world, expecting looking for the blessed hope and the brightness (**epiphaneia**) of the glory of our great God and Savior Jesus Christ.* The **hope** of every person of God is the return of Jesus and all connected with those events. Understand, *hope* in the bible is not *wishful thinking*, like, *I hope it doesn't rain tomorrow.* Rom 8:24ff says, *we are saved by hope: but hope that is seen is not hope: for who hopes for what he sees? But if we hope for that we don't see, then we with endurance expectantly look for it.* **It is something that is absolutely going to happen, we just don't see it happening yet**.

Having learned of the imminent wedding of the Lamb, which assumes the return of Jesus Christ, John now receives a vision of the event of His return. As you may notice, only one aspect of Christ's coming is emphasized: His victory over the forces of evil. The concept of a warrior-Messiah is seen in the Old Testament prophets (Is 13:4; 31:4; Ez 38–39; Joel 3; and Zech 14:3) and in apocalyptic literature. The second Psalm prefigures Armageddon:

*Why do the heathen rage, and the people imagine a vain thing? The kings of the earth set themselves, and the rulers take counsel together, **against the Lord, and against his anointed**, saying , Let us break their bands asunder, and cast away their cords from us. He that sits in the heavens shall laugh: the Lord scoffs at them. Then shall he speak unto them in his anger, and terrify hem in his wrath. Yet have I set my king upon my holy hill of Zion. I will declare the decree: the Lord said unto me, You are my Son; this day have I begotten you.* (used in Heb 1:5 to refer to the incarnation of Jesus as human) *Ask of me, and I will I give you the heathen for your inheritance, and the uttermost parts of the earth for your possession. You will break them with a rod of iron, you will smash them in pieces like clay pots Be wise now therefore, O you kings, be instructed, you judges of the earth. Serve the Lord with fear, and rejoice with trembling.* ***Kiss the So**n, lest he become angry, and you perish from the way, when his wrath is kindled but a little.* **Blessed are all they that put their trust in him. (KJV)**

SUDDENLY, *And I saw heaven opened, and behold a white horse; and he that sat upon him was called Faithful and True, and in righteousness he judges and wages war. His eyes were as a flame of fire, and on his head were many diadems; and he had a name written, that no man knew, but he himself. And he was clothed with a robe dipped in blood: and his name is called The Word of God.* The genuine, true, rightful rider on the white horse as opposed to the false one who appeared when the first seal was opened.

He judges and wages war. Mt 25:31ff states: *When the Son of man shall come in his glory, and all the holy angels with him, then shall he sit upon the throne of his glory: And before him shall be gathered all nations: and he shall separate them one from another, as a shepherd divides his sheep from the goats.* Jesus will judge. Paul, in Ac 17:31 tells the people of Athens, that God has appointed a day on which He will judge the world in righteousness by the Man whom He has ordained. He has given assurance of this to all by raising Him from the dead. The punishment inflicted on the beast and his followers is not arbitrary nor an act of personal vengeance; it is perfectly compatible with righteousness, truth and justice.

Jesus is not only the judge, he is the standard of judgment! That is why no matter how righteous we think we are, compared to Him we are not righteous. That's why we need His Righteousness put down to our accounts. In Hebrews 2, comparing Adam and Jesus, Both were *crowned with glory,* Adam sinned, and we know, *all have sinned and come short of the glory of God.* Hebrews goes on to say that Jesus life and death results in *bringing many sons to Glory,* back to the true image of God. Paul, in Col 2:25ff, says *the mystery which has been hidden...but is now revealed...is Christ in you, the hope of glory.*

As the vision John saw in ch I, *Eyes like a flame of fire.* He sees to the heart of things and people. He will make no mistakes at judgment time. Unlike the false rider, who had the **stephanos**, *victors crown,* and unlike Satan who had **seven diadems**, He has **many diadems!** He is the Ruler over everything and everyone. Remember that the next time you feel discouraged, or the enemy tries to convince you you're not going to make it........ **Hear Him say to you**:

Fear not, for I have redeemed **you***; I have called* **you** *by* **your** *name;* **You** *are Mine. When* **you** *pass through the waters, I will be with* **you***; And through the rivers, they shall not overflow* **you***. When* **you** *walk through the fire,* **you** *shall not be burned, Nor shall the flame scorch* **you***. For I am the Lord your God, The Holy One of Israel, your Savior (Is 43:1ff NKJ.) I am with you always, even to the end of the age (Mt.28:20). So When I walk through the valley of the deepest darkness I will not fear the evil one for you are with me. (Ps 23:4)*

The *end of the age* is now happening before our eyes. *He had a name written, that no man knew, but he himself.* The Names given to God frequently, partially, explain who He is, His character, His nature. As discussed previously, to try to explain The Trinity, or even, God the Son by Himself, is beyond our comprehension.

The last part of the scripture quoted says *His name is the Word of God.* I wrote a lengthy paper for a theology class, as a sophomore in Bible College, on Jesus being *the* **logos,** *the word.* My instructor was Earnest S. Williams, who had been General Superintendent of the Assemblies of God for 20 years. Brother Williams graded papers on a percentage grade. He told me, *This is the first 100% grade I have ever given...***but we don't really know a whole lot more than we did before, right?** I agreed!

I like what the author of Hebrews says to open the book, *God who at various times and in bits and pieces spoke in times past to the fathers by the prophets, has in the end of these days, spoken to us* **in/by Son** *Whom He has appointed heir of all things, through whom also He made the worlds; who being the brightness of His glory and the express image of His person, and upholding all things by the word of His own power, when He had all by Himself purged our sins, sat down at the right hand of the Majesty on high.* **Jesus is what God has to say.**

He was clothed with a robe dipped in blood shows us that what was mentioned previously, in ch 14, about Armageddon, was about to happen *the armies which were in heaven followed him upon white horses, clothed in fine linen, white and clean.* Zech 14:5 says, *The Lord my God will come, and all the holy ones with him.* Jude adds, *Behold, the Lord comes with ten thousands of his saints, To execute judgment upon all, and to convince all that are ungodly among them of all their ungodly deeds which they have ungodly committed, and of all their hard speeches which ungodly sinners have spoken against him.* (v 14-15)

And out of his mouth goes a sharp sword, that with it he should smite the nations: and he shall rule them with a rod of iron: and he treads the winepress of the fierceness and wrath of Almighty God. And he has on his robe and on his thigh a name written, King of Kings, and Lord of Lords. In the place where the warrior keeps his sword, on his thigh, was the title *King of Kings, and Lord of Lords,* which was also on His robe. No doubt about Who He Is! The armies need no weapons. **The Battle is the Lords!**

Ezekiel had prophesied, '*Speak to every kind of bird and to every beast of the field, Assemble and come, gather from every side to My sacrifice which I am going to sacrifice for you, as a great sacrifice on the mountains of Israel, that you may eat flesh and drink blood. You will eat the flesh of mighty men and drink the blood of the princes of the earth, as though they were rams, lambs, goats and bulls, all of them fatlings of Bashan. So you will eat fat until you are glutted, and drink blood until you are drunk, from My sacrifice which I have sacrificed for you. You will be glutted at My table with horses and charioteers, with mighty men and all the men of war, declares the Lord God. And I will set My glory among the nations; and all the nations will see My judgment which I have* executed and My hand which I have laid on them. And the house of Israel will know that I am the Lord their God from that day forward. (39:17ff NASB_)

Using some of the language of Ezekiel's picture of Armageddon, John says, *And I saw an angel standing in the sun; and he cried with a loud voice, saying to all the birds that fly in the midst of heaven, Come and gather yourselves together unto the supper of the great God; That you may eat the flesh of kings, and the flesh of captains, and the flesh of mighty men, and the flesh of horses, and of them that sit on them, and the flesh of all men, both free and bond, both small and great.* I have heard some preachers try to say after the next war, everything will be so destroyed the final war will be fought on horses. Of course not. This is a picture of great armies as armies are described throughout the Old Testament.

Now, this Huge, Gigantic, War. Try to picture This world with its military technology, multitude of lasers, multi-nuclear missiles, and probably weapons we know nothing about, saying, *We will not have him rule over us. We'll blast him out of the sky when he comes. He has no weapons like ours. We've seen our leader get killed and come back to life, we've seen the signs proving his power. What s weapons does Jesus Christ have to balance this?*

THE ONLY WEAPON MENTIONED, OR NEEDED, BY JESUS IS THE TWO EDGED SWORD THAT PROCEDES OUT OF HIS MOUTH. HE SPEAKS AND IT IS DONE

All those armies , all those weapons, and the text says simply, *and the beast was taken,* and with him the false prophet that wrought miracles before him, with which he deceived them that had received the mark of the beast, and them that worshipped his image. These both were cast alive into a lake of fire burning with brimstone. And the rest were killed with the sword of him that sat upon the horse, which sword proceeded out of his mouth: and all the birds were filled with their flesh. The armies are killed by him merely speaking.

A centurion approached Jesus to heal his servant. *Jesus said to him, "I will come and heal him." But the centurion said, Lord, I am not worthy for You to come under my roof, but just say the word, and my servant will be healed. For I also am a man under authority, with soldiers under me; and I say to this one, 'Go!' and he goes, and to another, 'Come!' and he comes, and to my slave, 'Do this!' and he does it. Now when Jesus heard this, He marveled and said to those who were following, Truly I say to you, I have not found such great faith with anyone in Israel (Mt 8:5ff) (NASB. The Centurion is saying, I understand authority...you have it. All you need to do is speak and it will happen.)* We need to trust what God tells us the same way. If God gives you a promise, it has

His authority...it will happen The things He speaks in His word are Truth and spoken with His authority, and they will certainly happen.

The battle belongs to Jesus alone, but we share in His victory. The Beast and False prophet, Satan's masterpieces of political and religious power, will be *cast alive into a lake of fire burning with brimstone,* where their leader, Satan, will meet up with them 1000 years later. Jesus will rule with a *rod of iron.* Armageddon is the end of this age, but the dawning of a new age during the next 1000 years, where Jesus will have absolute rule.

CHAPTER 20

Satan Bound, the First Resurrection, the Millenium, Satan Loosed, Gog and Magog, Satan Cast Into Lake of Fire, the Great White Throne, Resurrection of the Ungodly, Final Judgments, the Second Death

The Chapter division should really have been placed at 20:4. And I saw an angel coming down out of heaven, having the key to the Abyss and holding in his hand a great chain. He seized the dragon, that ancient serpent, who is the devil, or Satan, and bound him for a thousand years. He threw him into the Abyss, and locked and sealed it over him, to keep him from deceiving the nations anymore until the thousand years were ended. After that, he must be set free for a short time. 1-3

As we saw, the demons in the Abyss were loosed during the blowing of the fifth trumpet. We don't know if they are all incarcerated back in the Abyss, or, possibly they have already ended up in The Lake of Fire. We are simply not told. The same four names for Satan are used here that were used in Ch 12.

THE FIRST RESURRECTION

*Then I saw thrones and they sat on them and judgment was given to them **even** the souls of The ones who were beheaded on account of the witness of Jesus and on account of the word of God and anyone who had not worshipped the beast neither his image and had not received the mark upon the forehead and upon their right hand, and they lived and reigned with Christ a thousand years. But the rest of the dead did not live again until the thousand years were finished.* Most translations insert a second, *I saw,* which is not in the Greek text, *as if he's describing a second group..* The Greek, *kai,* may accurately be translated *and, also, or even.* I translate it as *even.* Just read the flow of my translation word for word from the Greek text above. The ones sitting on thrones were the martyrs, and anyone who had not given into the requirements of the Beast, or who possibly died from natural or because of the plagues, or were still alive. (I don't want to get too technical.. this is for the Greek students.. if an *ingressive Aorist* it would be translated, *came to life,* But if the *constative aorist* it simply means *they lived.* -the form is identical.)

So all the above, whether they had been martyred, had simply died, or were living at the time Christ returns, would live and reign for the 1, 000 years. The Israelites in Petra had not died. I remind you what the elders say of the saints in heaven in Ch. 5, *Worthy are You to take the book and to break its seals; for You were slain, and purchased for God with Your blood men from every tribe and tongue and people and nation. You have made them to be a kingdom and priests to our God; and they will reign upon the earth.* So at this point all the righteous: those in heaven in Ch 5, those martyred, those who have died from other causes during the Tribulation, and those who happen to be still alive will all be joined together to reign during the 1,000 years.

This is the first resurrection. Those who believe the church will go through the Tribulation point to this statement as proof that up to this point no one has been raised from the dead. However, we saw the two witnesses were raised from the dead long before this and were then caught up to heaven (11:11–12). Obviously, these verses show us plainly that this statement is not teaching there have been no previous resurrections. Paul reminds the Corinthians, *But now Christ is risen from the dead, and has become the* **firstfruits** *of those who have fallen asleep. For since by man came death, by Man also came the resurrection of the dead. For as in Adam all die, even so in Christ all shall be made alive. But each one in his own order: Christ the* **firstfruits***, afterward those who are Christ's at His* **parousia** *.* (ICor 15:20-22) *The first resurrection* began with Jesus, Himself, as the **firstfruits**; Mt 27:50ff, talks about when Jesus died there were earthquakes *, and the graves were opened; and many bodies of the saints who slept arose, and came out of the graves after His resurrection, and went into the Holy City and appeared to many;* The raptured saints, who are in heaven in ch 5; The two witnesses; then, this final raising of the righteous comprise the *first resurrection.* And, as stated, *The rest of the dead did not live again until the thousand years were finished.* **The use of First is not like first, second, etc., but First As opposed to Last. The first one is now complete!**

John continues, *Blessed and holy is he who has part in the first resurrection. Over such the second death has no power, but they shall be priests of God and of Christ, and shall reign with Him a thousand years.* So the result of the first resurrection is living and reigning during the Millennium, and, as priests, having access to the throne of God. The final one, which is 1,000 years later, results in *the second death-eternal death;* being thrown into the lake of fire forever. The first death is physical death. These blessed ones have resurrected bodies, whereas the people of the nations will have natural bodies. Jesus stayed here, among His disciples, for forty days in His resurrected body.

THE MILLENNIUM

Millennium,. It is a theological term and comes from two Latin words **mille,** thousand, and **annum**, year. It is used to refer to the thousand-year period of Christ's future reign on earth in relation to the establishment of the Kingdom over Israel. I am not going to discuss or debate the various interpretations of the *Millennium.* For that there are numerous books, and my Global University book *Daniel and Revelation.*

The Millennium is the fulfillment of many promises given in the Old Testament, including the one given to David that, a descendent of his would sit on his throne for ever. And that his kingdom would continue forever. Is 9:6-7 promises the Messiah would sit on the throne of David for ever.. The thousand years is a literal period of time. It is a period in which Christ will literally rule on earth as supreme ruler. Israel will thus occupy a prominent place in this kingdom, and the Gentiles will also be blessed.

While verses 4–6 give us some information about the Millennium, other Scripture passages give us characteristics of the kingdom age. The form of government will be *Theocracy* because Christ will rule, and the capital of His kingdom will be Jerusalem. Christ will thus have an earthly center in the Holy City in the Holy Land. Other characteristics are as follows: There will be

- universal peace (Ps 46:9; Is 2:4, 9:6–7; Mi 4:3–4).

- universal prosperity (Is 65:21–24; Am 9:13–15; Mi 4:4–5).

- universal justice (Is 11:3–5; Je 23:5).

- universal knowledge of the Lord (Is 11:9; Ha 2:14; Zech 8:22–23).

- a restoration of the earth to its first state of fruitfulness (Is 35:1–2; Am 9:13–15; Ez 36:8–12).

- no ferocious nature in animals (Is 11:6–9; 65:25).

- a change in the way earth receives the light of the sun and the moon (Is 30:26).

- a greatly increased life span (Is 65:20-22).

Notice in the descriptions in Isaiah, the popular conception that *the lion and the lamb will lay down together* is not there. The two scriptures actually, say the *wolf and the lamb shall dwell together and the wolf and the lamb shall feed together.*(11:6, 65:25) In the middle east the greatest danger to the lamb was the wolf. More details on some of the characteristics of the Millennium are found throughout the writings of the prophets.

Chapters 40–48 of Ezekiel give a detailed description of Israel after the nation's people have returned to the land promised to Abraham: (see Charles Feinberg's books on Ezekiel and Millennialism) The size of Jerusalem and the priests portion will be greatly increased. Some of the feasts and sacrifices of the Old Testament will be celebrated as a memorial to what God has done, in the same way the communion service is remembrance of what Jesus did.

Several things and ceremonies from the Old Testament are not included in Ezekiel's descriptions: There will be no High Priest, no Day of Atonement, no Passover Lamb, no Ark of the Covenant, so no Aaron's Rod, No Tables of the Law, No Mercy Seat, no Golden Candlestick, no Showbread, no Altar of Incense, no Atonement for Sin, No Veil, No hidden Holy of Holies. The Millennium will make possible the fulfillment of the promises, and after the Millennium, Abraham's descendants will dwell in this land forever. *God keeps His promises.*

SATAN LOOSED FOR HIS LAST STAND—GOG AND MAGOG

Now when the thousand years have expired, Satan will be released from his prison and will go out to deceive the nations which are in the four corners of the earth, Gog and Magog, to gather them together to battle, whose number is as the sand of the sea. They went up on the breadth of the earth and surrounded the camp of the saints and the beloved city. And fire came down from God out of heaven and devoured them. The devil, who deceived them, was cast into the lake of fire and brimstone where the beast and the false prophet are. And they will be tormented day and night forever and ever.

Satan immediately sets out to deceive the nations of the entire earth described as *Gog and Magog.* Not the same *Gog and Magog* as in Ezekiel; A different time in History. With long life during the Millennium, the population of the earth will have grown considerably. The people he attempts to seduce are the natural people who survived the Great Tribulation and their descendants born during the Millennium.

Why would God allow Satan to be loosed? God will allow Satan to be loosed because those born during the Millennium will not have had the opportunity to choose to live either for or against Jesus Christ, since He has been *ruling with a rod of Iron.*

Nevertheless, God gives every person the right of free choice. *Let us make man in our image, after our likeness, ...and God created man in His image, male and female he created them. Gen 1:26-27)*

God wanted someone to love, and who could love Him in return. As I said earlier, A robot cannot love; you can buy one, put batteries in it, it will say *Beep Beep Beep, I love you, I love you*, but it doesn't. Love is a matter of choice. We are made in the image of God, and thus have a free will, and this includes the ability to choose. Throughout Scripture, God has allowed individuals to choose whom they will serve. Adam and Eve made their choice, and every one of their descendants has made his or her choice either for or against God. Satan's presence among those born during the Millennium will give them an opportunity to choose. And, in a sense, the outcome is a foregone conclusion. People will still like to have their own way, to run their own lives.

As a result, multitudes, *as the sand of the sea*, believe his deception and will follow him in a rebellion against God, and surround Jerusalem. However, no battle will actually take place, for as they surround the city He loves, God will intervene and destroy the entire rebellious force with fire.

Thus Satan's last stand will become history, and he, *will be cast into the lake of fire where the beast and false prophet are.* Some like to debate, since the last word in the English translations is *are*, and it is not in the Greek text, they take it to imply that they were cast in, were burn up and are no longer there. However, not only is the absence of *are* common in *Street Greek* in such cases, here it is followed by a plural verb, *and __they__ shall be tormented day and night forever and ever*. So the insertion of *are* in the translations is proper. The Beast and False Prophet, have been there 1,000 years, and they are still there, along with Satan, being tormented.

THE GREAT WHITE THRONE JUDGMENT 11-15

Then I saw a great white throne and Him who sat on it, from whose face the earth and the heaven fled away. And there was found no place for them. What picture John sees. As the throne appears, all of creation runs away and hides. It's obvious this is a picture showing the importance of the Great White Throne, and there is not even the presence of any part of creation to turn attention away from it. *And I saw the dead, small and great, standing before God, and books were opened. And another book was opened, which is the Book of Life. And the dead were judged according to their works, by the things which were written in the books.* God has other books. *Then those who feared the Lord spoke to one another, And the Lord listened and heard them; So a book of remembrance was written before Him For those who fear the Lord And who meditate on His name. They shall be Mine, says the Lord of hosts, On the day that I make them My jewels. And I will spare them As a man spares his own son who serves him.*(Mal 3:16-17 NKJV) We are not told how many books.

If you are a Christian you will not be judged at the great white throne. Your sin was judged at Calvary. All the dead from all walks of life and degrees of importance appear before the throne. There are no mistakes. Each person is judged on the basis of his or her works. Of course, works do not save anyone, but your works demonstrate it whether you know God or not, they demonstrate who you are serving.

All has been recorded, and the record does not lie. Yet beyond one's works there is another fundamental basis for judgment: *The Book of Life*. All whose names are not recorded in this book are sentenced to eternal damnation and consigned to the lake of fire. Death and Hades are personified, just as they are under the fourth seal. As you read about Hades, did you think about who will be there to be resurrected? It is a sobering thought; however, only those who have died in an unsaved condition will be there. Death and Hades are now thrown into the lake of fire. The lake of fire indicates not only the severe punishment awaiting the enemies of the righteous, but also, their full and final defeat. It is the second death, that is, the destiny of those whose temporary resurrection results only in return to death and its eternal punishment.

CHAPTER 21-22:5

The New Heaven and Earth and the New Jerusalem

NEW HEAVEN AND EARTH v. 1

I saw a new heaven and a new earth, for the first heaven and the first earth had passed away. Also there was no more sea. In the last two chapters of his book, Isaiah foretells the creation of new heavens and a new earth that will endure forever. It now begins to take place before John's eyes.

In 20:11, John described the dissolution of the old heaven and earth. In graphic language he described their flight from the presence of God. Now John sees a new heaven and a new earth. Some teach that this is a totally new earth and heavens, a whole new creation, that this earth has ceased to exist at this point.

But throughout the Bible the destiny of God's people is an earthly destiny. The prophecies show God's people living on a redeemed earth, Ecclesiastes 1:4 states, *The earth abides forever.* And, God promises to give to Abraham and his seed, *all the land of Canaan for an everlasting possession.* (Gen 17:8) So , what does it mean, *The first heaven and the first earth were passed away?*.

In the Bible, three Greek words are translated *world*: **aion,** which is more accurately translated *age*; **kosmos,** which refers to the *structured society*; (Jesus called Satan, *The ruler of the kosmos in Jn 12:31, and 14:30, and The ruler of this kosmos in 16:11* and Paul calls Satan *The god of this aion (2 Cor 4:4)* and *You walked according to the age of this kosmos, according to the ruler of the authority of the air, the one who now is energizing in the sons of the disobedience (Eph 2:2.)* and **ge**, which means *earth* (always means earth when it is not referring to Canaan)

The terms **aion** and **kosmos** are frequently spoken of as *going to cease to exist* or *having ceased to exist*, but the term **ge** is never referred to as having ceased to exist. When Paul says *Therefore if any man be in Christ, he is a new creature:* **old things are passed away (parerchomai)***; behold, all things are become new (II Cor 5:17),* it is the identical word and meaning as used here.

When a person receives Jesus Christ, does that person . cease to exist in order to make way for the new person he or she is to become after accepting Christ? Of course not! Still, when one is made new, he or she is changed. Likewise, *the first earth had passed away* simply indicates the first earth will be changed—not that it ceases to exist. Rom 8:21 states, *the creation itself shall be delivered from the bondage of corruption.* Then Peter paints a graphic picture of the process by which the change will occur (2 Peter 3:10–13). He talks about the elements (**stoicheia**) being destroyed. In this context, the word translated *destroyed* can also be translated *loosed,* which harmonizes more completely with our concept of a changed earth. Peters descriptions of noise, fire, melting, reminds me of Armageddon, and Gog and Magog, which finally ends the old order of things. Of course there will be physical changes to the creation.

The use of the word, **stoicheia,** *elements,* in every other occurrence in the New Testament has to do with basic things like lists of 1.2.3.4, a.b.c.d. Paul uses it twice in Gal4:3, 9, to refer to the letter of the law, with the same concept in Co. 2:20.

In Col. 2:8 he uses it to refer to the *philosophical and traditional elementary systems of this kosmos.* In Heb. 5:12 it is used about the basic principles of Christianity. So the use every other place in the new Testament has to do with the change of the *kosmos,* the structures of this world, political, economic, religious and moral.

Verse 10 of Peter's discussion in the older translations of the Bible, KJ, NASB. Says *both the earth and the works that are in it will be* **burned up.** Since those two bibles were translated, i.e. the KJ from a 12th century manuscript, most of the newer translations are based on the older manuscripts which have been discovered since then. The ESV, English Standard Version, says *the earth and its works will be* **exposed.** The Greek word is **heurisko** which means *to find or discover.*

Our English word, *eureka,* meaning *I've found it* comes from this Greek word. The NIV says, *laid bare.* The NLV , says, *found to deserve judgment.* The basic idea is that when the new heavens and the new earth happen, there will be nothing hidden that is not revealed, or nothing that deserves judgment that will escape judgment. It will be a new *aion—age,* and a new *kosmos— structured society.* Thus, Peter's conclusion to his picture of the change climaxes with *a new heavens and earth* **wherein dwells righteousness.**

THE NEW JERUSALEM-GOD LIVING WITH HIS PEOPLE

And I John saw the holy city, new Jerusalem, coming down from God out of heaven, prepared as a bride adorned for her husband. While we often think of the heavenly Jerusalem as the permanent dwelling place of God and His departed people (Gal 4:26; Ph 3:20; Heb 12:22), it is only the temporary home of God's people between their death and the resurrection (2 Co 5:8; Phi 1:23; Rev 6:9–11). In the new order, however, the heavenly Jerusalem will be relocated on earth. The fact the New Jerusalem is said to come down out of heaven from God indicates it is already in existence.

It has been preached, in this area of the country, based on this verse and v 9, that the Bride of Christ is not the believers, but the city, the New Jerusalem. But, it is obvious, from the descriptions already given that it is the believers. In Lk 13:34 when Jesus said, *O Jerusalem, Jerusalem, the city that kills the prophets and stone those who are sent to it,* He was not indicating that the walls, buildings, gates, and streets of the city were responsible for killing the prophets. It was the people who lived there about whom He was speaking. Thus the New Jerusalem will not be the bride of Christ, but it is and will be the home of believers who will make up that bride.

God Living With His People

And I heard a great voice out of heaven saying, Behold, the tabernacle of God is with men, and he will dwell with them, and they shall be his people, and God himself shall be with them, and be their God. And God shall wipe away all tears from their eyes; and there shall be no more death, neither sorrow, nor crying, neither shall there be any more pain: for the former things are passed away .

In the new eternal order of things, the New Jerusalem will be God's dwelling place with people. In the Old Testament His presence was manifested in the tabernacle and later in the temple by the *shekinah,* or glory. In Johns Gospel, *In the beginning was the word and the word was with God and the word was God, the same was in the beginning with God, All things through him came into existence and apart from him not even one thing which has come into existence came into existence.*

John's thinking must have gone back to the Exodus, when, after deliverance they pitched a tent, The Tabernacle, and all the tents of the people of Israel surrounded that tent. Every person could stand in their tent door and look in that tent and see the Glory of God as a cloud by day and pillar of fire by night.

Then John says, *The Word became flesh and pitched his tent in our midst, and we beheld His glory, glory as the unique one from the father, full of grace and truth.* In the same way they could look into that tent and see God's Glory, Jesus is God we can see in action, hear his voice. He, Himself is God's Glory. He lived for a while physically in Israel. Presently He lives in us by His Spirit, and we know His presence. But in the future eternal order we will see His face.

At this future time, God will wipe away every tear from His people's eyes. There will be no more tears, for all the evils and ills that have oppressed humanity will be forever banished as the curse is lifted

The emphasis here is not on people's remorse but on the comfort God gives. God will even wipe away the tears of believers that result from the sorrow for those who are dear to them who have been cast into the lake of fire at the final judgment. Not only will tears be no more but also death, mourning, crying, or pain. All these tragic emotional experiences will have passed, for they are associated with the old order of things

And he that sat upon the throne said, Behold, I make all things new. And he said unto me, Write: for these words are true and faithful. And he said unto me, It is done. I am Alpha and Omega, the beginning and the end. He who is seated on the throne told John that He was making everything new (v. 5). *Everything new* indicates things new in character and new in the sense of being recently made. Drastic change is indicated. Thus the physical world will be liberated from the bondage of the curse. John is therefore instructed to record what he has seen and heard, for that which has been revealed is trustworthy. Moreover, the phrase **It is done** signifies God is bringing to a conclusion His work concerning the whole history of humanity until the eternal state. Not only has God's program of redemption been completed, but also the future has been made secure by the One who is the First and Last, the Author of creation and redemption

I will give unto him that is thirsty of the fountain of the water of life freely. He that overcomes shall inherit all things; and I will be his God, and he shall be my son. The one who thirsts is promised a satisfying drink of the water of life. Thirst here depicts the desire of the soul for God. David reflected this in Ps 42:1: *As a deer pants for flowing streams, so pants my soul for you, O God.* (See also Ps 36:9; 63:1; and Is 55:1.) God is *the fountain of living waters (Jer 2:13) that satisfies thirst.* Jesus told the woman of Samaria, *Whosoever shall drink of the water that I will give him, will never thirst, for the water that I will give him will be in him a spring of water springing up unto eternal life.* Not only does the living water satisfy. Jesus, at the Feast of Tabernacles, *on the last day, that great day of the feast;* which was the day the High Priest would go to the Pool of Siloam, fill the golden censor with water, and the people would follow him back up to the temple singing the psalm of Isaiah 12:3, *with joy shall we draw water out of the well of salvation,* that Jesus stood and said, *If any man thirst, let him come unto me, and drink. He that believes in me, as the scripture said, out of his belly shall flow rivers of living water. (But this he spoke concerning the Holy Spirit, which they that believe on him would receive: for it was not yet Holy Spirit time.; because Jesus was not yet glorified.) (Jn 7:37ff.)*

Not only does the Christian have the living, satisfying, water inside, but, in addition, those who truly believe in and commit their lives to Him will have streams of living water flowing from within them. **They will become a source to other people:** Will be able to minister to others by the power of the Holy Spirit within them. I pray God will give you such a thirst for the power of the spirit working this way in your own life that you will be filled with Him, so the overflow will then flow out like a river and influence others. The promise to the *overcomer*, remember the *overcomer is the believer* is to be God's son/ heir and inherit all things.

But the cowardly and unbelieving and abominable and murderers and immoral persons and sorcerers and idolaters and all liars, their part will be in the lake that burns with fire and brimstone, which is the second death. Eight types of ungodly people who will be placed in the lake of fire are listed: The *cowardly*, who head the list, are those who are afraid to accept Christ, live for Him, and let it be known. I had a young adult man say to me years ago, *I'm too cool to be a Christian.* I answered him, *No, you're too much of a coward to be one.*

The second class, The *unbelieving*, remind us that more is required in believing than mental assent., as mentioned earlier in this book, the very word translated *believe* is also translated *commit.* Jn1:12 indicates to *believe* means *to receive* Him. Believing demands that one make Christ the Lord of his or her life and live consciously and actively for Him.

The third group, The *abominable.* The word is used in the Greek translation of the Old Testament to pollute or become polluted. It refers to those who have become defiled by the impurities of false religion.

Murderers make up the fourth group. The fifth are *fornicators*—sex outside marriage between one man and one woman. *Sorcerers, pharmakois,* Make up the sixth group. The word is commonly used for those who do sorcery and witchcraft using drugs. However, I'm convince, since this is a prophecy of the end time, *druggers*, would be a more fitting translation. The seventh group is *Idolaters*, which in scripture seems to be associated with all the others listed, and finally, all *liars*. Obviously here those whose very life is a lie. God is true, so expects us to be true. And here *The Second Death.* Is used for the second and final time.

DESCRIPTION OF THE EXTERIOR THE NEW JERUSALEM

Then one of the seven angels who had the seven bowls full of the seven last plagues came and spoke with me, saying, "Come here, I will show you the bride, the wife of the Lamb. And he carried me away in the Spirit to a great and high mountain, and showed me the holy city, Jerusalem, coming down out of heaven from God, having the glory of God. Her brilliance was like a very costly stone, as a stone of crystal-clear jasper. It had a great and high wall, with twelve gates, and at the gates twelve angels; and names were written on them, which are the names of the twelve tribes of the sons of Israel. There were three gates on the east and three gates on the north and three gates on the south and three gates on the west. And the wall of the city had twelve foundation stones, and on them were the twelve names of the twelve apostles of the Lamb. (21:9-14 NASB)

The scene is identical with that in 17:1, where John was caught away to view Babylon. John undoubtedly intends a deliberate contrast between the harlot city and the heavenly city where God dwells. Most striking is the fact that the city bears the glory of God. Scintillating in the reflected light of God, the city sparkles like a many-faceted diamond.

Some have wondered why the city has a wall. We must remember this may simply be part of the description of an ideal city as conceived by ancient people who were accustomed to the security of strong outer walls. The city also has gates of pearl, in fact, twelve of them, and *each one of the gates was a single pearl* (v 24) 1. And on the gates are written the names of the *twelve tribes of Israel*. This stresses the continuity of the church of the New Testament with the people of God under the old covenant. And the names of *the twelve apostles* on the twelve foundations emphasizes once again the unity of ancient Israel with the church. It is very clear from the description of these gates and foundations that both the Old Testament and New Testament people of God are in the bride of Christ.

I pointed out, in the opening chapter, that the number twelve means *final completion*. Notice throughout this description the repetition and significance of the number twelve and its multiples in regard to the New Jerusalem.

Measurements of The New Jerusalem

The one who spoke with me had a gold measuring rod to measure the city, and its gates and its wall. The city is laid out as a square, and its length is as great as the width; and he measured the city with the rod, fifteen hundred miles; (Gk 12,000 stadios) its length and width and height are equal. And he measured its wall, a hundred and seventy-two yards, (Gk 44 pechus) according to human measurements, which are also angelic measurements. (vs 15-18 NASB) The measuring is done to show perfect completion in addition to the immense size, perfection, and beauty of the city. The KJ text uses *furlong*, (*stadios*) to measure the city and *cubit* (*pechus*) to measure the wall. The furlong equals 1/8 of a mile, thus 12,000=1500 miles. A *pechus*, technically, is the length of a man's arm from his elbow to the tip of his longest finger. Babylonians established a *Royal Cubit*, of about 20.2 inches, but a *Regular Cubit*, of at 17.6 inches. The length is generally figured to be 18 inches.

Thus the translation above. There is some controversy over the shape of the city. We are told it *is laid out as a square*. And in connection with that he says, *its length is as great as the width*. So at its base it is 1500 miles square. Then we are told, *its length and width and height are equal*. He does not say it's a cube. A pyramid would have the same description. A pyramid at its base is square. The question has been asked by many, *If it's a cube, where does the throne sit?* Of course *if it's a pyramid, the throne is at the top*.

One author I read many years ago , mentioned that, *If it's a cube and the streets are one mile apart and one mile high, it would have 2,250,000 streets 1500 miles long.* He went on to say how many if they were only ½ mile apart, etc. Which ever it is, Its going to take our breath away. Paul indicates, in 2 Cor 12, when he was *caught up to heaven*, he saw things *impossible to describe*. Imagine how long its going to take to explore that city, after we have worshipped the Lord for long periods, met our loved ones...It's a good thing we have forever. (Literally: 12,000 x12,000 Stadia...final completion)

Additional Description of The New Jerusalem

And the building of the wall of it was of jasper: and the city was pure gold, like unto clear glass. And the foundations of the wall of the city were garnished with all manner of precious stones. The first foundation was jasper; the second, sapphire; the third, a chalcedony; the fourth, an emerald; The fifth, sardonyx; the sixth, sardius; the seventh, chrysolite; the eighth, beryl; the ninth, a topaz; the tenth, a chrysoprasus; the eleventh, a jacinth; the twelfth, an amethyst. And the twelve gates were twelve pearls; every several gate was of one pearl: and the street of the city was pure gold, as it were transparent glass.

The 216-foot high wall of jasper that rests on twelve foundations, each of which is a precious gemstone. The twelve gates are made of twelve immense pearls, and the streets are of transparent gold. The colors of the foundations, *Jasper, brilliant like a diamond, Sapphire-blue, Chalcedony-green or blue, Emerald-bright green, Sardonyx-red and white, Sardius-blood red, Chrysolite-transparent golden, Beryl-golden green, Topaz-transparent yellow, Chrysoprasus-green, Jacinth-violet, Amethyst-purple.* One may only contemplate the effect of the light in the city as it filters through the various colors of the foundations and the crystal-clear jasper wall itself and then diffuses in lustrous softness on the golden pavement. People sell souls for a little gold here. There we will be surrounded by it.

I saw no temple in it, for the Lord God the Almighty and the Lamb are its temple. And the city has no need of the sun or of the moon to shine on it, for the glory of God has illumined it, and its lamp is the

Lamb. The nations will walk by its light, and the kings of the earth will bring their glory into it. In the daytime (for there will be no night there) its gates will never be closed; and they will bring the glory and the honor of the nations into it; and nothing unclean, and no one who practices abomination and lying, shall ever come into it, but only those whose names are written in the Lamb's book of life.

The temple was supremely the place of God's presence in the Old Testament. But now the symbol has given way to reality. Nor is there any need of stellar light, for the glory of God enlightens the city. This city is also unique by the very things that are missing:

There is no temple, no sun, no moon, no darkness, no abomination, no tears, no parting, no pain, no thirst, no hunger, and no death. In God's Word darkness is the usual metaphor for life apart from the presence of God; So all darkness will be abolished in the presence of God and the Lamb. Paul puts it this way, in Eph 5:6ff *you were formerly darkness, but now you are Light in the Lord; walk as children of Light (for the fruit of the Light consists in all goodness and righteousness and truth), trying to learn what is pleasing to the Lord. Do not participate in the unfruitful deeds of darkness, but instead even expose them; for it is disgraceful even to speak of the things which are done by them in secret.*

The passage shows there will be *nations,* in eternity, for there are *people and kings and nations who bring their glory and honor into that city.* It will be open day and night. And the final phrase, *no one who practices abomination and lying, shall ever come into it, but only those whose names are written in the Lamb's book of life.* There is no one who fits *unclean, abomination and lying* categories any more at this point. They are all in The *lake of fire.* Only the saved will walk in that city.

Then he showed me a river of the water of life, clear as crystal, coming from the throne of God and of the Lamb, in the middle of its street. On either side of the river was the tree of life, bearing twelve kinds of fruit, yielding its fruit every month; and the leaves of the tree were for the healing of the nations. There will no longer be any curse; and the throne of God and of the Lamb will be in it, and His bond-servants will serve Him; they will see His face, and His name will be on their foreheads. And there will no longer be any night; and they will not have need of the light of a lamp nor the light of the sun, because the Lord God will illumine them; and they will reign forever and ever.

A river of life as clear as crystal flows from the throne of God down the middle of the great street of the city. The river is thus central in the city. Humanity's earthly story initially began beside a river (Gen 2:10), and the history of civilization has progressed along this world's rivers, and now continues eternally beside the source of life. The tree of life from which Adam and Eve were driven now reappears, producing a different fruit each month). It will not have to go through the cycle of budding, blossoming, fruitbearing, and harvest, giving but one or two crops per year. Rather, it will be weighted down with fruit every month, *for the healing of the nations,* but there will be no more sickness anyway; this represents the complete triumph of life over death. This fruit will promote the enjoyment of life to the full. Moreover, the curse will be lifted! As J. B. Smith (1961) wrote describing in eternity:

And there shall be no more curse. . . . . perfect restoration.

But the throne of God and of the Lamb shall be in it. . . . . perfect administration.

His servants shall serve him . . . . perfect subordination.

And they shall see his face . . . . perfect transformation.

And his name shall be in their foreheads. . . . . perfect identification.

And there shall be no night there; and they need no candle,
    neither light of the sun; for the Lord gives them light. . . . . perfect illumination.

And they shall reign forever and ever . . . . perfect exultation.

While Moses could not see God's face and live, the redeemed will see God's face. His name will be on their foreheads. In their glorified state the redeemed will be fully transformed; they will be like Him, and they will reflect His likeness. The seal on their foreheads indicates ownership and likeness. He adds we *will reign for ever and ever.* No explanation is given as to who or what the saints will reign over. Have to wait and see!

CHAPTER 22:6-21

A Reminder and Warning About Jesus Sudden Coming

The story part of CHAPTER 66 is finished, but the chapter is not yet. He adds a very important postscript:

Then he said to me, These words are faithful and true. And the Lord God of the holy prophets sent His angel to show His servants the things which must quickly (suddenly) take place. Behold, I am coming quickly (suddenly)! Blessed is he who keeps the words of the prophecy of this book.

In verse 6 the message-bearing angel describes the nature of the message he is declaring: *These words are trustworthy and true.* Moreover, the angel's statement that the Lord is *the God of the prophets* indicates the relationship between prophets and prophecy: All true prophets are voices or channels of the Spirit of God because they yield their spirits to His direction and control. Finally, the angel indicates he has been sent to *show his servants what must soon (suddenly) take place. Must soon take place* is the same expression we saw in Revelation 1:1 and discussed in an earlier lesson.

The word *soon* is emphasized again in verse 7 in Jesus' statement, *Behold I am coming soon. Soon* means certainly and suddenly in both verses 6 and 7. The church of all times has been encouraged to live in a state of expectancy. A. T. Robertson, reminds us *soon* is God's time not ours. (Word Pictures in the New Testament)

As mentioned in connection with chapter 1, there are seven beatitudes in Revelation. Here, the sixth one, pronounces a blessing on those who *keep the words of this prophecy*, that is, do God's commandments. *be ye doers of the word, and not hearers only, deceiving your own selves* (Ja 1:22). As mentioned previously, God's primary purpose in giving us all scripture, including the prophecies in Revelation, is to show us how to live and not simply to fill us with information.

And I John saw these things, and heard them. And when I had heard and seen, I fell down to worship before the feet of the angel which showed me these things. Then he said to me, See you don't do this: for I am thy fellow servant, and of your brothers the prophets, and of those who are keep-

ing the sayings of this book: worship God. And he said to me, Don't seal the sayings of the proph-
ecy of this book: for the time is at hand. He that is unjust, let him be unjust still: and he which is
filthy, let him be filthy still: and he that is righteous, let him be righteous still: and he that is holy,
let him be holy still

John identifies himself. Since he is well known to all the churches, he needs no other identify-ing names. He does, however, verify the visions and experiences recorded here. John made the same mistake he had made earlier by trying to worship the angel/messenger, who, again, here is human not an angel.

Daniel, in Ch 12, was told *shut up the words and seal the book, until the time of the end* However, with reference to the same prophetic message John is told: *Do not seal up the words of the prophecy of this book* Why was Daniel told to seal up the message while John was told to make it known? Quite obviously, Daniel's prophecy was obscure until John wrote **CHAPTER 66**. Until then it was beyond human understanding.

John's message is a revelation that was to be heard throughout the Church Age. Its warnings are important to every church of every age. The book of Revelation shows what God expects of His people, and it warns His people to obey His Word. This message is to be proclaimed even if the proclamation of the prophetic message does not cause people to repent, it will encourage the true believer to continue to do right and to be holy. So, regardless of the response of peo-ple, continue to proclaim God's message. That is our responsibility.

The Arabs have a saying, **the greatest sin is to find water in the desert and keep it secre**t. You and I have found the greatest water ever in the middle of the desert of this world, don't keep it secret, proclaim it, regardless of how others accept or reject it.

Behold, I am coming suddenly, and My reward is with Me, to render to every man according to what he has done. I am the Alpha and the Omega, the first and the last, the beginning and the end.

Again, the Lord stresses that His coming will be without warning and that He will bring His reward with Him to repay everyone according to what he or she has done. We have seen the reward of the both the godly and ungodly in these closing chapters. It is obvious there are many wonderful rewards for serving God. Moreover, it is equally clear that judgment on the basis of works, because you live what you are, so He adds:

Blessed are those who wash their robes, so that they may have the right to the tree of life, and may enter by the gates into the city. Outside are the dogs and the sorcerers and the sexually immoral persons and the murderers and the idolaters, and everyone who loves and practices lying. I, Jesus, have sent My angel to testify to you these things for the churches. I am the root and the descendant of David, the bright morning star.

The contrast is between those who will spend eternity feasting on the rich presence of God, and those who are in the lake of fire. The term *dogs,* is used several ways in scripture: Mt 7;6, Jesus used it to refer to those who reject His teaching, Ps 22:16 to represent the wicked; Is 56:10 calls the *Watchmen, dumb dogs, who cannot bark, lying down, loving to slumber, greedy dogs who can never have enough, they are shepherds that cannot understand; they all look to their own way....;* Paul, in Phi. 3:2, uses it for false teachers who are trying to put the law on the Philippians. Many authors quote, in this connection. Deut 23:17-18 says, *there shall be no whore of the daughters of Israel, nor a sodomite of the sons of Israel. You shall not bring the hire of a whore, or the price of a dog, into the house of the Lord your God for any vow: for even both these are abomination unto the Lord your God.*(KJV) Rom 1:24–27 and 1 Cor 6:9–10 explain what the term *sexually immoral* includes.

Jesus declares the angel/messenger who revealed these things to John was sent by Jesus Himself, and he mentions two of His titles; *the root and the descendant of David,* Jesus fulfills the prophecy in 2 Samuel 7:16 in which David was promised an eternal heir for his throne. The term *root* speaks of Jesus as God who gives the family tree of David unending life. The term *descendant* speaks of Jesus as a man who is the rightful, legal heir to David's throne. And *The bright morning star,* which speaks of Jesus who will bring about first the Millennium and then the new, eternal order of things. This star anticipates the coming dawn of a glorious day. In order to experience that day, however, we must know Jesus, the bright morning star.

THE FINAL INVITATION IN THE BIBLE TO COME TO JESUS

The Spirit and the bride say, Come. And let him that hears say, Come. And let him that is thirsty come. And whosoever will, (whosoever will exercise his or her will) *let him take the water of life freely.* The New Testament makes it clear that God wants everyone to be saved. He does not desire for anyone to end up in the lake of fire. The choice is ours. Paul reminds Timothy, that God *desires all men to be saved and to come to the knowledge of the truth* (1 Ti 2:4), and Peter states, *The Lord...is not wanting that any should perish, but that would come to repentance.* (2 Pet 3:9). Jn 3:16 tells us that God's love in sending Jesus was for *the world.* Paul rephrases the same idea in 1 Tim 4:10, when he says, *we have fixed our hope on the living God, who is the Savior of all men, especially of believers.* Jesus died for everyone...the choice is ours. Those who are to give this last invitation to people are the Holy Spirit and the Bride of Christ, and anyone who hears the invitation.

Here the word *hears* refers not only to physical hearing but also to mental and spiritual acceptance of Christ. Thus anyone who accepts Jesus should immediately invite others to accept Him. As was mentioned, The church, the believers, empowered and inspired by the Spirit, are *the salt of the earth,* the antiseptic against the spread of evil, so that the Antichrist cannot make his appearance, according to 2 Thes, as we saw earlier, until the church is removed from the earth. The Holy Spirit will still be here.

God then gives a warning, *I testify to everyone who hears the words of the prophecy of this book: if anyone adds to them, God will add to him the plagues which are written in this book; and if anyone takes away from the words of the book of this prophecy, God will take away his part from the tree of life and from the holy city, which are written in this book.*

This is a warning against tampering with the divinely inspired prophetic record. In the Old Testament Israel was admonished along these same lines (Deut 4:2). What John is speaking to here is deliberate distortions and perversions of the divinely authenticated Word. **It is not only a warning against tampering with CHAPTER 66, It is a warning against tampering with all 66 chapters of God's Word.**

CHAPTER 66 closes God's Story by reminding about the suddenness of his return. *He who testifies to these things says,* **Yes, I am coming quickl**y. Knowing that His return is going to end all sin, sorrow, pain, suffering, oppression, prejudice, deceiving lying, and get rid of Satan and his influence once for all, the response of every child of God should be to invite others to receive Jesus Christ and to pray:

Amen. Come, Lord Jesus!
The grace of the Lord Jesus be with all, AMEN!

APPENDIX A
The Misuse of Firstborn

While the New Testament was being written there started a primitive form of what later came to be known as Gnosticism. The basic premises of the teaching were that God is Holy and anything material is evil, therefore a Holy God could not have created this evil universe, so He created a Lesser God, or Top Angel, who created everything else. This developed in several directions: That any sin you commit with the body is ok. I Cor 6:8-20 argues against this. Another was that anything done with the body is sin, so there should be marriage without sex, and Paul deals with that in I Cor 7:1-8 Denying the resurrection of the body was another, which is dealt with in I Cor 15:1-58 Another is that Jesus didn't have a real body, but that is dealt with in First John 1:1-4, 4:2. **But the main one I wish to deal with here is the false teaching that Jesus Christ is not really God, but a lesser created God or the top angel.**

As a result of this philosophy rather than translate John 1:1 like every good translation of the Bible: **In the beginning was the Word, and the Word was with God, and the Word was God**. The gnostic version of the bible translates the final phrase *the word was* **A God**, which is a totally indefensible translation. Since I taught New Testament Greek for 25 years: (levels 1st-4th year) I want to give a Greek Lesson. The word for word translation, as it stands in the original text is: *in beginning was* **The** *Word and* **The** *Word was with* **The** *God and God was* **The** *Word.*

In The Original Language Of The New Testament The Definite Article...**The** Is Extremely Important By Its Presence or Its Absence.

in beginning was **The Word**....*There is no* **the** *before* **beginning.** *The absence of* **the** *emphasizes the nature and character of the following word ..it is not referring only to THE beginning in Genesis, but rather anything that ever had the nature of a beginning the Word was already there.* **SO THE WORD DID NOT HAVE A BEGINNING.**

The Word was with **The** God..... **The** used with **God** and with **Word** Indicates Two separate Persons.... **The Word** and **The God.** The Father and the Son as we learn later in the chapter when **The Word becomes flesh.**

and God was The Word...The absence Of The Article **the** before **God,** Indicates The Very Nature Of The One Called **The Word**...is Identical In Nature, Character, Eternal Existence As The One Called **The God,**.....**The Word** is just as totally **God**, As Much **God**, As **The God**, but He is not **The God,** He is **The Word**. So the father is not the Son, nor the Son the Father.......

The Fact That **God** Comes BEFORE **Word** Makes The Translation *The Word Was* **A God** Impossible. Greek had no indefinite article , **A**. But, to insert it required it coming immediately prior to the word it modified. To translate as, *The Word Was A God*, **God** would have to come after **Word**. The Holy Spirit Was Careful To Have John Write It The Way He Did.

A Second Erroneous Translation Based On The Gnostic Philosophy Is From The Book Of Colossians,1:13-19, where the word *other* is inserted into the same translation referred to above which is not in the Greek Text.

The Greek Poet, Homer, who wrote the Odyssey and the Iliad several hundred years before the birth of Jesus Christ, coined a term in Greek, **ta panta**, literally meaning, **the all things**. He used it to refer to *everything that exists*. It was a common phrase in New Testament times. Paul uses it in Colossians, which is written to oppose every part of this false teaching, to indicate Jesus Created **the all things (Ta Panta)** . So I have included it where it exists in the passage below.

HE has rescued us from the dominion of darkness and brought us into the kingdom of the Son he loves, in whom we have redemption, the forgiveness of sins. The Son is the image of the invisible God, the **Firstborn** *over all creation* **FOR By Him The All Things (Ta Panta)** *were created (Here Is Where The Word* **Other** *Is incorrectly Inserted Based On Gnostic thinking and says He Created All* **Other** *Things) things in heaven and on earth, visible and invisible, whether thrones or powers or rulers or authorities;* **The all things (Ta Panta)** *have been created through* **Him** *and for* **Him. He, Himse**l*f, is before all things, and* **by Him the all things (Ta Panta)** *hold together. And* **He** *is the head of the body, the church;* **He** *is the beginning and the* **firstborn** *from among the dead, so that in everything* **He** *might have the* **supremacy** *(Many Translations Say* **preeminence**). *For it pleased God to have all the fullness dwell in* **Him**.*(NIV)*

So Colossians is saying that everything that has ever been created, He created it all...**so He Himself is not created.** Jn 1:3 says: *All things came into being through Him, and apart from Him nothing came into being that has come into being. (NASB) All things came into being through Him, and apart from Him there came into being not even one thing that has come into being. (My Trs)*

A second error based on the erroneous philosophy is the use of the term **firstborn** in this passage, It is used to say he was first one created, and from that the error inserted above, *He created all other, things.* Israel is Called **the firstborn**. (Ex 4:22) Obviously Israel was not the first nation on earth. Other were raised from the dead before Jesus. Jacob elevated his son Joseph to the position of **firstborn** by giving him a double portion for his sons, after Jacob rejected Reuben from the first-born position. *Now the sons of Reuben the firstborn of Israel (for he was the firstborn, but because he defiled his father's bed, his birthright was given to the sons of Joseph the son of Israel; so that he is not enrolled in the genealogy according to the birthright. Though Judah prevailed over his brothers, and from him came the leader, yet the birthright belonged to Joseph (I Ch. 5:1-2)*

The Firstborn was the primary heir, held the leadership position. The key word in the above translation is **supremacy/preeminence.**

APPENDIX B
Jehovah or Jesus, Which is Correct

I was asked on local radio program (November 2017) to comment on Psalm 83:18, *That men may know that You, whose **NAME** alone is **JEHOVAH**, are the most high over all the earth.* The question was obviously asked by someone who is convinced that the name by which people are saved and come into a relationship with God is the NAME **JEHOVAH.**

Since the person quoted the King James Edition of the Bible, I also referred to Isaiah 42:8, *I am the **LORD**, that is my **NAME*** in the King James. Both of these words, **JEHOVAH** AND **LORD**, are the English of the same name of God, **YHWH**, in the original Hebrew.

The name of God in the Original Hebrew Old Testament was simply **YHWH.** Ancient Hebrew had no written vowels. There is no way sure to pronounce it. Many say YAWEH...but, , that would be the translation if it followed rules for other than proper names, but this is a noun...a proper name, so any variety of vowels could be used, consequently there is no way to determine the correct pronunciation.

In the 9th or 10th century a group of scholars, The Masorites, invented written vowels and produced the Masoretic Text of the Old Testament using vowels so later generations would know how to pronounce the language of the Bible.

The name of God, **YHWH**, was considered so holy that it was not only never to be pronounced; if a scribe would write it he would purify himself seven times before writing it. As a result, they took another important word, **ADONAI**, (LORD) and inserted the vowels from *ADONAI, A, O, A*, Into YHWH, resulting in **Y A H O W A H**. Because English Language has Anglo influence, the Y was changed to a J, and the W to a V resulting in the name **JEHOVAH.**

HOWEVER: When this word is read in the original language, Hebrew, it is not pronounced **YAHOWAH**, but **ADONAI**–LORD. **THE VOWELS FROM ADONIA ARE THER TO REMIND THEM THE SACRED NAME, YHWH IS NEVER TO BE PROUNOUCED, AND THE WORD LORD, ADONAI, IS TO BE USED IN ITS PLACE. THUS, JEHOVAH IS A NON-WORD.**

Does God get upset when we sing songs, like Jehovah Jireh? God is not as legalistic as people are. As I mentioned earlier, If God was as legalistic as people, no one would ever be right with God. To repeat from earlier: When people would call on the TV program and ask *Do we keep the Jewish Sabbath.. Sundown Friday to Sundown Saturday, or The Lords Day, Sunday? "* I would say **YES!** We are not saved by what day we keep but Who We Know....See Romans 14, were Paul explains it doesn't matter. And I would be asked, *Do we have to be baptized in Jesus' Name only, or in the Name of the Father, Son, and Holy Spirit?* And I would give the same answer, **YES!** We are not saved by a formula but by a Relationship with Jesus Christ...I can give you all the reasons why I used the latter.

There are many now who say we must use the Hebrew word **Yeshua, the Hebrew name of Jesus,** when we pray or cast out demons, etc. etc. But people are set free, healed, delivered, in various languages around the world, the name of Jesus but pronounced as **Iasous** in Indonesia, **Hasous** in Latin America, **Iasous** Greece, (and the Greek New Testament) and **Jesus** in English. Regardless of how you pronounce it, demons know it, and the power of the Holy Spirit within you, and flee at your command. Jesus Said, *I give you authority over all the power of the enemy (Lk 10:19)* Understand that last phrase. I have mentioned to the congregation, *a huge truck can drive down the street shaking the houses because of its power.....a man with a badge can get in front of that truck and it will come to a halt...that is authority.* You, my brother and sister have authority over the Devil.

When the Old Testament Was Translated Into Greek (known as the Septuagint abbreviated by LXX) In The Second Century BC, The Greek Word **kurios**, **LORD** was The Translation Given To **YHWH**. This Is Why In Your King James Bible, and others, in the Old Testament, it Is written in English, as **JEHOVAH** Or **LORD**. **JEHOVAH** is Simply A Transliteration of the letters, and **LORD** the translation assigned to **YHWH.** By New Testament times Common Greek had been the language of Western Civilization for over 300 years since the conquests of Alexander the Great. People spoke their own language plus Greek. As mentioned earlier, most of the quotes from the Old Testament in the writings of Paul are from the Septuagint not the Hebrew Old Testament. Any quote from the Old Testament in the New, where the name **YHWH** is used in in the Old Testament the New Testament Greek uses **kurios**,

JOHN 1:18 SAYS: *No One Has Seen God At Any Time, The Unique God, Who Continually Exists In The Bosom Of The Father, He Has Revealed Him.* (NASB but substitute reveled for explained)

THIS MEANS EVERY APPEARANCE IN THE OLD TESTAMENT WHERE MEN SEE GOD... IT IS ALWAYS GOD THE SON.

ISAIAH 6:1-5 SAYS:

*In the year of King Uzziah's death I saw the Lord (**adonai**) sitting on a throne, lofty and exalted, with the train of His robe filling the temple. Seraphim stood above Him, each having six wings: with two he covered his face, and with two he covered his feet, and with two he flew. And one called out to another and said "Holy, Holy, Holy, is the <u>LORD</u> (**YHWH**) of hosts, The whole earth is full of His glory. "And the foundations of the thresholds trembled at the voice of him who called out, while the temple was filling with smoke. Then I said, Woe is me, for I am ruined! Because I am a man of unclean lips, And I live among a people of unclean lips; For my eyes have seen THE KING, THE <u>LORD</u> (**YHWH**) OF HOSTS.* (NASB)

In verse 1 Isaiah says he saw **adonai**, and the Saraphim refer to HIM as **YHWH**, in verse 5, Isaiah says he saw **YHWH**. And, in Jn 12:36-41, John speaking of the rejection of Jesus by the religious leaders, he refers to Isaiah 6 9-10 (LXX) quotes from it, and says:

But Though HE Had Done So Many Miracles Before Them, Yet They Believed Not On HIM: That The Saying Of Isaiah The Prophet Might Be Fulfilled, Which He spoke , Lord, Who Has Believed Our Report? And To Whom Has The Arm Of The Lord Been Revealed? therefore *They Could Not Believe, Because That Isaiah said Again, He Has Blinded Their Eyes, And Hardened Their Heart; That They Should Not See With Their Eyes, Nor Understand With Their Heart, And Be Converted, And I Should Heal Them.* ***THESE THINGS SAID ISAIAH , WHEN HE SAW <u>HIS GLORY</u>, AND SPOKE OF <u>HIM.</u>***

Make Is Clear That Who Isaiah Saw, Whom He Called both *adonai* and **YHWH** was God The Son, Jesus, Not God The Father. **GOD THE SON IS THE *YHWH* OF THE OLD TESTAMENT that men see.** He is the one they see in various manifestation, (preincarnate appearances), such as appearing to Abraham and Sarah as a man and as a man Not only gave promise of a son, said, *At the time appointed I will return to you , according to the time of life, and Sarah shall have a son. An angel cannot do that.* He appeared as Melchizedek, (name means King of Righteousness), and is called that in English Bibles, and also King of Shalom...King of Peace. No one else in history could ever be called that.

PHILIPPIANS 2:5-11:

Let this mind be in you, which was also in Christ Jesus: Who, being in the **form** *of God, did not think he had to seize equality with God, but emptied (ekenosen) Himself and took upon himself the* **form** *of a servant, and was made in the* **likeness** *of men: And being found in* **fashion** *as a man, he humbled himself, and became obedient unto death, even the death of the cross. Wherefore God also hath highly exalted him, and given him a NAME WHICH IS ABOVE EVERY NAME: That AT THE NAME OF JESUS every knee will bow, of things in heaven, and things in earth, and things under the earth; And that every tongue will confess that JESUS CHRIST IS LORD (**KURIOS**) , to the glory of God the Father.*

This means, prior to his birth as a child, the Angels looking at **him**, by his very **form** knew he was **God**. He emptied himself of his **form,** not his deity; He was 100 percent God and 100 percent man. (likeness and fashion—-looked human and was totally human) Thus Isaiah said **his name would be Emmanuel...God with us**. Isaiah 9 Referring to His birth said *for unto us* **a child is born**, *unto us* **a son is given**: *and the government shall be upon his shoulder: and his name shall be called Wonderful, Counselor, The mighty God, The everlasting Father, The Prince of Peace*. **At His birth GOD, the son was given and born as a child.**

I Jn 5:12 says: *Whoever has the son has life; whoever does not have the son of god does not have life.* Ac 4:12 says: *Salvation is found in no one else, for there is no other name under heaven given to man- kind by which we must be saved.* As john 1:12 teaches *As many as received him, to them gave he power to become children of God, even to them who are believing(continuous action verb, not a one time event only)into his name:* the Greek New Testament never says to believe on Him, nor in Him, but into Him.

Belief in the New Testament is not mere mental assent to the fact that Jesus is the Son of God. It is defined here as receiving Jesus Christ. In addition, the very Greek word translated **believe**, *pisteuo*, is also translated __commit__ throughout the New Testament. (Jn2:23-24 it is translated **believed** in v 23 and **commit** in 24) Thus to be a Christian means to **receive** Jesus Christ and make a **commitment** of your life to him. And, as Romans 8:15 Indicates, you will **know** you are saved because the Holy Spirit bears with witness with your spirit that you are a Child of God.

APPENDIX C
Additional Information about the Antichrist from Daniel 8 and 11

IN DANIEL 8, Daniel sees a vision of A Ram with two horns, *one being higher than the other, and the higher came up last.* Then he sees a goat with a notable horn is attacking the ram and defeating the ram. We don't have to wonder what these represent for we are told in verses 20-21 that the Ram is Media and Persia, and the Goat is Greece. In the case of The Ram, Persia developed later but became the more powerful, thus the one horn that came up last is higher than the other The notable horn, we are told is the King of Greece, who was Alexander the Great. The horn is broken off and 4 other horns take the place of the one. When Alexander died, his kingdom was divided between his four generals; Cassander ruled Macedonia and Greece, Lysimacus ruled Thrace, Bithynia and Asia Minor, Ptolemy ruled Egypt, and Selecus ruled Syria and Babylon. The only two we are concerned about is Ptolemy in Egypt and Selecus in Syria. These are referred to as *The King of North, Syria,* and *The King of the South, Egypt.* The two fought for about 200 years, and Israel was the battleground. Which ever had the strongest army controlled Israel. The last of the Ptolemy Dynasty of Egypt was Cleopatra.

We are primarily interested in the King of the North. Daniel 8:9ff, talking about the 4 horns, says: *out of one of them came a little horn which grew exceedingly great toward the south, toward the east, and toward the Glorious Land. And it grew up to the host of heaven; and it cast down some of the host and some of the stars to the ground, and trampled them. He even exalted himself as high as the Prince of the host; and by him the daily sacrifices were taken away, and the place of His sanctuary was cast down. Because of transgression, an army was given over to the horn to oppose the daily sacrifices; and he cast truth down to the ground. He did all this and prospered. Then I heard a holy one speaking; and another holy one said to that certain one who was speaking, How long will the vision be, concerning the daily sacrifices and the transgression of desolation, the giving of both the sanctuary and the host to be trampled underfoot? And he said to me, For two thousand three hundred days; then the sanctuary shall be cleansed.*(NKJ)

Scholars agree that the *little horn* is the King of the North, Syria, Antiochus IV Epiphanes (the Bright One, the name he added to himself) took control of the vacant throne of The Seleucid Empire. He came to the throne by flattery, bribery and deceit. He began in a small way, but soon became powerful. After having ruled for 8 years, he turned his attention to *the Glorious Land.* From 168 BC, for the next three and one half years, using military power, he tried to destroy the religious root of the Jewish People by forbidding Jewish worship. This included the reading of the Torah (Law), Jewish Feasts, and the rite of circumcision. All temple offerings were prohibited. They were forced to eat pig meat. He killed anyone who observed Jewish Feasts. I Maccabees 1:61 indicates many mothers who had their son's circumcised were killed with their dead sons hung around their neck. . He forced them to attend pagan feasts and ceremonies. The statements about *The Stars* and *The Prince of the Host*, are generally considered to refer to the priesthood, and the High Priest. He killed the High Priest, Onias, III, and set up his own High Priest and priesthood. There are many various opinions about the reference to 2300 days. Having read a lot of material over many years, I agree with the opinion that the 2300 days refer to 171 BC when the High priest was killed, to the death of Antiochus in 164 BC. The Climax of his destruction of Judaism, and contempt for the God of Israel, was when He defiled the Torah and coating it with the grease of a Pig before he destroyed it, and He offered a Pig on the altar in the temple. The Pig on the Altar is what is called in Daniel 11, *The Abomination of Desolation.*

The Apocryphal Book of I Maccabees give the details of what he did, and then what followed. Maccabees is good history, but it is not Scripture. It is part of the 13 books called the Apocryphal. They are in the Catholic Bible, but were never considered to be part of Scripture until the Council of Trent , 1545-1563 added them to Scripture because they seem to support some of the traditions. However, The Maccabees are excellent history.

So what happened to rid Israel of this pollution? Many Israelites did their best to oppose what was happening. One group, after having disobeyed the orders, went to the desert. So Antiochus had soldiers attack them on the Sabbath, and they refused to fight on the Sabbath and were all killed., Word of this reached Matthias, who had previously killed the kings messenger, announced *If anyone attacks us on the Sabbath day, whoever he may be, we shall resist him; we must not all be killed, as our brothers were in the hiding places.* (I Mac 2:41) When he died, his Son, Judas Maccabaeus, *The Hammer,* led the revolt that drove the Syrians out. When confronted about the size of their little band against the Syrian Army, Judas Said: *Victory in war does not depend on the size of the fighting force: Heaven accords the strength* (3:19). They won over the enemy, Purified the Sanctuary, pulled down the polluted altar and built a new one of unhewn stones, made new sacred vessels, set up the Menorah,. They found enough oil for the Menorah to last one day, and proceeded to dedicate the altar...but the Oil lasted 8 days, thus the 8 day Feast of Dedication today called Hanukah.

NOW...THE REST OF THE STORY.

The prophecy now goes way beyond Antiochus, who was a picture of one coming in the latter days; *And in the **latter time** of their kingdom, when the transgressors are come to the full, a king of fierce countenance, and understanding dark sentences, shall stand up. And his power shall be mighty, but not by his own power: and he shall destroy wonderfully, and shall prosper, and practice, and shall destroy the mighty and the holy people. And through his policy also he shall cause craft to prosper in his hand; and he shall magnify himself in his heart, and by peace shall destroy many: he shall also stand up against the Prince of princes; but he shall be broken without hand. And the vision of the evening and the morning* *which was told is true: wherefore shut thou up the vision; for it shall be for many days. And I Daniel fainted, and was sick certain days; afterward I rose up, and did the king's business; and I was astonished at the vision, but none understood it.*(KJV) These descriptions fit the the *Man of Sin, The Antichrist* in the New Testament. It is from this and Daniel 11 that I gave some of his characteristics in connection with Rev. Ch 6.

IN DANIEL 11, In this chapter there are 135 prophecies that were fulfilled during the period between the Old and New Testaments. The Global University Book I authored gives a list of some of these, and web sites also give lists. These prophecies are so literally fulfilled that they cause Liberal Theologians, who deny prophecy, to call Daniel a Historian. I reminded a professor in a Liberal Seminary that Jesus Called Daniel a Prophet not a historian. When the professor had spent weeks trying to prove Moses didn't really write the Pentateuch, I reminded him, *Jesus, when quoting from it, always said, Moses said.* His answer was, *Jesus was going along with popular opinion.* I answered back, *Jesus never went along with popular opinion, He was and is the truth.* That's the class from which I received a B.

However in chapter 11, at verse 36 there is a remarkable change, similar to the one in Ch 8. *And the king shall do according to his will; and he shall exalt himself, and magnify himself above every god, and shall speak marvelous things against the God of gods, and shall prosper till the indignation be accomplished: for that that is determined shall be done. Neither shall he regard the God of his fathers, nor the desire of women, nor regard any god: for he shall magnify himself above all. But in his estate shall he honor the God of forces: and a god whom his fathers knew not shall he honor with gold, and silver, and with precious stones, and pleasant things. Thus shall he do in the most strong holds with a strange god, whom he shall acknowledge and increase with glory: and he shall cause them to rule over many, and shall divide the land for gain. And at the time of the end shall the king of the south push at him: and the king of the north shall come against him like a whirlwind, with chariots, and with horsemen, and with many ships; and he shall enter into the countries, and shall overflow and pass over. He shall enter also into the glorious land, and many countries shall be overthrown: but these shall escape out of his hand, even Edom, and Moab, and the chief of the children of Ammon. He shall stretch forth his hand also upon the countries: and the land of Egypt shall not escape.*(KJV)

Jerome 347-420 AD, bible translator, said: *We...understand this to refer to Antichrist.* There is no correspondence in history of this part of Daniel 11 having fulfillment. Notice a couple of things about this chapter, first, it shows the *King of the South and King of the North* against him. This, again, is Syria and Egypt. Arab nations fighting the Antichrist. This is the passage also that indicates, as mentioned in the discussion of Ch 12. He will not control the three nations that make up modern Jordan; Edom Moab, Ammon. This chapter ends with the following, *But tidings out of the east and out of the north shall trouble him: therefore he shall go forth with great fury to destroy, and utterly to make away many And he shall plant the tabernacles of his palace between the seas in the glorious holy mountain; yet he shall come to his end, and none shall help him.* This fits with the 6th Trumpet judgment. It also agrees that Jerusalem will be world headquarters, and how the Antichrist is simply *taken* at Armageddon and *cast into the lake of fire.*

APPENDIX D BRIEF OUTLINE OF MATTHEW 24-25